THE CONSTITUTION OF INDIA

This book provides an overview of the content and functioning of the Indian Constitution, with an emphasis on the broader socio-political context. It focuses on the overarching principles and the main institutions of constitutional governance that the world's longest written constitution inaugurated in 1950. The nine chapters of the book deal with specific aspects of the Indian constitutional tradition as it has evolved across seven decades of India's existence as an independent nation. Beginning with the pre-history of the Constitution and its making, the book moves onto an examination of the structural features and actual operation of the Constitution's principal governance institutions. These include the executive and the parliament, the institutions of federalism and local government, and the judiciary. An unusual feature of Indian constitutionalism that is highlighted here is the role played by technocratic institutions such as the Election Commission, the Comptroller and Auditor General, and a set of new regulatory institutions, most of which were created during the 1990s. A considerable portion of the book evaluates issues relating to constitutional rights, directive principles and the constitutional regulation of multiple forms of identity in India. The important issue of constitutional change in India is approached from an atypical perspective.

The book employs a narrative form to describe the twists, turns and challenges confronted across nearly seven decades of the working of the constitutional order. It departs from conventional Indian constitutional scholarship in placing less emphasis on constitutional doctrine (as evolved in judicial decisions delivered by the High Courts and the Supreme Court). Instead, the book turns the spotlight on the political bargains and extra-legal developments that have influenced constitutional evolution.

Written in accessible prose that avoids undue legal jargon, the book aims at a general audience that is interested in understanding the complex yet fascinating challenges posed by constitutionalism in India. Its unconventional approach to some classic issues will stimulate the more seasoned student of constitutional law and politics.

Constitutional Systems of the World
General Editors: Benjamin L Berger, Rosalind Dixon, Andrew Harding, Peter Leyland and Heinz Klug

In the era of globalisation, issues of constitutional law and good governance are being seen increasingly as vital issues in all types of society. Since the end of the Cold War, there have been dramatic developments in democratic and legal reform, and post-conflict societies are also in the throes of reconstructing their governance systems. Even societies already firmly based on constitutional governance and the rule of law have undergone constitutional change and experimentation with new forms of governance; and their constitutional systems are increasingly subjected to comparative analysis and transplantation. Constitutional texts for practically every country in the world are now easily available on the internet. However, texts which enable one to understand the true context, purposes, interpretation and incidents of a constitutional system are much harder to locate, and are often extremely detailed and descriptive. This series seeks to provide scholars and students with accessible introductions to the constitutional systems of the world, supplying both a road map for the novice and, at the same time, a deeper understanding of the key historical, political and legal events which have shaped the constitutional landscape of each country. Each book in this series deals with a single country, or a group of countries with a common constitutional history, and each author is an expert in their field.

Published volumes

The Constitution of the United Kingdom; The Constitution of the United States; The Constitution of Vietnam; The Constitution of South Africa; The Constitution of Japan; The Constitution of Germany; The Constitution of Finland; The Constitution of Australia; The Constitution of the Republic of Austria; The Constitution of the Russian Federation; The Constitutional System of Thailand; The Constitution of Malaysia; The Constitution of China; The Constitution of Indonesia; The Constitution of France; The Constitution of Spain; The Constitution of Mexico; The Constitution of Israel; The Constitutional Systems of the Commonwealth Caribbean; The Constitution of Canada; The Constitution of Singapore; The Constitution of Belgium; The Constitution of Taiwan; The Constitution of Romania; The Constitutional Systems of the Independent Central Asian States; The Constitution of Pakistan

Link to series website

www.bloomsburyprofessional.com/uk/series/
constitutional-systems-of-the-world

The Constitution of India

A Contextual Analysis

Arun K Thiruvengadam

B L O O M S B U R Y
NEW DELHI • LONDON • OXFORD • NEW YORK • SYDNEY

Bloomsbury Publishing India Pvt. Ltd
Second Floor, Building No.4 ,DDA Complex LSC, Pocket C – 6 & 7
Vasant Kunj, New Delhi 110070
www.bloomsbury.com

First published in India 2018
First published 2017

This edition published with permission from Bloomsbury Publishing Plc,
50 Bedford Square, London, WC1B 3DP, UK

Published in North America (US and Canada) by Hart Publishing
An imprint of Bloomsbury Publishing Plc
HART PUBLISHING, the Hart/Stag logo, BLOOMSBURY and the Diana logo are trademarks of Bloomsbury Publishing Plc

 British Library Cataloguing-in-Publication Data. A catalogue record for this book is available from the British Library.

Library of Congress Cataloging-in-Publication Data
Names: Thiruvengadam, Arun K., author.
Title: The constitution of India : a contextual analysis / Arun K Thiruvengadam.
Description: Portland, Oregon : Hart Publishing, 2017. | Series: Constitutional systems of the world | Includes bibliographical references and index.
Identifi ers: LCCN 2017042042 (print) | LCCN 2017042423 (ebook) |
ISBN 9781849468695 (Epub) | ISBN 9781841137360 (pbk. : alk. paper)
Subjects: LCSH: India. Constitution. | Constitutional law—India.
Classifi cation: LCC KNS1744.5195 (ebook) | LCC KNS1744.5195 T49 2018 (print) |
DDC 342.5402—dc23
LC record available at https://lccn.loc.gov/2017042042

ISBN: 978 93 87146 55 6

For sale in the Indian subcontinent only

Typeset by Compuscript Ltd, Shannon

Printed and bound in India by Replika Press Pvt. Ltd.

To find out more about our authors and books visit www.hartpublishing.co.uk.
Here you will find extracts, author information, details of forthcoming events and the option to sign up for our newsletters.

For
Sanjana and Ghazal:
cherished lodestars

Acknowledgements

This book has been seven years in the making, and owes its origin, content and final form to a variety of encounters, both professional and personal. My biggest debt is to Andrew Harding, who persuaded me to take on this assignment, was its driving force (especially in periods when I myself did not believe I was the person to complete it), and used an intriguing array of manoeuvres to ensure that it *was* completed, even if well beyond the original timeline. For his patience, unwavering support and belief I shall remain grateful to Andrew.

This book project was conceived while I was based at the National University of Singapore (NUS), and was supported by a research grant from the Singapore Ministry of Education's Academic Research Fund (MOE AcRF #R-241-000-104-112). Colleagues at NUS who provided support in multiple ways include Ho Hock Lai, Kevin Tan, Arif Jamal, Umakanth Varottil, Victor Ramraj, Gary Bell, Tracey Evans Chan, Michael Hor, Terry Kaan, Alex Loke, Michael Ewing-Chow, Michael Dowdle, Jaclyn Neo, Swati Jhaveri, Tony Anghie, and M Sornarajah. I completed much of the writing of this project at the School of Policy and Governance (SPG), Azim Premji University (APU), Bangalore. I presented drafts of two chapters of this book at the weekly Faculty SPG seminar and received excellent feedback from the following colleagues: Sitharamam Kakarala, A Narayana, Srikrishna Ayyangar, Mathew Idiculla, Vishnupad, Malini Bhattacharjee, Nigam Nuggehalli and Sudhir Krishnaswamy.

Communities of scholars are vital to sustain both the spirit and material output of research and writing. I am fortunate to have found such support beyond the institutional and university settings mentioned earlier. I thank Vikram Raghavan, V Venkatesan, Nick Robinson, Madhav Khosla, Douglas McDonald-Norman, Arvind Narrain, Tarunabh Khaitan, Clark Lombardi, Sitharamam Kakarala, Mathew John, Victor Ramraj, Sunil Khilnani, Jothie Rajah, Philipp Dann, Siddharth Narrain, Mayur Suresh, Asanga Welikala, Harshan Kumarasingham, Lawrence Liang and Rohit De, who have been fellow travellers on a range of academic and intellectual projects, including those that fed this specific assignment.

This book project has benefited from the synergies between teaching, research and writing. It was the joy of exchanging ideas and debating with students while teaching as a graduate student that convinced me to become an academic. The book's content was formatively influenced by the course on the 'Contemporary Indian Legal System' that I taught at NUS between 2007 and 2015. I remain grateful to the many students who took this course across several years, and particularly to N Sandeepan, Nancy Lalruatkimi and Devashish Dhar, who served as my earliest research assistants. The book has similarly benefited from courses on the Indian Constitution that I taught at the Central European University, the University of Toronto and the University of Trento. At APU, students in two batches of the MPG course on 'Constitutional Foundations of the State in India' helped me in ways that they may never fully know. Students in the inaugural batch of the LLM in Law and Development helped me polish some of my overall themes by their active participation. A motivating hope for this book, given the dearth of such works, is that it will aid other students in grappling with the complexities of Indian constitutionalism.

My work as a teacher makes me acutely aware of the formative roles performed by teachers in my own intellectual development. The influence of my first constitutional law teachers—Professors T Devidas, VS Mallar and V Vijayakumar—at the National Law School, Bangalore bears mentioning because they instilled in me a lifelong fascination for the subject. Other teachers who provided stimulation and models to emulate in teaching, writing and living include: Professors Babu Mathew, A Jayagovind, G Ajjappa, Sitharamam Kakarala, Frank Upham, Holly Maguigan, Diana Hortsch, Derrick Bell Jr, Mattias Kumm, Pasquale Pasquino, Burt Neuborne, Joseph Weiler and Thomas M Franck. We often gain teachers in persons who never taught us formally. Foremost among these is Professor MP Singh, whom I was fortunate to meet at a pivotal time and has been a constant source of encouragement and support across a dozen years. Professor Singh was an early and enthusiastic supporter of the book project and egged me on to complete when my spirits were flagging. I have been similarly fortunate in my associations with Michael Hor, Victor Ramraj and Roberto Toniatti.

Ashna Ashesh, Anshuman Singh, Douglas McDonald-Norman and Prarthana Krishnamurthy read several draft chapters and offered constructive criticism, and morale-boosting praise. Benjamin Berger's editorial comments were similarly extremely valuable. The opportunity of working with Putachad Leyland on the cover was a major incentive to complete the writing. Her novel and unique interpretations of Indian culture, art and constitutional experience bring a freshness to these themes which are as vibrant as the colours she weaves into her paintings.

I am deeply grateful to the librarians at the CJ Koh Law Library at NUS (and to Carolyn Wee in particular) and the APU library (and to Suresh B Balatugi, Sachin Tirlapur and Praveena CS in particular). Carolyn Fox improved the text considerably during the copy-editing process and deserves special mention. Anne Flegel managed the publication process adroitly, and I thank her and the entire Hart Publishing team for their help in facilitating the final form of the book. Prarthana Krishnamurthy provided crucial inputs at the copy-editing and proofreading stages.

A number of friends contributed through their support and camaraderie to the completion of the book project. They include NK Dilip and Arpita Sen; RV Anuradha and Piyush Joshi; Swapna Umakanth and V Umakanth; Shona Malvi and Senthil Ramamoorthy; Jayna Kothari and Sudhir Krishnaswamy; Esha Shah and Sitharamam Kakarala; Sanjay Awasthi and Prarthana Krishnamurthy; Sridhar Arunachalam; and Karthik Chandresekaran. Members of my immediate family deserve special mention for their fortitude and for assisting the project in myriad ways. My mother, Chandraleka Thiruvengadam, fostered my love of reading and will, I hope, be happy to see this in its final form. My brother, Ajay Thiruvengadam, had to bear burdens that should have been mine and I am grateful to him. My parents-in-law, Sudha Baweja and Brij Mohan Baweja, pitched in on multiple occasions and through various ways, as did Shebani and Mohit Baweja.

This book is dedicated to Sanjana and Ghazal who, through their presence and love, provided the motivation for persevering with it. They have come to view the project as an inanimate competitor for the time that they have a legitimate claim upon. I fervently hope they will see this book differently when they are old enough to engage with its content. At that time, I hope it will enable them to appreciate some aspects of the exasperating but ceaselessly fascinating nation that they are bound to by the bonds of descent.

Contents

Table of Cases

Table of Legislation

Other Jurisdictions

Introduction

Scope and principal themes of the book – Its approach and orientation

I. THE CONSTITUTION OF INDIA AND ITS SPECIAL SIGNIFICANCE

THIS BOOK, IN keeping with the mandate of the series to which it belongs, seeks to provide a contextual account of the Constitution of India, the foundational document of the world's largest democracy. The Constitution of India has been the framing device for many crucial debates that have been central to India's evolving culture of constitutionalism and governance, even as it has endured and established its legitimacy over the last seven decades. It is, in form, the longest written Constitution in the world. More significantly though, it is the substantive governing document of the world's most populous democracy, whose diversity and other complexities result in extraordinary challenges for governance and regulation.

The Indian Constitution was exceptional in relation to previous attempts at Constitution making because it sought to attain several goals simultaneously. At the first level, the Constitution of India sought to deliver political freedom after two centuries of colonial rule—when many basic civil and political rights and freedoms had been unavailable to ordinary people—while simultaneously ensuring national unity and security. At the second level, the Indian Constitution sought to lay the blueprint for economic development of the vast subcontinental nation, which was an imperative for a populace that was largely illiterate, poor and disproportionately situated in rural societies that had limited access to many essential social goods and infrastructural facilities. At the third level, it sought to tackle deeply entrenched social practices that had existed in pre-colonial India for centuries. The more pervasive problems—such as discrimination on the basis of caste, religion and gender—preceded colonialism but their prevalence was exacerbated by colonial practices. Tackling this third set of issues was also an imperative if the constitutional goal of creating an overarching sense of national unity and identity was to be achieved. In seeking to address these varied objectives simultaneously, within the constraints of a system of governance founded upon a written Constitution that was itself based on principles of liberal constitutionalism (though the nature of that liberalism has, as we shall see, many unique and distinctive elements), the Constitution of India was indisputably an ambitious project. What *is* disputed, nearly seven decades after its adoption, is how successful it has been in achieving all or any of these goals.

The text and the jurisprudence that has evolved around the Constitution of India bear significance for those interested in comparative constitutional law as well as for those who study practices of governance and constitutionalism within India. The Indian Constitution was perceived by many in the post-colonial world to be a revolutionary document. In the era of decolonisation that followed the aftermath of the Second World War, India was one of the earliest of the colonies to gain independence. Moreover, it was rare among the many post-colonial states of Asia and Africa in being able to decide its own constitutional fate. As analysed at length in Chapter 1, Indians designed their own Constitution over a period extending across nearly three years. Scholars have noted that as the process of decolonisation wound along, this became rarer still. In Japan, Malaysia and Singapore, for instance, the Constitutions currently in force were crafted with little or no involvement of locals. The 'Lancaster House' Constitutions that were drafted for many African nations were, as the name suggests, conceived in London and had little legitimacy and credibility in the newly inaugurated constitutional orders of these nations.

Apart from having had considerable influence on the drafting of several other post-colonial Constitutions across Asia and Africa, the Constitution of India continues to be studied by more contemporary Constitution makers as is clear from more recent experiences in South Africa and Nepal. This is in part because the Indian Constitution is unusual in the post-colonial world for having endured across nearly seven decades, and for having engendered a robust constitutional culture. Constitutional democracy was formally suspended only once—from 1975 to 1977—in what is referred to by Indians as 'the Emergency'. Though there have been other problems in its operation, the Constitution of India has taken hold in the political and legal culture of the country.

Many of the core problems that the framers of the Indian Constitution grappled with, and which continue to be pressing issues in contemporary India, are also the concern of constitutionalists elsewhere. A focus on the way Indian constitutionalism has sought to address these issues should be of interest to anyone convinced of the value of comparative insight. Given that the Indian Constitution was framed by explicit reference to comparative experience, and sought to gain insights into how other countries had grappled with comparable constitutional problems, its body and text offer lessons on how to adapt and integrate ideas of constitutional design from elsewhere to attend to very particular issues within a specific context.

In August 2017 India completed seven decades of existence as a free and independent nation state. Its Constitution, which was adopted some time after independence, on 26 January 1950, will reach that milestone in 2020. Within India, the meaning, impact and legacy of the Constitution are sites of severe contestation. Supporters of the Constitution—and the tradition of constitutional democracy it has sought to engender—note the huge challenges involved in conceiving and implementing a foundational vision for a subcontinental nation that had never been a single political entity prior to colonialism. To its supporters, the fact that the Constitution has managed to keep the Indian nation together for nearly 70 years as a single national entity is an achievement in itself. That apart, they note the constitutional order's relative success in bringing about economic development, which is causing poverty rates to decline consistently, amidst the challenge of a constantly growing population. Supporters also point to the social reform programmes that have been initiated to tackle entrenched problems of discrimination based on caste, class and gender, the successful establishment of political institutions and a move away from the feudalistic, hierarchical and oppressive patterns of individual and governmental conduct that were pervasive at the time of independence.

Critics of the contemporary legal and constitutional order question whether it has been able to make significant progress on any of the three founding objectives outlined earlier. They note that large sections of India's territory, estimated at about one-fifth of India's total land mass, are under the control of insurgent groups, raising doubts about the nation's territorial integrity. On the issue of economic development, such critics draw attention to high levels of absolute poverty in contemporary India. Based on reports of official government sources and of global bodies such as the United Nations Development Programme and the World Bank, the number of people living below the poverty line ranges between 250 million and 320 million (exceeding the population of India at the time of independence and constituting a high proportion of its current population, which stands at about 1.2 billion). Finally, the critics point to regular outbursts of communal violence and continuing discrimination on the basis of caste and gender to raise doubts about constitutionally sanctioned efforts to tackle these issues. The critics also blame the constitutional order for many other ills that afflict the Indian nation: fundamental problems of governance stemming from the absence of basic forms of infrastructure (roads, sanitation, public health facilities); rampant and widespread corruption; high rates of violence against women, religious and ethnic minorities; and inadequate systems of accountability across legal and governance systems among others. Other persisting problems—such as the unresolved constitutional status and frequent bouts of violence in the State of Jammu and Kashmir—give pause to anyone who considers the condition of the Indian constitutional system to be stable. Some other critics believe that alternative models of constitutionalism may be more appropriate for India.

In developing the narrative for this volume, my attempt will be to present the Indian Constitution as a site for continuing contestations of the sort described above. There is a tendency (evident particularly in early scholarship, but one that continues in some contemporary strains) in Indian constitutional scholarship to write about the Constitution in celebratory terms, to present it as a complete product in itself, awaiting only implementation. This trend may have been caused by the perception among a group of constitutional scholars that such a portrayal was necessary to secure the Constitution's legitimacy. However, such attempts have had the unintended effect of portraying the Constitution as being a far more definitive and decisive document—and system—than is the case in reality. By presenting the Constitution as a 'living' text, I will attempt to emphasise the many ambiguities and gaps that it contains—sometimes by deliberate design, at other times by unintended omissions—and its innate flexibility, which is not surprising given how different in form it is from pre-existing Constitutions.

In recounting the story of Indian constitutionalism, this book seeks to account for the role that the Constitution of India played in two important moments in modern India's history. These are, respectively, 1947 and 1991. The first marks the year of political independence. The second marks the date when, in the view of a number of scholars and citizens, India became 'economically free' and initiated policies that have led to a transformation of the nature of the Indian state and polity, leading to its much-vaunted economic might. The second period is also significant because it witnessed a range of social and political events that brought about monumental changes in the way social relations and politics are conducted in India. Much conventional constitutional scholarship in India has focused on the role that the Constitution played in 1947 and the crucial four decades that followed. The formal Constitution has played a less prominent but nevertheless critical role in shaping events that have occurred since 1991. The change in the nature and shape of the regulatory state in India since 1991—a transformation that has been brought about while ostensibly staying within the terms of the existing constitutional order—is a significant focus of the book. While issues of development have always been a central part of constitutional debates in India, they have taken on a different dimension in the era of globalisation and neoliberalism that characterises post-1991 India.

II. APPROACH AND ORIENTATION OF THE BOOK

Taking its cue from the series of which this book is a part, one objective of the book project is to provide an account of Indian constitutionalism that is both sensitive to, and oriented towards, comparative analysis. This goal is pursued not so much by drawing explicit comparisons with other constitutional systems (which are covered in relevant places where the framers referred to comparative experience), but by seeking to describe developments in India in terms that go beyond the doctrinal focus that domestic lawyers would employ to address them. Instead, the book seeks to locate the events being described and analysed within their broader political and socio-economic context. This, it is hoped, will make the book accessible to audiences within India beyond the legal community, such as students from the social sciences and the humanities, and the curious but uninformed ordinary citizen who seeks a succinct base of knowledge about the evolution of India's constitutional culture and traditions.

I have made some specific choices which shape the way the book addresses the vast range of issues it could potentially cover. The first of these is that the book steers clear of a tendency in Indian legal and constitutional scholarship to focus almost exclusively on the Indian judiciary—and more specifically, on the case law of its Supreme Court—when addressing constitutional issues. This is true of the celebrated commentaries on the Constitution of India from soon after its adoption right through to the present day. These works, while often of great technical ability, and demonstrative of fascinating insights and industry, are almost wholly focused on the judgments and orders of the Supreme Court of India. This apex court-centric nature of Indian legal scholarship has been noted by both foreign scholars and non-legal scholars, who often find the mass of cases and conflicting decisions bewildering and are puzzled by the almost complete lack of reference to the wider socio-economic context that informs these cases. Indeed, very little attention is paid in the mainstream works of constitutional scholarship to the actual conditions of the citizens who bring the cases to the Court and to the impact of the decisions on the lives of citizens in their wake. This is not a malady that is peculiar to India: many other jurisdictions have had to confront such criticism of doctrinal, court-centric scholarship. I should clarify that this book does not entirely avoid doctrinal developments, which are extremely important to understand how constitutional text has evolved and been interpreted across time. Nevertheless, this book has far less doctrine than might be expected in a book on the constitutional law of India.

My choice is dictated by two considerations. The first is that there is, by now, a considerable body of scholarship which provides reasonably good resources to obtain an understanding of the doctrinal output of the judiciary on important constitutional questions. In the main this consists of several practitioner-oriented commentaries that are frequently revised to take account of the constant updating of the judiciary's case law. In addition, the recently published *Oxford Handbook of the Indian Constitution* is an excellent resource which meticulously and comprehensively covers the most significant doctrinal developments in Indian constitutional law up to 2015 across its 56 chapters. This book relies heavily on several of these chapters where necessary.

The second reason for preferring a wider view of constitutional issues in India is the insight offered by a respected scholar of comparative constitutional law on this issue. In a short but compelling essay written in the early part of this century, Kim Lane Scheppele urged scholars to reach beyond 'constitutional case law and the operation of a high court' to obtain a more profound understanding of constitutionalism. This is because, Scheppele emphasises, 'the fundamental features of a constitutional order are the results of political bargains that go beyond the interpretive capacities of courts'.[1] I should clarify that I am not a political scientist by training and do not adopt an exclusive focus on 'political bargains' on every constitutional issue that is the focus of the book. I take the 'contextual' part of the title of the series to mean a nod to the wider socio-economic and political context of the nation under focus. Each chapter of the book does focus on the motivations and concerns of the framers of the Constitution, which go beyond the strictly legal reasons offered by them. But they also go beyond to look at the way the political system in India has evolved over time and how the policies of the particular government in power at the Centre influence the legal and constitutional stances adopted by it.

A second general point about the methodological orientation of the book needs to be emphasised here. The book is about the Constitution of India, which is the longest Constitution in the world. It therefore contains an enormous amount of text. However, as is commonly known and is once again not unique to the Indian context, much of what becomes constitutionally salient is derived from a very small proportion of the actual text of the Constitution. Consequently, even seasoned lawyers and legal academics are quite unaware of large portions of the text of the Constitution. I seek to address this lacuna by drawing attention specifically to the textual provisions relating to the thematic subject of each chapter. I also focus much more attention than is usually accorded to the constitutional history of the provisions, relying upon the development of ideas and concepts across the colonial period and through the various stages of the Constituent Assembly. This is to emphasise the vast range of materials that are available on the making of the Indian Constitution, which are much neglected and have not yet been sufficiently mined and studied. The material

[1] Kim Lane Scheppele, 'The Agendas of Comparative Constitutionalism' (2003) Spring *Law and Courts* 5, 15.

available to the student of the Indian Constitution in understanding why it contains what it does and the reasons for such choices may well be unprecedented in the annals of the history of Constitution making. It is therefore a pity that this has not been adequately focused upon. My hope is that by drawing upon these materials in a systematic way, a signal can also be sent out on further research that needs to be conducted on the Indian constitutional tradition. I should add the caveat that my methodological choices should not be read as signalling my interpretive preference for text or for privileging the original intent/ vision of the framers. Nevertheless, both text and original intent gain enormous importance in Indian constitutional interpretation because of the length and relatively recent origin of that document.

III. BRIEF OUTLINE OF CHAPTERS

The book consists of nine chapters. This brief Introduction is followed by Chapter 1, which sets out the historical context necessary for appreciating the drafting of the Constitution of India, paying particular attention to the processes adopted by the Constituent Assembly of India for drafting the text of the Constitution across the nearly three-year period from November 1946 to 1949. While this broad history is reasonably well known to scholars of the Indian constitutional tradition, an aspect that I seek to emphasise here is the repeated efforts by Indian nationalists at Constitution making that occurred during the period between 1895 and 1946. The remaining chapters adopt a predominantly institutional approach to issues of constitutional law and politics, focusing on the major constitutionally created institutions and structures to channel and control the exercise of political authority. Chapters 2–5 cover the major institutions of Indian constitutional governance—the Executive and Parliament; federalism and local government; the Judiciary (with its guardianship role of the fundamental rights and directive principles); and technocratic institutions (covering the Election Commission, the office of the Comptroller and Auditor General and new regulatory institutions). Chapter 6, the longest in the book, focuses on India's unique challenges in regulating its multiple diversities and identities. Chapter 7 addresses the issue of constitutional change and amendment. This is followed by the concluding chapter, which focuses on the contemporary period in Indian constitutionalism before attempting an overall assessment of the Indian constitutional experience in dialogue with selected scholarly accounts. A number of topics that could be covered in a discussion of constitutionalism in India have been excluded for the sake of thematic and analytic coherence and due to constraints of space. The references for further reading aim to guide the interested reader to other resources, including for allied topics that could not be covered here. This book covers legal and political developments until May 2017.

1

Origins and Crafting of the Constitution

Pre-colonial forms of governance – Constitutional forms of government under the East India Company and The British Raj – Nationalist efforts at Constitution making – Crafting a Constitution for the new republic

I. INTRODUCTION

INDIA HAS A long civilisational history dating back to ancient times. Historians have noted how the many kingdoms and dynasties that ruled over parts of the Indian subcontinent from 500 BC onwards experimented with and implemented many innovative features of law and governance.[1] As we will see later in this book, some aspects of the older traditions of the law survive in the contemporary legal system, especially in the realm of religious laws, and have influenced the nature of multiculturalism in Indian constitutionalism in significant ways. These ancient traditions of law and governance are often invoked in contemporary political and constitutional discourse, sometimes by judges and Cabinet Ministers, and accounting for them is important to understand contemporary constitutional discourse. However, all these measures were engineered while staying broadly within the structural framework of monarchical and dynastic systems, which, despite their many variations, did not impose constitutional limits upon the authority of the ultimate power holder. Nevertheless, some scholars have sought

[1] See generally, PV Kane, *History of Dharmasastra: Ancient and Medieval Religious and Civil Law*, 2nd edn, (Pune, Bhandarkar Oriental Research Institute, 1968–1975); John Keay, *India: A History* (New York, Gloria Press, 2000).

to argue that ideas similar to modern notions of constitutionalism existed in India from very early times.[2]

This chapter adopts the stance that while law and governance in India have a long pedigree, and one can find instances of many innovative forms of legal thinking in ancient and medieval India until the Mughal period, constitutionalism in India, as in other parts of Asia and Africa, is a modern project, whose origins can be traced to much more recent times. The chapter thus focuses on the colonial period, particularly since 1857, when, in the aftermath of an event that the British colonial regime referred to as the Mutiny and the nationalist movement would term the First War of Independence, the British government formally took over charge from the East India Company. Soon thereafter, the demand for forms of constitutional government was increasingly articulated by leaders of the nascent Indian nationalist movement starting from the late nineteenth century. In response to such demands, the colonial authorities ceded constitutional powers to the representatives of the people of the Indian subcontinent gradually over a period of half a century, culminating in the independence of the new nations of South Asia through the Indian Independence Act 1947. There is a rich body of work that documents this complex narrative.[3] My goal is to sketch the broad contours of that narrative, with a focus on specific parts that are relevant for the purposes of this book project.

Specifically, the chapter seeks to track two parallel lines of development—the gradual ceding of constitutional powers by the colonial government from 1861 onwards, and the increasingly sophisticated constitutional demands raised by the nationalist movement (represented principally by the Indian National Congress, which was formed in 1885). A focus on both tracks is essential for understanding the

[2] See, eg, M Rama Jois, *Legal and Constitutional History of India* (Gurgaon, Universal Law Publishing, 2012, first edition 1984). For a contrary view, see Arun K Thiruvengadam, 'Excavating Constitutional Antecedents in Asia: An Essay on the Potential and Perils' (2013) 88(1) *Chicago-Kent Law Review* 45–61.

[3] See generally, WAJ Archibald, *Outlines of Indian Constitutional History* (London, Curzon Press, 1926), AB Keith, *A Constitutional History of India 1600–1935* (Delhi, Pacific Publication, 1937, reprinted 2010) and MP Singh, *Outlines of Indian Legal and Constitutional History*, 8th edn (New Delhi, Universal Law Publishing, 2006).

complex ways in which the crafting of the Constitution of India of 1950 sought, simultaneously, to achieve two seemingly contradictory objectives: the adaptation of colonial structures of governance that were premised on efficiency in achieving imperial, exploitative goals, with the insertion of new instruments and institutions to usher in an egalitarian and democratic spirit within the new constitutional order. While seeking to provide a chronological account that spans three-and-a-half centuries, my goal will be to focus on key moments that help set out the overall narrative in order not to overwhelm the reader with historical detail.

Descriptively, the chapter begins with a short section on the entry of the East India Company into India towards the end of the Mughal Empire, and the legal rules and systems it established to initially supplement and eventually supplant the system that existed in India during the Mughal era. This is followed by an overview of the reforms brought about in the post-1857 era when the British government formally took over charge of the Indian colony. Section III analyses the significant period of about 90 years during which many constitutional ideas and reforms were discussed and introduced, focusing on the perspective of the colonial authorities. Thereafter, Section IV details the early attempts at Constitution making by the Indian nationalists. Section V describes the making of the Constitution of India in the Constituent Assembly during its nearly three-year tenure between 1946 and 1949.

II. THE MUGHALS AND THE EAST INDIA COMPANY (1550–1857)

The Mughals were the last of the great empires to control large portions of the territory of modern-day India before the advent of colonial rule. The Mughal Empire was at its zenith from the middle of the sixteenth century until the early part of the eighteenth century, shortly before the death of Emperor Aurangzeb in 1707. Although it covered a vast territory across present-day India, the Mughal Empire was primarily concerned with issues of commerce, trade and taxation. Ideas of constitutional governance, as understood in the contemporary modern sense, were not well developed in any of the pre-colonial regimes in India. As in many other parts of Asia and Africa, such ideas were often developed by leaders of anti-colonial movements whose introduction to ideas of nationalism, liberalism and constitutional democracy emerged through their exposure—either through education or through texts—to discourses in the metropolitan centres of colonial rule.

The Portuguese were the first Europeans to arrive in India in 1503, followed successively by the French, the Dutch and the English. By the early part of the seventeenth century, several European trading posts had been established in India. By the time the Mughal Empire went into active decline around the middle of the eighteenth century, the struggle for control over trade between the European powers was largely between the British and French as other European powers had been marginalised. Eventually, the British became the dominant European power in the Indian subcontinent.

The British presence in India was established through the East India Company, which had been created through a Royal Charter issued by Queen Elizabeth in 1600 as a mercantile body that was to possess a trading monopoly in the East. Soon after its creation, the East India Company was able to obtain a toe-hold in India during the reign of the Mughal Emperor Jahangir and initially focused on expanding its commercial and mercantile activities in India. The East India Company was initially granted certain limited powers of a legislative character, including the power to impose penalties, to enable it to perform its commercial functions.[4] As the Company's operations expanded, it demanded and obtained greater legislative, executive and ultimately, judicial powers. The initial laws issued by the Company sought to establish courts and other institutions of English/continental law in several of the territories under their control. This led later to the codification of criminal, civil and 'personal' laws of various Indian religious communities. Over time, the Company officials obtained powers similar to legislators for India, but continued to deny the responsibilities that came with exercising effective State authority in India.[5]

[4] Keith (n 3) 5–6.

[5] See generally, Ramkrishna Mukherji, *The Rise and Fall of the East India Company: A Sociological Appraisal* (New York, Monthly Review Press, 1974); Cyril Henry Philips, *The East India Company, 1784–1834* (Manchester, Manchester University Press, 1961); Tirthankar Roy, *The East India Company: The World's Most Powerful Corporation* (New Delhi, Penguin Books, 2012).

For nearly a century before its formal control over India ended, from about the middle of the eighteenth century until the middle of the nineteenth century, the Company conducted itself as a proxy for the British government. The foundation of the colonial legal order was established in India during this period. The Company followed a practice of governing the Indian colony through a Governor-General and his Legislative Council at the Central level, and through a Governor and his Legislative Council at the level of the provinces. Appointments to these offices were based on nominations, which in turn depended on the judgement of the Company and its supervising governmental authorities.

By the late eighteenth century, the East India Company adopted the coercive, administrative and financial processes typical of contemporaneous empires, and gradually took on more of the functions of sovereignty, such as collecting revenues, making treaties or fighting wars with regional potentates and exercising juridical authority.[6] This was accompanied by high levels of corruption, acts of despotism, and a growing perception that the officials of the Company were exploitative and immoral in their extractive zeal. This led to demands, primarily from within Britain, that the British Parliament intervene to remedy the situation, which in turn led to legislative acts to regulate the functioning of the East India Company. In response, the British Parliament enacted the Regulating Act 1773 to overhaul the management and operations of the East India Company. A decade later, to rebut the perception that the Regulating Act was not effective in its mission, the East India Company Act 1784 sought to further these reforms by establishing a Board of Control and by strengthening the British government's regulatory powers over the Company. The clamour against company misrule also resulted in the impeachment of the former Governor-General, Warren Hastings, which, while ultimately unsuccessful, ignited a heated domestic debate championed by figures such as Edmund Burke on empire, liberalism and its consequences for ideas of British governance and democracy.

[6] Jane Burbank and Frederick Cooper, *Empires in World History* (Princeton, NJ, Princeton University Press, 2010) 170–78, 240–45.

III. THE BRITISH RAJ AND COLONIAL FORMS OF CONSTITUTIONAL GOVERNMENT (1858–1947)—A BIRD'S EYE VIEW

> It was the aim of the greatest among the early British administrators in India to train the peoples of India to govern and protect themselves … rather than to establish the rule of a British bureaucracy.
>
> Arthur Berridale Keith[7]

This statement captures, in overarching terms, the view of a section of the British colonial administrators about the overall objective of colonial government in India during the period of direct British rule. This 'pedagogical' self-perception of the colonial role was severely contested by the growing nationalist movement and, in the next section, we will see how it led the nationalists to develop constitutional documents that set out a competing vision for constitutionalism in India. At the same time, each constitutional development initiated by the colonial authorities across this period was at least in part a response to the nationalist movement's criticism of the previous initiative. In what follows, due to constraints of space, I focus on significant legislative instruments enacted by the British Parliament during this period, rather than other events that were also salient. This survey of laws enables one to appreciate how the colonial forms of constitutional government evolved over this nine-decade period.

The Great Indian Mutiny of 1857, or the First War of Independence as it came to be called by the nationalists, spelt the death-knell of the rule of the East India Company, which had faced criticism domestically within Britain for over a century. Through the enactment of the Government of India Act 1858 by the British Parliament, the task of governing India was formally transferred to the British Crown, acting through the Secretary of State. The colony of India was formally ruled by the British government for 90 years (from 1858 to 1947), a period which is also referred to as the 'British Raj'. One major change made to the structure of the Governor-General's Legislative Council from the time of the rule of the Company was that under the new regime, an Executive Council was also set up to aid the newly created office of the Viceroy, which replaced the office of the Governor-General of India.

[7] Keith (n 3) 1.

A. Early Constitutional Developments in the Indian Councils Acts

Despite the formal change, little of substance changed on the ground in colonial India, at least initially. The Indian Councils Act 1861 made a few technical changes to the governmental superstructure that had been used by the East India Company to govern India, without addressing the increasing demand for representation in the Councils by Indians. The demand for real change became more pressing after the formation of the Indian National Congress in 1885. This event represented the growing clout of the emerging Indian middle class, which was still small in numerical terms but whose growth was a consequence of the introduction of schools, the press and associational forms facilitated by the policies of the East India Company. Initially, the Congress was dominated by a moderate wing, led by Gopal Krishna Gokhale, who chose the path of negotiating with the colonial authorities through the route of petitions to seek incremental reforms, while engaging in social service alongside.

The Indian Councils Act 1892 sought to respond to the demand of the nationalists seeking greater representation for Indians in the Legislative Councils by making some more minor administrative changes. However, the worsening economic and political situation, caused by famine, the spread of bubonic plague and the growing popularity of the leader of the extremist wing of the Congress, Bal Gangadhar Tilak, led to the perception that these were feeble attempts to assuage a rising tidal wave of demands for reform. These rising demands were not satisfied by the next legislative measure, the Indian Councils Act 1909, which increased the representative capacity of the Legislative Councils, extended their powers and also recommended that Indians be appointed within the Governor-General's Council. However, like its predecessor enactments, it effectively left control in the hands of the executive, with little restraint on its powers. It therefore lacked credibility as a serious initiative towards constitutional reform, if measured by the introduction of effective checks and balances on the power of the imperial authorities. Keith approvingly notes that the authors of this particular reform 'absolutely disclaimed the idea of introducing responsible government or parliamentary institutions within India'.[8]

[8] ibid 258.

They did, however, seek to 'consult' Indians in matters affecting their interests. The overall approach of British administrators (and scholars such as Keith who recorded their efforts) was to oppose the introduction of representative politics of the British type in India, convinced as they were, along with leading British liberals like JS Mill, that Indians were not ready, because of the stage of their civilisation, for full liberal democratic politics.

To understand why there was a mismatch between the approaches of the colonial administrators and the growing nationalist movement, it is important to recall that the Indian nationalists were closely following developments across the globe, and especially in other British colonies. The granting of Dominion status, with concomitant concessions to autonomy and self-rule, to Canada in 1867, to Australia in 1901 and to South Africa in 1910 emboldened the nationalists to seek similar concessions from the British for Indians as had been made for white settler populations in these colonies. However, the British were not willing to concede such a status to Indians for a much longer time to come. Among the first to understand this was Mohandas Gandhi, who had struggled unsuccessfully in South Africa through much of the 1890s and the 1900s to seek parity with the white settler population for his fellow Indians in South Africa. Upon his return to India in 1915, Gandhi began a process of self-discovery and re-examination of his beliefs in relation to his approach towards British colonial authorities. He ultimately concluded by 1919 that the British would never treat Indians on a par with the white settler colonies and that a different approach would be required.

B. The Government of India Acts of 1909 and 1919

To return to the chronology of colonial concessions to constitutional governance for Indians, Keith notes that the reforms of 1909–12 were 'clearly unlikely' to satisfy the demands of the extremist wing of the Congress party led by Bal Gangadhar Tilak, and 'in fact went but a small way to conciliate the moderates'[9] led by Gopal Krishna Gandhi, who had become a mentor to Mohandas Gandhi. The First World War and the stellar role played by Indian soldiers in the important theatres

[9] ibid 264.

of the war, made it imperative that the colonial government be seen to be responsive to the growing demand of Indians for representative government.

It was against this context that the Government of India Act 1919 was enacted in December 1919, which promised some significant changes 'with a view of the progressive realization of responsible government in India'.[10] In its details, the Act sought to fulfil its promises by emphasising greater autonomy to the provinces, and by making changes to the powers of the Secretary of State and his Council, and those of the Central and provincial governments. The Act introduced a system of 'dyarchy' in the provinces, whereby for some subjects in a 'transferred list' authority to legislate would be subject to scrutiny and accountability by the Provincial Council. These reforms were truly significant in that they held the prospect of enabling Indians to exercise real legislative power, especially at the provincial level. However, the Act offset the impact of these changes by providing a very restricted franchise, by making very small budgets available to provincial legislatures, and by including rural and special-interest seats that were perceived as amenable to control by the colonial authorities. The reforms sought to be ushered in by the Act of 1919 were diluted by the near simultaneous enactment of the draconian Rowlatt Act 1919 and the brutal massacre ordered by General Dwyer at the Jallianwala Bagh, which turned public opinion against the colonial authorities in a definitive manner. Although the Government of India Act 1919 did not have a great impact in practice, its innovations were later discussed for inclusion in the text of the Constitution of independent India, and for this reason it remains a significant constitutional landmark, apart from being an improvement on its predecessor enactments.

By 1920 Mohandas Gandhi had emerged as the undisputed leader of the Congress. Although he started as a protégé of Gokhale, his experience of following 'moderate' politics in South Africa appears to have convinced him of the limitations of such an approach. After his return to India in 1915, Gandhi began to initiate campaigns that had seeds

[10] This quotation is taken from the statement of the newly appointed Secretary of State, Edwin Montague, who took office in June 1917. Montague, together with Lord Chelmsford, the erstwhile Viceroy of India, authored the Montague-Chelmsford report, which formed the basis of the Government of India Act of 1919.

in the experiments that he had begun while in South Africa. These campaigns, built on the strategies of *satyagraha* ('striving for truth') and *ahimsa* ('non-violence'), in turn converted the Indian National Congress from an elite group of middle class intellectuals to a mass movement with deep roots across the Indian subcontinent. In the aftermath of the Jallianwala Bagh massacre, Gandhi started a Non-Cooperation movement which found support across the whole of British India and signalled to the colonial authorities that a new kind of anti-colonial movement had emerged.

C. The Government of India Act 1935 and the Indian Independence Act 1947

The next significant law to be passed by the British Parliament to regulate constitutional development in India was the Government of India Act 1935. This law made some pivotal changes and introduced many elements, especially in relation to its federal provisions, that were ultimately retained by the Constitution of India. The Act of 1935 introduced direct elections and expanded the franchise, enabling several million Indians to exercise voting rights. It also established the Federal Court in India, which became an important judicial institution, and was both the predecessor and a role model of sorts for the Supreme Court that was instituted by the eventual Constitution of India. Indeed, one respected scholar has asserted that as much as 'seventy-five percent' of the Government of India Act 1935 was to find place in the new Constitution of independent India.[11] However, this should not lead to the impression that the Act of 1935 was a document that actively sought to secure 'responsible government' for Indians. While it had several notable features, the Act of 1935 was apace with other colonial constitutional documents in empowering the colonial executive with supreme powers, including the power to take back any of those conferred upon

[11] Subhash C Kashyap, *Our Constitution: An Introduction to India's Constitution and Constitutional Law* (New Delhi, National Book Trust, 2004) 4–5. See also Arvind Elangovan, 'Provincial Autonomy, Sir Benegal Narsing Rau, and an Improbable Imagination of Constitutionalism in India, 1935–38' (2016) May, *Comparative Studies of South Asia, Africa and the Middle East* 66–82 (noting that the continuity can also be explained by the fact that Sir BN Rau was an important contributory draftsperson of both constitutional documents).

bodies where Indians were allowed to exercise legislative and executive power. The Act of 1935 abolished the system of dyarchy introduced by the Act of 1919, which had proven to be both unpopular and impractical. It went further than any other colonial statute in empowering provincial governments but, as mentioned earlier, also enabled the colonial executive to step in and retrieve powers should it perceive any threat. This was viewed as paternalistic and an incurable flaw by the nationalist movement. As we will see in the next section, by this time the nationalist movement had experimented with several constitutional documents and had presented them to the colonial authorities. What is striking about the Act of 1935 is how completely it ignored the demands of the nationalist movement on many fronts, including their demand for a Bill of Rights, and how it represented a step back even from the Act of 1919. It is important to recall that the Act of 1935 was the result of a compromise between those who sought to advance responsible government in India and those who were completely opposed to it. Since the law was enacted by a Conservative government, it was perhaps to be expected that those opposed to granting any meaningful concessions to the Indian nationalist movement won out.

As it happened, the federal provisions of the Act of 1935 never came into effect. The Act of 1935 came into force in relation to the provinces only in 1937. In elections held in 1937, Congress governments were elected in eight out of 11 provinces. For two years until 1939, when the Indian National Congress decided that its governments in the provinces would resign en masse in protest against the British government's unilateral decision that British India was to join the Allied cause in the Second World War, the Congress had, for the first time, direct experience of governance. This was to prove crucial for many reasons and also explained why, despite their awareness of the flaws of the Act of 1935, the Congress was willing to retain elements of the scheme of the Act of 1935 in the Constitution of independent India.

As noted above, the start of the Second World War in 1939 affected the implementation of the Act of 1935. As in the case of the First War, Indian soldiers were used extensively in the major theatres of the war, and India's involvement in the war once again led to demands for the grant of independence in exchange for loyalty to the Allied cause.[12]

[12] See generally, Srinath Raghavan, *India's War: The Making of Modern South Asia*, 1939–45 (New Delhi, Allen Lane, 2016).

These efforts did not yield much result due to opposition from Conservative politicians in England.

Once the Second War ended in 1945, a Labour government under Clement Atlee was elected. Atlee's government brought about radical reforms within the UK and presided over the start of the decolonisation of the British Empire in South Asia. Prime Minister Atlee's government took a realistic view of the following factors in reaching its decision to exit from the colonies: the state of the UK's poor finances in the post-War era; the international pressure that the UK was facing for the hypocrisy between its rhetoric against the Axis powers and its own oppressive conduct in its colonies; and the lack of confidence expressed by imperial generals about the ability of the Indian army to remain impervious to the call of nationalism.

The Indian Independence Act 1947 was the principal legal instrument by which the new nations of Pakistan and India came into being in August 1947. Its effect was to formally bring to an end 182 years of British rule in India, confer the status of dominions upon the new nations of Pakistan and India from 15 August 1947, and provide for legal and administrative continuity until the new constitutional orders in both nations emerged. In India the process of creating a new Constitution had begun formally on 9 December 1946, when the Constituent Assembly held its first sitting. Section V of this chapter will delve into the details about the body and its processes. However, since this factor is underemphasised in the current literature, it is important to acknowledge that the intellectual groundwork for the process of crafting a new Constitution for independent India was a process that began at least half a century before the first sitting of the newly constituted Constituent Assembly. It is to this important historical aspect that we turn in the next section.

IV. THE NATIONALIST MOVEMENT AND THE BUILD-UP OF ATTEMPTS AT CONSTITUTION MAKING (1895–1947)—A WORM'S EYE VIEW

As noted in the previous section, the Indian National Congress had been through a process of change and evolution since its founding in 1885. At first, it was a small organisation formed of middle and upper class Indians and was derisively referred to as a 'debating club'. By 1920, under Gandhi's charismatic leadership, it had transformed into a mass movement that grew in numbers and popularity almost continuously until India gained independence in 1947. In the previous section it was noted how the Congress resisted and opposed the incremental and often painfully slow concessions made by the British colonial regime towards providing autonomy and self-governance to Indians. However, the Congress was not just an oppositional force; it was equally a constructive force, and was simultaneously involved in creating a new vision for the independent country that India would eventually become. This nation- and Constitution-building aspect of the Congress's workings has been relatively neglected in contrast to the large body of work that has studied its resistance to colonial constitutional statutes by demanding greater autonomy as a means towards *Swaraj* or self-rule. This section seeks to focus on the constitutional documents that were drafted by the Congress from fairly early on in its history. The focus will be on the evolution of this constitutional vision as the Congress's own sense of what the independent Indian nation would represent and symbolise changed over time.

A. The Earliest Attempts at Constitution Making (1885–95)

An early example of the first phase of the Congress is to be found in two resolutions passed by the 1889 session of the Indian National Congress that was held in Bombay. These resolutions, passed within five years of its inception, saw the Congress seeking more representation for Indians in the Legislative Councils, which were important legislative institutions created under the Indian Councils Act to govern India.[13]

However, soon thereafter, in 1895, came the Constitution of India Bill. While its author remains unverified, the document states that it had been prepared after a study of the Constitutions of the US and Brazil, and contained provisions relating to the government of India which were housed in separate chapters detailing provisions relating to the legislature, executive and judiciary.[14] The Bill also contained a set of rights provisions which primarily sought guarantees of civil and

[13] The full text of the two resolutions is reproduced in B. Shiva Rao (ed), *The Framing of India's Constitution: Select Documents*, vols I–V (New Delhi, Universal Law Publishing, 1967, Reprint 2010) vol I, 3–4.

[14] The full text of the Constitution of India Bill is set out in ibid 5–14.

political rights. This was, from the point of view of the tradition of British constitutionalism, a radical demand since British constitutional culture, even today, is very sceptical about constitutionalised Bills of Rights. The Bill further sought to catalogue the issues that could potentially form the subject of legislation (an early form of the List system that would be used in the final Constitution to classify subject matter competence between the Central and State legislatures) and also made a bold attempt to catalogue the departments within the executive (equivalent to Ministers in our time). Consisting of 111 provisions, this Bill represented an early yet sophisticated attempt at drafting a Constitution for independent India. What is striking is that this document, conceived more than a half century before the eventual Constitution for independent India was drafted and adopted, anticipates many of the institutional issues that would come to dominate the imagination of the framers of the eventual Constitution.

B. Evolution of Constitution-making Efforts: The Commonwealth of India Bill 1925 and the Motilal Nehru Report 1928

As the Congress continued to grow and debates within it became more sophisticated, more resolutions, declarations and models continued to emerge. In 1918, at another annual session held in Bombay, the Congress issued a Declaration of Rights that sought a statute from the British Parliament recognising a series of rights for Indians on a par with British citizens. In the early 1920s, under the leadership of Annie Besant and the respected lawyer, Tej Bahadur Sapru, the Commonwealth of India Bill was drafted by a convention consisting of 255 persons endorsed by the Congress, and introduced into the British House of Commons in 1925 (where, once the first elected Labour government which took office in 1923 fell after the elections in 1924, its fate was sealed). Nevertheless, the contents of the Bill are noteworthy also because they influenced models of Constitutions that emerged in its wake. The Commonwealth of India Bill conceived of the right to local self-government and envisaged five levels of government across the village, taluk, district, province and Central level.[15] It guaranteed a set of rights which went beyond the classic civil and political rights

[15] For the full text of the Bill, see ibid 43–50.

(including the right to liberty, property, freedom of conscience and free expression) to social rights (specifically the right to free elementary education).

Shortly afterwards, at the Madras session of the Congress in 1927, it was resolved that a Swaraj Constitution would be drafted for India. This eventually led to the creation of a committee led by the senior Congress leader, Motilal Nehru, and consisting of others such as Tej Bahadur Sapru. The Nehru Report, as it came to be known, set out the text of a Constitution that was based on the principle of Dominion status for India (seeking parity with the colonies of Canada, Australia, New Zealand, South Africa and the Irish Free State) and devised a responsible government on the parliamentary model. As Niraja Jayal has argued, the Constitution set out in the Nehru Report was 'a rather exceptional document' as it envisioned many novel aspects.[16] It contained extensive provisions on rights, which directly inspired many provisions in the Fundamental Liberties chapter (Part III) of the eventual Constitution, while some others inspired provisions in the chapter on Directive Principles of State Policy (Part IV). The Nehru Report had more elaborate provisions on the structure and form of the three wings of government than any previous Constitution-making effort and also sought to tackle the thorny issue of communal representation explicitly.

C. Alternative Conceptions of the Constitution and the Sapru Committee Report (1945)

In the period after the Nehru Report was published in 1928, the Congress continued to demand greater autonomy from the colonial regime while also investing in developing its own constructive vision of what a Constitution for independent India should consist of. Once the Second World War began, followed by the 'Quit India' movement launched by the Congress in 1942, attempts at Constitution making in order to influence the new Constitution became even more urgent. Before turning to the Congress's attempts, it is worth taking note of three attempts by non-Congress individuals and groups which sought to provide alternative conceptions of the new Constitution.

[16] Niraja Gopal Jayal, *Citizenship and its Discontents: An Indian History* (Cambridge, MA, Harvard University Press, 2013) 138–39.

These include: MN Roy's *Constitution of India: A Draft* (1946), SN Agarwal's *Gandhian Constitution for Free India* (1946) and the Socialist Party's *Draft Constitution of Indian Republic* (1948).[17] Roy, a former Communist, authored a radical and populist Constitution which contained many guarantees of social rights. Agarwal's Constitution drew from Gandhian ideas of village-based decentralised governance. The Socialist Party's Constitution conspicuously left out the right to property. These alternative conceptions are worth emphasising to draw attention to the fact that while the Indian National Congress enjoyed great popular support, it had to contend with many other streams of opinion and thought, which often clashed with its own ideas and were difficult to build consensus upon given the wide range of interests and ideologies represented within the Congress itself. Recalling these facts is necessary to appreciate the importance of the inclusive style of decision making followed in the Constituent Assembly.

In December 1945 a committee under the leadership of Tej Bahadur Sapru and consisting of members including N Gopalaswami Ayyangar (who would play a pivotal role within the Constituent Assembly) was constituted to deal with the growing problem of communalism and the significant issue of minority rights. The Sapru Committee Report placed considerable emphasis on minority protection and the rights of minorities and became an influential model for these provisions in the eventual Constitution of India.[18]

V. CRAFTING A CONSTITUTION FOR INDEPENDENT INDIA: THE WORK OF THE CONSTITUENT ASSEMBLY

A. Background and Origin of the Constituent Assembly

The work of the Constituent Assembly of India has been described in laudatory, even heroic, terms.[19] It has also been the subject of strong

[17] ibid 143.

[18] This voluminous report also saw several notes of dissent drafted by some of the committee members. The full text of the report, being too large to be included in its entirety in the B Shiva Rao papers, is available online at <https://ia801407.us.archive.org/19/items/saprucommittee035520mbp/saprucommittee035520mbp.pdf>.

[19] The most prominent of these adulatory accounts is still Granville Austin, *The Indian Constitution: Cornerstone of a Nation* (New Delhi, Oxford University Press,

criticism, both contemporaneous and recent.[20] Regardless of whether one thinks of it as broadly positive or not, the result of the efforts of the framers of the Indian Constitution has been markedly influential across the post-colonial world, and its provisions came to be emulated in many other Constitutions. This section focuses on the origins of the Constituent Assembly, its processes and the main themes that it dealt with. In each subsequent chapter of the book the substantive work of the Constituent Assembly will be examined closely within the rubric of specific constitutional issues. Here, the purpose is to provide a broad, descriptive overview of some foundational matters.

As noted in the previous section, many Indians—and not just the leaders of the nationalist movement—had focused on the nature and type of Constitution that independent India should be governed by for a considerable period of time before independence was actually achieved. The Indian National Congress's previous efforts at Constitution making were marked by robust debate among several contending positions and had reached an advanced stage of deliberation whereby consensus was reached on some broad issues such as the need for a strong Bill of Rights, agreement that a parliamentary system would work best for India's many needs, and the need for a federal system which would guard against fissiparous tendencies while allowing India's diversity to flourish.

It is important to consider the backdrop against which the Constituent Assembly was established in December 1946. After the Second War and the election of Prime Minister Atlee's Labour government, Great Britain was finally willing to grant independence to India, albeit on its own terms. By the mid-1940s, the differences between the Indian National Congress and the Muslim League had become unbridgeable, in part because Mohammed Ali Jinnah, the leader of the Muslim League, who had been a prominent and important member of the

1966). Austin's account of the making of the Indian Constitution is regarded as authoritative, five decades on, but is written in stirring, adulatory tones which, even as it seeks to critique several aspects of the working of the framers, has a consistently positive appraisal of the process and the results reached.

[20] See generally, Shibanikinker Chaube, *Constituent Assembly of India: Springboard of Revolution*, 2nd edn (New Delhi, Manohar Publishers, 2000). A recent work which is scathing in its criticism of the overall 'imperial' approach of the Constituent Assembly is Mithi Mukherjee, *India in the Shadows of Empire* (New Delhi, Oxford University Press, 2010).

Congress during its crucial foundational period, was deeply sceptical that the Congress would successfully represent India's diversity beyond its own constituency, the dominant sections of the Hindu population. In 1945 Jinnah had expressed scepticism about the idea of a single Constituent Assembly, demanding two separate Assemblies for the new nations of India and Pakistan. For its part, the Congress, which had the backing of many Muslims, regarded Jinnah as unfairly attacking its secular character and exploiting long, simmering, communal tensions to build his 'two-nation' theory. The primary reason for Partition was undoubtedly the fact that these two significant political groupings could not come to an agreement on the future of colonial India. Their differences notwithstanding, there were several rounds of negotiations between the Congress and the Muslim League to begin the process of Constitution making even as such tensions persisted.

In May 1946 the Cabinet Mission, which had been established by the Atlee government to effect the transfer of power from the British to the Indians, delivered its report. Although both the Congress and the Muslim League had reservations, both formally accepted the plan, following which elections for the Constituent Assembly of India were held in July 1946. The Congress had long demanded a Constituent Assembly elected on the basis of universal adult suffrage. However, it gave in to the Cabinet Mission plan's proposal that the Constituent Assembly be indirectly elected, through the existing provincial legislatures, because it recognised that holding general elections on the basis of universal franchise would delay the important task of convening the Constituent Assembly. In addition, the Constituent Assembly also had representation from 600-odd Princely States. Of the 389 seats in the Constituent Assembly, 93 were accorded to the representatives of the Princely States, while the Congress (208) and the Muslim League (73) emerged as the dominant political parties.[21]

The first session of the Constituent Assembly was held on 9 December 1946 but given the tense atmosphere, not much business was transacted. On 13 December 1946 Nehru moved the 'Objectives Resolution', which set out the broad objectives and contours of the Constitution-making process. The Constituent Assembly also started

[21] Barbara N Ramusack, *The Indian Princes and their States* (Cambridge, Cambridge University Press, 2004) 8.

identifying the various working committees that would do the major work of drafting portions of the eventual Constitution but discussions did not begin in earnest until after independence. The Muslim League participated only half-heartedly in the Assembly's initial sessions; even this stopped after Jinnah instructed its members to boycott the Assembly in July 1947. The second and third sessions of the Constituent Assembly were held in January and April 1947 but the prospect of Partition ensured that substantive deliberations on important issues were minimal. Once the Indian Independence Act 1947 came into force on 15 August 1947, the Constituent Assembly was formally granted legal recognition, enabling it to move much faster towards its goal.

B. The Ambient Atmosphere of Constitution Making

The immediate effect of the Indian Independence Act 1947 was to make the Constituent Assembly also the Dominion Parliament. Members of the Assembly were simultaneously converted into parliamentarians and they spent half of their time dealing with day-to-day matters of government. Being seized of immediate problems inevitably affected their long-term constitutional vision, especially on crucial issues such as the powers that the executive and Parliament should have to restrict the rights of citizens. Awareness of the broader context at the time will help us situate their decisions better.

The Indian subcontinent in the period 1946–50 was, to put it mildly, in a state of turmoil. Although the Atlee government was praised for its decision to free India and its other South Asian colonies, this decision was made in an overly hasty manner, which made the by-then inevitable partition of the Indian subcontinent into the Muslim-dominated Pakistan and the Hindu-dominated India more messy and violent than it had to be. The British government had originally announced in February 1947 that it would quit India by June 1948. However, in June 1947 the newly appointed Viceroy, Lord Mountbatten, announced that Partition would come into effect not after a year, but in two months. This led to a sense of panic that historians—both British and Indian—believe exacerbated the problems involved. The subcontinent had been roiled by communal riots since August 1946. After starting in the eastern city of Calcutta, the riots had spread westwards through the State of Bihar, and to the capital in Delhi. By 1 November 1946 the death toll across India had reached 5,000. Once Partition was effected in August 1947 the subcontinent bore witness to 'the greatest mass migration in history': between 10 and 15 million people emigrated in response to the physical dismembering that led to the creation of the new State of Pakistan out of parts of the eastern and western perimeters of British India. Both new nations had to scramble to prevent mass carnage. In the latter, they were only partly successful: erstwhile estimates of the killings put the deaths at 1 million, while more recent historians believe that the death toll reached 2 million. On 30 January 1948, after he had made valiant efforts to quell the communal killings, Gandhi was assassinated in Delhi by a Hindu fundamentalist, who later blamed him for causing the partition of India by conceding to demands from Muslims.

There were other monumental problems. It is often forgotten that British India was not a cohesive political entity. The British governed a large portion of their territory in India indirectly, large pockets of which were constituted by the assorted chiefdoms and states of what were known as 'Princely States', of which there were 600-odd in existence. The new governments of India and Pakistan had to negotiate with each of these rulers in a bid to persuade them to join their territories or face the prospect of 'balkanisation' of the subcontinent. While most rulers eventually agreed to join the new States, some rulers held out: Junagadh (in western India), Hyderabad (in southern India) and Kashmir (in northern India, with a shared border with Pakistan). While the ruler of Junagadh eventually agreed to join India in November 1947, the Indian government had to send in its military to overwhelm the defiant ruler of Hyderabad in September 1948. Kashmir would prove to be a much harder case. It has been a continuing source of strife between India and Pakistan and has resulted in armed skirmishes on several occasions, including for many long months in 1947–48. The terms under which Kashmir joined India have led to continuing legal uncertainty and social and political strife nearly continuously to the present time.

In the immediate aftermath of Partition, many of the major Indian cities were flooded with refugees: the numbers ranged from half a million each in Delhi and Bombay to 1.7 million in Calcutta. In all, 8 million refugees are estimated to have entered India. What made the problem worse was the serious shortage of food, coupled with an inflationary crisis across the nation. These were only some manifestations of the grave economic problems that the British Empire had bequeathed to the subcontinent. Exploitative economic policies over two centuries resulted in a huge mass of the population being left in the grip of poverty, illiteracy and severe forms of underdevelopment. To address these issues, Nehru's government was determined to carve out space for a strong, centralising government in the Constitution that would be able to undertake the massive social development programmes that were urgently needed.

Those broader problems were made more acute because of the effects of Partition, the influx of refugees and the continuing spectre of communal and other forms of violence. The Communist parties in India, which enjoyed popular support in the Telangana region of the State of Hyderabad and in parts of Bengal, had, in February 1948, proclaimed the start of a general revolution in India and advocated forms of violence against the Indian State. The Indian government responded with propaganda and repression, causing their support to dwindle temporarily. The government also turned its instruments of force upon members of the Hindu fundamentalist groups in the wake of Gandhi's assassination, banning the Rashtriya Swayamsevak Sangh (RSS) and arresting several of its cadres. Having to deal with the threat posed by the RSS and Communists gave many of the leaders of free India an appreciation of the police powers enjoyed by the colonial State, and this appreciation is also reflected in their attitude towards restrictions on fundamental liberties that were then under discussion in the Assembly.

As we will see in subsequent chapters, these factual circumstances resulted in substantive and structural responses and solutions by the framers, which influenced the broader constitutional vision and specific institutional arrangements in the new and independent India.

C. Processes, Modes of Functioning and Stages of Constitution Making in the Constituent Assembly

The Constituent Assembly of India was in existence for 2 years, 11 months and 18 days, between its first session, which was held on 9 December 1946, and its final session on 26 November 1949 when the final draft of the Constitution was adopted. A great deal of attention was paid to the processes and procedures that would be followed in order to make the 389-member body function efficiently and democratically. For this purpose, the Assembly had drafted the services of Sir BN Rau, who had recently retired from the judicial side of the Indian Civil Services and had considerable exposure to comparative trends in Constitution making, having been involved in the making of the Constitution of Burma of 1947. The level of preparation and planning is evident from a note prepared by him in September 1946, which contained comprehensive notes on the modes of voting, whether sessions should be open or held *in camera*, how the Chairman should be chosen, and the language to be used, and cited precedents from the Constitution-making exercises in the US, Canada and South Africa.[22] The Assembly had access to a well-staffed Secretariat which was paid out of Central revenues and was thus able to attract high-calibre officials.[23]

The Assembly constituted itself into several committees (more than 15 in total) to complete its work. Of these, eight handled the major issues: Rules, Steering, Advisory, Drafting, Union Subjects, Union Constitution, Provincial Constitution and States. These eight committees had approximately 36 members in all. Granville Austin notes that some of the members of the Assembly were more equal than others because of their stature as leaders of the nationalist struggle and their role in government. Austin refers to four of these—Jawaharlal Nehru, Vallabhbhai Patel, Abul Kalam Azad and Rajendra Prasad—as the 'oligarchy', who wielded enormous authority within the Assembly while also holding important positions in the Dominion government. Another prominent member of the Assembly was BR Ambedkar, who was appointed, at the instance of Gandhi, as the Chairperson of the Drafting Committee. Dr Ambedkar was the undisputed leader of the former Untouchables and his appointment was an important symbolic reminder of the diversity within India. Other influential Assembly members, representing a range of regional, linguistic, religious and intellectual strands, included KT Shah, KM Munshi, Syama Prasad Mukherjee, Purushottamdas Tandon, Rafi Ahmed Kidwai, Bakshi Tek Chand and AK Aiyar. Significantly, the Assembly had 15 women representatives, with Hansa Mehta playing a significant role in the

[22] 'A Note on points of procedure—Sep 2, 1946' in Shiva Rao (n 13) 405–18.

[23] 'Setting up the Constituent Assembly Secretariat: Correspondence and Notes' in Shiva Rao (n 13) 360–72.

Fundamental Rights Sub Committee, and Begum Aizaz Rasul being a consistent and vocal voice on the floor of the Assembly across a range of issues. As several commentators have noted, the Congress, particularly after Partition when the departure of the Muslim League members left it with an overwhelming dominance in the Assembly, took several concrete measures to ensure that the constituents of the Assembly represented, as far as practicable, the range of interests present in Indian society.

The Assembly completed its functioning in five stages:[24]

(1) The Working Committees for specific subject areas met, debated and deliberated, and prepared reports often requiring several revisions. This process lasted from December 1946 until August 1947.

(2) Sir BN Rau, the Constitutional Advisor, considered these reports and prepared a first draft of the Constitution in collaboration with the Assembly Secretariat between August and October 1947.

(3) The Drafting Committee, led by Dr BR Ambedkar, scrutinised the draft Constitution prepared by Sir BN Rau and produced its own revised draft through daily meetings between 27 October 1947 and February 1948. This revised draft was then made public, inviting comments, suggestions and criticisms. The phase of gathering public responses and responding to them lasted from February to November 1948.

(4) In November 1948 Dr Ambedkar introduced the draft Constitution on the floor of the Constituent Assembly, following which a clause-by-clause deliberation was conducted over an 11-month period between 15 November 1948 and 17 October 1949. Following this, the Drafting Committee met again to revise the draft Constitution, incorporating all the amendments that had been accepted and giving final shape to the Constitution.

(5) In November 1949 Dr Ambedkar presented the final draft of the Constitution before the Assembly. Amendments were considered by the Assembly between 14 and 16 November and on 26 November 1949 the final draft of the Constitution was adopted by the Assembly.

[24] 'Progress of the Constitution through the Assembly' in Shiva Rao (n 13) 107–18.

Two months later, the Constitution of India was formally enforced on 26 January 1950. In its initially adopted form, it contained 395 articles (divided into 22 parts) and eight schedules, and was one of the world's longest Constitutions.

D. A Summary of Important Provisions and Themes in the Text and Process

In the remaining chapters of the book, several significant aspects of the Constitution of India will be focused upon at length. This section takes note of some striking aspects of the Constitution as a whole.

The Constitution of India established a modified version of the British Westminster form of parliamentary democracy in India. India is both a republic and a federal state, albeit with a stronger central authority than is the case in most federations. Important changes to the colonial order include a constitutionally entrenched Bill of Rights, an independent judiciary and a range of constitutionally empowered technocratic institutions (including the Election Commission, and the Comptroller and Auditor General) which are to serve as guardians of the constitutional order. The Constitution of India has been described as a 'transformative' document, given its commitments in relation to secularism, the removal of untouchability, and gender equality. The framers of the Indian Constitution made an important departure from the American model by providing a relatively easy amending procedure, which has, predictably, resulted in more than a 100 amendments to the Constitution in the six decades that it has been in force. What may not have been predictable is the innovation of the 'doctrine of basic structure' that came to be evolved by the Indian judiciary and will be examined more closely in Chapter 7.

On the substantive content and themes of the Constitution, Upendra Baxi has argued that the Indian Constitution can be viewed as oriented towards four goals: 'rights, justice, development and governance'. Baxi argues that each of these goals is 'intertwined and interconnected with the rest and in contradictory combination … with both the constitutional and social pasts and their images of the future'.[25]

[25] Upendra Baxi, '"A Known but Indifferent Judge" Situating Ronald Dworkin in Contemporary Indian Jurisprudence' (2003) 1(4) *International Journal of Constitutional Law* 557–89, 582.

Similarly, Uday Mehta has argued that the framers were guided by three broad objectives: (i) an overriding concern with national unity; (ii) a deep and anxious preoccupation with social issues such as poverty, illiteracy and economic development; and (iii) an intense concern with India's standing in the world.[26] Mehta, like Baxi, suggests that the first two goals identified by him in particular have the potential of moving towards ends which are quite different from those of the anti-colonial struggle which emphasised ideas of freedom. Benjamin Zachariah's tracing of the intellectual history of ideas of 'development' among the nationalist elites between 1930 and 1950 indicates that the term had an ambiguous quality and could encompass goals that were seemingly common among imperialists, capitalists and socialists.[27] These multiple understandings of 'development' had a role to play in the constitutional entrenchment of the goal of 'development' in the text and institutional structures of the Constitution of India.

The length of the Indian Constitution has been the subject of much commentary and speculation. It must be noted that unlike in the case of many federal states, where state Constitutions are housed separately, the Constitution of India sets out the provisions in relation to both the federal and State units. Its length has also been attributed to the anxiety of its framers to set out even minute details in black letter law for fear that failing to do so would lead to the constitutional order being dismantled quite early on. This is a reference to the many factors not conducive to constitutionalism in India: its long history of communal violence, the rampant illiteracy and underdevelopment that characterises its populace, the inequality in caste Hindu society which was exacerbated under the exploitative practices of colonialism, and the persistence of feudal mindsets in large parts of the country. That length has also enabled, as noted in the previous paragraph, the co-existence of many contradictory features within the overall model of Indian constitutionalism. Careful historical research is beginning to reveal that perhaps inevitably, the many different actors who contributed to the process had multiple motivations which were very often at odds with each other. The implementation of the Constitution has

[26] Uday Mehta, 'Constitutionalism' in Niraja Gopal Jayal and Pratap Mehta (eds), *The Oxford Handbook to Politics in India* (New Delhi, Oxford University Press, 2007) 16.

[27] Benjamin Zachariah, *Developing India: An Intellectual and Social History* (New Delhi, Oxford University Press, 2005) xv–xvii.

led to some portions of the text gaining more importance over others. Equally, as the practical politics of Indian constitutionalism has worked itself out, some of the expectations of the framers have been defied by the realities of politics, while some other expectations have proved to be very accurate. In its various chapters, this book seeks to highlight examples of both tendencies. This analysis seeks to emphasise the point that the framers of India's Constitution were extraordinary men and women, who often acted with great insight into the human condition but were not seers or astrologists. The cases where the framers misread expectations are nearly always as interesting as when they did foresee what would be required to regulate the constitutional politics of a specific issue.

An important issue that was much debated within the Constituent Assembly, and is also relevant for comparative audiences, was the heavy reliance on foreign models. This gave rise to several heated debates on the importance of autochthonous models of constitutional governance for securing both credibility and durability. Such debates have continued across the working of the Indian Constitution as the foreign origins of some provisions and institutions in the constitutional order have been attacked from time to time by a range of forces on the political Left and Right. The Indian Constitution-making exercise provides a valuable resource for those seeking to evaluate the perils and promise of cosmopolitanism in the art of Constitution making. What is striking about the Indian constitutional order is that it has not only survived, but also thrived across the relatively long period of its existence.

VI. CONCLUSION

This chapter has sought to provide an overview of forms of governance during the pre-colonial and colonial periods of Indian history. It has focused in particular on critical constitutional developments that occurred across a hundred years, from the middle of the nineteenth century to the middle of the twentieth century, to track significant events in the shaping of the constitutional order of India. While providing a broad overview of historical events, the chapter has sought to emphasise the interplay between the efforts of the colonial authorities to govern India while ceding to the increasingly vehement demands of the nationalist movement in respect of constitutional governance.

It has also focused on the themes and processes that characterised the working of the Indian Constituent Assembly as it designed and deliberated upon the content of its Constitution. An important theme that has been emphasised is the complexity of interactions between the forces of colonialism and constitutionalism, and the need to be alive to the motivations of these forces, which act in surprising and unexpected ways at times.[28]

Having obtained a sense of the overall nature of the Constitution and its making, we turn, in Chapter 2, to a focus on the most important institutions of governance under the Constitution of India: the Executive and the Parliament.

FURTHER READING

Granville Austin, *The Indian Constitution: Cornerstone of a Nation* (New Delhi, Oxford University Press, 1966).

Shibanikinker Chaube, *Constituent Assembly of India: Springboard of Revolution* 2nd edn (New Delhi, Manohar Publishers, 2000).

Rohit De, 'Constitutional Antecedents' in Sujit Choudhry, Madhav Khosla and Pratap Bhanu Mehta (eds), *The Oxford Handbook of the Indian Constitution* (Oxford, Oxford University Press, 2016) 17–37.

Arvind Elangovan, 'The Making of the Indian Constitution: A Case for a Non-Nationalist Approach' (2014) 12(1) *History Compass* 1.

Niraja Gopal Jayal, *Citizenship and its Discontents: An Indian History* (Cambridge, MA, Harvard University Press, 2013).

AB Keith, *A Constitutional History of India, 1600–1935* (New Delhi, Pacific Publications, reprint 2010).

Uday Mehta, 'Constitutionalism' in Nirja Gopal Jayal and Pratap Mehta (eds), *The Oxford Handbook to Politics in India* (New Delhi, Oxford University Press, 2007) 15–27.

Barbara D Metcalf and Thomas R Metcalf, *A Concise History of India* (Cambridge, Cambridge University Press, 2002).

[28] In this regard, the emerging historical work of Arvind Elangovan is significant. Among other issues, Elangovan focuses on the separate importance of the category of 'nationalism', which adds further complexity to this mix.

Mithi Mukherjee, *India in the Shadows of Empire: A Legal and Political History, 1774–1950* (New Delhi, Oxford University Press, 2010).

Barbara N Ramusack, *The Indian Princes and Their States* (Cambridge, Cambridge University Press, 2004).

B Shiva Rao (ed), *The Framing of India's Constitution: Select Documents*, vols I–V (New Delhi, Universal Law Publishing, 1967, reprint 2010).

MP Singh, *Outlines of Indian Legal and Constitutional History*, 8th edn (New Delhi, Universal Law, 2006).

2

The Executive and Parliament

Constitutional provisions – Pre-history, and debates in the Constituent Assembly – Evolution of the political order (1947–2017) – The changing role of the Indian Parliament – Significant rulings of the judiciary on the executive and legislature

I. INTRODUCTION

THE FRAMERS OF the Indian Constitution adopted a modified Westminster form of executive and legislature. Thus, while the Constitution provides for a parliamentary system of government of the British type with an executive responsible to Parliament, it also stipulates that the head of state would be an indirectly elected President, thereby departing from the British model of having a monarch as the formal head of state. In India too, while the President is the head of state, it is the Prime Minister who is the head of government. However, the Constitution does set out powers and functions of the office of the President, making it a more powerful office than that of the British monarch. In addition, the federal system adopted by the framers of the Indian Constitution, analysed in greater depth in Chapter 3, resulted in further adaptations to the unitary form of government adopted in the UK. The States are formally headed by Governors, but the government in the States is headed by the Chief Minister and her Council of Ministers. A significant difference from the Central level is that the Governors are not elected, but are nominated by the Central government, which gives them less legitimacy than that enjoyed by the President. In many other respects, though, the nature of the executive at the State level mirrors that which exists at the Union level.

While the form of the legislature adopted in the Indian Constitution resembles that in the UK, it is quite different from the colonial legislature that was incorporated by the imperial regime in India. The colonial legislature in India was riddled with undemocratic features and was designed to suit imperial interests. The framers of the Constitution made several drastic changes to the form and structure of the legislature in independent India in order to make it adhere to democratic principles of constitutional governance. However, their final choices were still more in line with principles of constitutional governance drawn from Euro-American experience. The framers were urged to hark back to ancient Indian practices of governance and to Gandhian ideas that emphasised decentralised, village-based systems. Their eventual choices marked a decisive rejection of these models and their reasons for such choices are important to examine, given that calls for 'indigenising' the constitutional tradition are a regular and recurrent feature of political discourse in contemporary India.

This chapter provides an overview of the constitutional provisions relating to the legislature and the executive (with a primary focus on the Union level). Section II sets out the bare provisions and conducts a textual examination of the overall structure and formal design of the executive and legislature as envisaged by the framers. Section III then moves on to a discussion of the constitutional pre-history of these institutions in colonial India and the debates among the framers that led to the eventual adoption of the model in the original Constitution. It is important to appreciate the originalist history of these provisions also because the debates among the framers became crucial for resolving post-independence disputes, many of which resulted in landmark court decisions. Section IV of the chapter focuses on the evolution of the post-independence political system, which inevitably shaped the post-colonial trajectories of the institutional structures of the executive and Parliament in India. This section covers the tenures of successive governments (identifying them through the Prime Minister who held the reins of executive power) and the political-party formations that were involved. This narrative will help the reader access the background political context for the remaining chapters as well, and is more detailed than would be necessary for the purpose of this chapter alone. Section V follows up on the analysis in Section III to highlight the changes in the nature and role of Parliament in response to the changes in the political landscape. Section VI highlights some key areas where the judiciary has been called upon to resolve interpretive disputes relating to the powers of the executive and the legislature.

II. BRIEF OVERVIEW OF RELEVANT CONSTITUTIONAL PROVISIONS

Provisions relating to the executive and the legislature in the Union and the States are housed in Parts V and VI of the Constitution. Extending from Articles 52 to 237, these 185 provisions detail the elements of the most significant institutions of constitutional governance (they include provisions relating to the judiciary which are examined separately in Chapter 4). Part V of the Constitution, entitled 'The Union', contains five chapters, outlining provisions relating to the Union Executive, the Union Parliament, Legislative Powers of the President, the Union Judiciary and the office of the Comptroller and Auditor General. Part VI of the Constitution, entitled 'The States', contains the analogue provisions for the State Executive and the State Legislature housed in six chapters. What follows is a brief survey of the most significant among these provisions, relying also on the constitutional practice that followed in later years.

We begin with an examination of the provisions relating to the executive. Chapter 1 of Part V comprises 26 provisions (Articles 52–78). They deal, respectively, with the offices of the President and the Vice-President, the Council of Ministers and the Prime Minister, the Attorney-General for India and conduct of government business. As we will see in the next section, the framers wanted to entrench within India a modified version of the Westminster form of Cabinet government. Yet, this intent to vest real executive power in the Cabinet would not be entirely clear if one were to adopt only a textual reading of the relevant provisions, which focus, quantitatively, much more on the President and the Vice-President than on the Prime Minister and the Council of Ministers. This feature led to some avoidable confusion over the exact nature of executive power, and, more importantly, which office gets to wield that power.

Article 52 simply, starkly and somewhat peremptorily declares that 'There shall be a President of India'. This has been taken to mean that the existence of a President is a necessity for the constitutional scheme to function. Article 53 stipulates that the executive power of the Union government shall vest in the President of India, while the next nine provisions (Articles 54–62) set out the manner of election, term of office, qualifications for election as President, as well as the procedure for impeachment of the President. Articles 63–71 deal with analogue provisions for the office of the Vice-President. Article 72 details the important power of the President to grant pardons, etc. Article 73 provides that the extent of the executive power of the Union is co-extensive with the legislative power of Parliament.

After these 22 provisions relating to the President and Vice-President, only two provisions—Articles 74 and 75—deal with the important institutions of the Council of Ministers and the office of the Prime Minister. Significantly, Article 74(1) provides that the President is to act in accordance with the aid and advice of the Council of Ministers with the Prime Minister at its head. The original provision did not use language making the advice binding, but was amended by the Indira Gandhi Government through the infamous 42nd amendment in 1976 to its present form, in a bid to emphasise the primacy of the office of the Prime Minister and the Cabinet. Article 75(1) stipulates that the Prime Minister shall be appointed by the President and that other Ministers in the Cabinet are to be appointed by the President on the advice of the Prime Minister. This is clearly a practice continued from Westminster, as is the provision in Article 75(3) that declares that the Council of Ministers shall be collectively responsible to the House of the People (the lower house of Parliament). These last two provisions reflect, as we shall see in a subsequent section, the intention of the framers to incorporate in the constitutional order the fundamental principles of the Westminster form of government.

A controversial provision, which seeks to provide a link between executive and legislative power, has been Article 123. The sole provision in the chapter entitled 'Legislative powers of the President', it empowers the President to promulgate 'ordinances'. Conceived as temporary legislation to be issued when Parliament is not in session, the original check on this provision was the requirement that any such ordinance would have to be presented within six weeks of Parliament being back in session. In practice, however, ordinances have been used rampantly and have also been 'repromulgated' frequently, arguably defeating their original purpose.

We now turn to the provisions relating to the Parliament in India, where, as will be analysed in the next section, the contrasts with the colonial situation are more starkly evident. The Constitution establishes a Parliament consisting of two houses. Chapter II of Part V of the Constitution, consisting of Articles 79–122, sets out the relevant provisions. The more significant institution is the lower house, called the Lok Sabha or the House of the People. It has a membership of a maximum of 552[1] and has a term of a maximum of five years. Its members are elected from country-wide general constituencies on a first-past-the-post basis, which requires a win by simple plurality. The concept of separate electorates, which placed restrictions on voting rights on the ground of religion during the colonial period, was abolished. All citizens who are adults have the right to vote once they turn 18 (21 in the original Constitution, which was amended in 1988)[2] and the adoption of the principle of universal adult suffrage is regarded as one of the most crucial, revolutionary decisions taken by the framers in mid-twentieth-century India at a time when much of its population was wracked with illiteracy and poverty, and more 'developed' nations were yet to adopt such a measure.

The upper house, called the Rajya Sabha or the House of States, is an indirectly elected body with a maximum membership of 238.[3] Its members, except for 12 of whom are nominated by the President in a continuance of the colonial practice of 'functional representation',[4] are elected by the various State legislative assemblies and Union Territories. Members of the Rajya Sabha are elected through an indirect electoral process which relies on a single transferable vote. Unlike the Lok Sabha, the Rajya Sabha is a continuing house, with one-third of its members retiring every two years, while each member has a total term of six years.

Article 84 sets out the qualifications for membership of Parliament, which include being a citizen of India and minimum age qualifications for each house. Article 102, on the other hand, lays out disqualifications from membership, which include a bar against holding an 'office of profit' under the government. An unusual disqualifying factor in India, incorporated through a constitutional amendment in 1985 which inserted the Tenth Schedule into the Constitution, is a bar against

[1] To arrive at this figure one has to engage in a combined reading of Articles 81 and 331 of the Constitution.

[2] Articles 325 and 326 of the Constitution.

[3] Article 80 of the Constitution.

[4] Article 80 of the Constitution.

membership for those legislators who give up the political party on whose plank they were originally elected, or disobey a voting instruction issued by their parent political party. Interestingly, this is the only part of the Constitution which actively recognises and seeks to regulate any activity related to a political party. The silence of the text on regulating other aspects of political parties is both notable and consequential, as we shall discuss later in this chapter.

Article 105 of the Constitution lays out the powers, privileges and immunities of members of Parliament, while Article 194 is the corresponding provision for State legislatures. These provisions seek to enable parliamentarians and legislators to discharge their duties as representatives of their constituents and active legislators without intimidation or fear of reprisals. Article 105(2) therefore guarantees freedom of speech within Parliament and Article 105(3) immunises parliamentarians from legal action for anything said or any vote rendered in Parliament. In another nod to the continuity with British constitutional tradition, the original provision stipulated that Indian parliamentarians would enjoy the same privileges as those of members of the House of Commons of the UK Parliament at the time of commencement of the Constitution. This reference was later omitted but courts have continued to rely on British constitutional practice to interpret the privileges of parliamentarians, following the lead given by the framers.

The power of Parliament to enact laws, and the subjects upon which it can do so is dealt with in Chapter 3 while discussing issues of federalism.

III. PRE-HISTORY, COLONIAL EXPERIENCES AND DEBATES WITHIN THE CONSTITUENT ASSEMBLY

A perusal of the provisions in the previous section might give the impression that the framers of the Indian Constitution simply continued with the institutions and traditions of the colonial era. Indeed, as we saw briefly in Chapter 1, this is also the charge levelled against the Indian constitutional order by those who are its most bitter critics domestically, whether from the far left or the far right of the political spectrum. This section seeks to show that this simplistic impression misses the complexities involved in the process of making choices about the executive and the legislature for independent India.

As emphasised in Chapter 1, Indian nationalists had a long tradition, dating back to the late nineteenth century, of thinking about the constitutional order that would be inaugurated by them when they gained independence from colonial rule. There is an equally long tradition of thought, particularly in imperial scholarship on India, of the 'granting' of liberal constitutional ideas by the British to Indians ever since the enactment of the first local government Act of 1882, which was seen as heralding 'sixty five years of liberal constitutional reform' culminating in the granting of independence to India in 1947.[5] By contrast, the nationalists adhere to a narrative which describes how they demanded greater representative roles, especially in the legislative setting of the colonial authorities, which were grudgingly conceded over time through the Indian Councils Act 1909, the Government of India Act 1919, and the Government of India Act 1935. Recent scholarship has noted that there were further complexities involved beyond the binaries of colonialism and constitutionalism, and that nationalism brought its own problems for the emerging conceptions of constitutionalism being formulated by Indian nationalists.[6]

A. Gandhian Ideas About Decentralisation

An example of such a tension between the nationalists themselves relates to Gandhi's views on decentralisation. Gandhi's famous work, *Hind Swaraj*, published in 1910, argued that the goal for Indians should be to aspire to their ancient traditions of civilisation rather than to mimic Western modernity. Gandhi rejected the idea—commonly held by many nationalists within the Indian National Congress—that salvation for India lay in adhering to modern notions of governance. In later years, many Gandhians argued that independent India should reject top-down forms of governance that were most closely identified with Western civilisation and should opt for decentralised forms of

[5] Two exemplars in this tradition include AB Keith, *A Constitutional History of India, 1600–1935* (London, Metheun, 1936) and R Coupland, *The Indian Problem: Report on the Constitutional Problem* (London, Oxford University Press, 1944).

[6] Arvind Elangovan, 'Constitutionalism, Political Exclusion and Implications for Indian Constitutional History: The Case of the Montague-Chelmsford Reforms (1919)' [2016] *South Asian History and Culture* 1–18.

governance by keeping the Indian village as the base for institutional development. A group of Gandhians within the Constituent Assembly also took this view.

However, despite the great awe and respect that many in the nationalist movement had for Gandhi, his views on this score had never found widespread support. Evidence for this can be found in the various constitutional documents that were drafted by the Congress, dating back to the Constitution of India Bill 1885, which adopted a rights-based approach and advocated civil and political freedoms. Other constitutional reforms suggested by the Nehru Report (1928) and the Sapru Committee Report (1945), which were important precursors to the drafts considered by the Constituent Assembly, reflected the same approach. Gandhi's influence on institutional thinking is absent in all these documents. It is important to recognise that while Gandhi had enormous impact on the nationalist movement, his ideas on governance found few takers within the nationalist elite who dominated the Constituent Assembly.[7] Another reason for rejecting the Gandhian decentralisation model was that the members of the Assembly had by then resolved to adopt universal adult suffrage for Indians. Gandhian models of decentralised governance were predicated on a system of indirect elections, which ran against the idea of a generalised system of universal adult franchise. Looked at retrospectively, the decision to grant universal adult suffrage seems both natural and inevitable. However, even at the time, this was a matter of considerable debate among Congress members and had been the subject of intense discussion for several decades. Many Congress leaders harboured doubts about vesting the all-important power of voting in the hands of the populace, substantial portions of which were functionally illiterate and mired in deep poverty. Many liberal thinkers, including followers of JS Mill, believed that constitutional democracy was unsuited for such a polity. That is why the decision of the Assembly to persist with universal suffrage is justifiably acknowledged as a visionary albeit risky move.

[7] See generally, Granville Austin, *The Indian Constitution: Cornerstone of a Nation* (New Delhi, Oxford University Press, 1966) 26–49.

B. The Reasons for Persisting with the British Westminster Model

The evolution of nationalist thinking on constitutional democracy and its institutions across the early part of the twentieth century is a better explanatory factor for the decision to persist with elements of the British constitutional tradition in India's independence Constitution. Many within the Assembly had had first-hand experience of governance under the constrained forms of representation that the British had imparted to Indians when the Congress was allowed to administer areas where it had won elections. Assembly members realised that faced with the severe challenges that awaited them in the aftermath of Partition, and the economic and security crisis of India in the mid-1940s, there was little space and time for drastic experimentation with institutions. They preferred to continue with modes that were familiar to them, though they took care to bring about important modifications to weed out what they knew to be impediments and drawbacks in the colonial model. The members of the Assembly were also influenced by larger trends of their age. The Second World War had just ended, the United Nations was being set up and constitutional democracy was enjoying a rare moment of great popularity across the world. In many parts of the colonised world, independence movements were structured around a narrative of freedoms and representative government. As we shall see, the modifications made by the Indians to the Westminster model resulted in drastic and fundamental changes to the old order,[8] giving credence to the claim that the Indian Constitution-making experience, while an evolutionary process in many ways, also had radical elements in its imagination and effect. As Austin notes, the coming of independence had marked the success of the political revolution that the nationalists had striven for. What remained to be achieved was the social revolution to liberate India's teeming masses from poverty and destitution. The framing of the Constitution and its institutions was motivated by that larger goal, even as this process had to concede to

[8] Harshan Kumarasingham terms the Constitutions of India and Sri Lanka 'Eastminster' Constitutions to denote the significant ways in which they departed from the Westminster model. See generally Harshan Kumarasingham, *A Political Legacy of the British Empire: Power and the Parliamentary System in Postcolonial India and Sri Lanka* (London, IB Tauris, 2013).

the demands of many sections, thereby remaining a conservative rather than a revolutionary process and text.[9]

Recent scholarship has noted that while the main elements of the Westminster model were retained, the framers of the Indian Constitution very much intended to make important modifications to it. Sir BN Rau, in particular, intended to make the office of the indirectly elected President far more powerful than the English monarch. Rau, who drafted the initial version of the Constitution that the Assembly worked from, initially sought to create a powerful Presidency which would have vast discretionary powers. Rau's intention appears to have been to create an institution that would be able to discipline the natural engine of government—the executive represented by the Prime Minister and his Cabinet—in crucial matters such as the appointment of judges, prevention of riots and safeguarding the rights of minorities, and protecting the financial stability of the country.[10] As the draft of the Constitution wound across the process of Constitution making, as we shall see below, Rau's position did not find complete favour and the powers of the President that he had in mind were either diluted or taken out. Yet, some of his vision was reflected in the final text, which is why the textual and originalist case for a President with meaningful constitutional powers is strong, both in theory and the eventual practice of constitutional politics in India.

C. Designing the Executive for a Free and Independent India

On the provisions relating to the future executive, the framers within the Assembly had considerable debate among themselves.[11]

[9] Austin describes this process in heroic, celebratory terms. See generally Austin (n 7) 26–49. Other commentators have been more guarded and sceptical about the motivations of the framers. See, eg, Rajeev Dhavan, *The Constitution of India: Miracle, Surrender, Hope* (New Delhi, Universal Law Publishing, 2017) (arguing that the Constitution of India, being a 'bourgeois constitution' has failed the poor and marginalised sections of Indian society).

[10] Arvind Elangovan, '"The Road Not Taken": Sir Benegal Rau and the Indian Constitution' in Sekhar Bandhyopadhay (ed), *Decolonisation and the Politics of Transition in South Asia* (New Delhi, Orient Blackswan, 2016) 146–49.

[11] Austin analyses the crafting of provisions involving executive power in Chapter 5, pp 116–43. See also B Shiva Rao (ed), *The Framing of India's Constitution: Select Documents*, vol V (New Delhi, Universal Law Publishing, 1967, reprint 2010) 334–81.

Some members, especially from minority communities, suggested that India emulate the Swiss or the American models of executive power. The Swiss model was seen as attractive because it would prevent concentration of power in an executive, which some minority members felt would be a threat to the rights of minority groups. On the other hand, some other members felt that having a US Presidential-style executive would empower the executive to effectively carry out the large socio-economic projects that were vitally needed. Ultimately, the Assembly rejected both these alternatives, and preferred to stay with the Westminster model of Cabinet government.

Even here there were differences. Some members suggested having an elected President. This was resisted, particularly by Jawaharlal Nehru in his capacity as the chair of the powerful Union Constitution Committee. Nehru explained that while the intention was to bestow 'great authority and dignity' on the office of the President, it was equally to 'emphasise the ministerial character of the Government that power really resided in the Ministry and in the legislature and not in the President as such'.[12] This is the position that was eventually accepted and which was strongly held by many of the framers, though, as we shall see, this was later challenged when the institutions came into being and were being worked in the first few decades after the adoption of the Constitution.

D. The Legislative Provisions and Changes from the Status Quo

In contrast to the provisions relating to the executive, the framers made several drastic departures from the colonial situation regarding the legislature. This is because the colonial legislatures lacked the elements of popular government. Franchise was restricted by property, educational and other qualifications and the electorate was thoroughly fragmented in communal and functional compartments. Seats in the lower house of the federal government were filled by indirect election, and on the basis of communal and functional electorates. The drastic cure adopted by the framers was to provide for universal adult franchise and to replace separate and communal electorates by joint and mixed electorates in

[12] Shiva Rao, ibid 340.

which all groups could contest for seats. The colonial legislatures had circumscribed powers and could be overshadowed quite easily by colonial executive authorities. By contrast, the Union Parliament and State legislatures created by the Constitution had much more robust powers.

A major concern while drafting the provisions relating to the legislature was in relation to the protection of minority interests. There was a near consensus against continuance of separate electorates but nearly all minorities wanted reservations to protect their interests. The decision to opt for universal adult suffrage and have direct elections to the lower houses at the Union and State level were significant decisions affecting all pre-existing dynamics. Ultimately, only Anglo Indians and Untouchables had reserved seats. Muslim and Sikh members espoused the value of proportional representation but this too was given up as incompatible with the parliamentary system. The fear was that this would lead to fragmentation. For the upper house, however, a form of proportional representation was adopted in part because this was the case under the colonial regime as well.

The Assembly members paid little attention to political parties and how to regulate them through the Constitution. This silence may be attributed to the awareness of Assembly members about the dominant role the Congress would play for the foreseeable future, which many felt would have a beneficial unifying effect on the country. In this, they may have been over-optimistic. It is important to remember that the German post-War Constitution recognised the importance of regulating political parties in the interests of maintaining strong traditions of constitutional democracy.[13] Awareness of the American case, where the failure of the Constitution to regulate political parties led to vital gaps in the public law regime,[14] should have sensitised the framers to the need to regulate political parties.

[13] See Werner Heun, *The Constitution of Germany* (Oxford, Hart Publishing, 2011) 92–100.

[14] See generally, Mark Tushnet, *The Constitution of the United States of America* (Oxford, Hart Publishing, 2009) 48–60.

IV. BRIEF OVERVIEW OF EVOLUTION OF THE INDIAN POLITICAL LANDSCAPE THROUGH THE PRISM OF ELECTORAL RESULTS AND PARTY POLITICS

This section seeks to provide a brief overview of the changes in the Indian political landscape across the seven decades since independence, with a specific focus on issues relating to executive power and legislative power (as reflected in majorities won through electoral contests). The purpose of this survey is also to highlight how changes in the political fortunes of parties across 16 general elections affected the strength and effectiveness of executive governments over time and led to major changes in other spheres of constitutional governance. The survey pays particular attention to restraints on executive power through the emergence of institutional changes, the impact of powerful political personalities, and swings for and against particular parties. Since this will also enhance appreciation of several subjects that will be covered in subsequent chapters, the survey is alive to influences beyond those that affect executive power.

A. Phase I—Dominionhood and the Making of the Constitution (1947–50)

Pursuant to the enactment of the Indian Independence Act, India became an independent Dominion with effect from 15 August 1947. The Constitution was still being drafted by the Constituent Assembly, which also functioned as a provisional Parliament. Jawaharlal Nehru, who was Gandhi's anointed heir and the most charismatic and popular leader across the nation, assumed office as India's first Prime Minister. His Cabinet comprised Vallabhbhai Patel (who had a powerful hold over the Congress party) as Home Minister and several non-Congress party Ministers, including BR Ambedkar as law minister and Syama Prasad Mookerjee (who later founded the Jana Sangh, a right wing party that was a precursor to the Bharatiya Janata Party) as minister of commerce and industry. Lord Mountbatten served as Viceroy and then Governor-General until 1948. In that year, C Rajagopalachari took over as the last Governor-General of India until 1950, when the Constitution was adopted and India formally became a republic. During this time, Prime Minister Nehru's power was counterbalanced by that of Patel as Home Minister. Lord Mountbatten and C Rajagopalachari shared in exercising executive power as Governors-General. However, they were both in tune with Prime Minister Nehru, who coordinated well with Home Minister Patel to consolidate the nascent Indian nation by alternately persuading and coercing the rulers of 552 Princely States to join the Indian Union. The period of crisis following Partition saw all constitutional actors working in harmony with each other towards crucial nation-building efforts.

B. Phase II: The Nehru Years of Dominant Congress Rule, Clashes with the President (1950–64)

With Patel's death in 1950, Nehru became the pre-eminent leader within the Congress and the nation, with few restraints on his power. He served as External Affairs minister and also directed economic planning in the country through the extra-constitutional but powerful Planning Commission. His power was consolidated when he led the Congress party to a massive win in the first general elections held in 1951–52. Under Nehru's leadership the Congress party won 364 of the 489 Lok Sabha seats at stake. Later that same year, Nehru was at the helm of the Congress party while it swept to victory in legislative assembly elections across all the States. This meant that the Congress was dominant both in Parliament and in the provinces. This state of affairs continued through much of Prime Minister Nehru's 17-year tenure, until his death in 1964. In the general elections of 1957 and 1962, the Congress was returned to power with majorities of 371/494 and 361/494 in the Lok Sabha.

These substantial majorities in Parliament and the State legislative assemblies enabled Prime Minister Nehru to unleash a flurry of economic policies and nation-building efforts that would take forward the Constitution's transformative agenda to bring about a social revolution in India, the effects and consequences of which are being felt—and hotly debated—to this day. Prime Minister Nehru's attempts at introducing a 'developmental state' in India were motivated by the goal of rapid industrialisation, which would, it was expected, enable India to 'catch up' with the developed economies. This was also an attempt at introducing the welfare state in a colonial economy which had been deprived of both phenomena. These policies resulted in massive changes in the Indian economy, including its planning and regulation, all of which were to be overseen by the State and its institutions. Many of the economic policies and institutions initiated in the Nehruvian era lasted until the early 1990s, when a process of dismantling them began in the era of liberalisation.

In these early years of the republic, the only real challenge to Prime Minister Nehru's power came from India's first President, Rajendra Prasad.[15] Nehru had wanted the last Governor-General of India, C Rajagopalachari, to become India's first President, but Rajendra Prasad thwarted this move and asserted his own claim to being President, for which he obtained the backing of the Congress party and the Constituent Assembly. Prasad assumed office in 1950 and after going through the constitutionally ordained process of an indirect election in 1951, was formally appointed as India's first elected President in 1951. Immediately after taking office, Prasad made it clear that he would assert the powers of his office and would not be content to be a figurehead. The flashpoint of tensions between the offices of the President on the one hand, and the Prime Minister and the Cabinet on the other, arose over the issue of the Hindu Code Bill. This was Nehru's attempt at reforming Hindu law through progressive legislation. Being a conservative Hindu, and representing the wing of the Congress that agreed with his sentiments, Prasad sought to counter the legislative initiative by raising substantive doubts about the legislative proposal. He relied on the various provisions in the Constitution which gave the office of the President more substantial powers than that of a titular head. Nehru enlisted the support of Attorney-General MC Setalvad and the distinguished jurist Alladi Krishnaswami Aiyer to argue that, despite the powers of the President enshrined in the Constitution, the intent and content of the provisions relating to the executive gave real power to the Cabinet to drive policy and the working of government. Aiyer, who had been an integral part of the Constituent Assembly, drew upon his knowledge of the actual intention of the Assembly to marshal arguments in favour of the primacy of the Cabinet and the Prime Minister. Prasad never challenged this position directly but continued to maintain

[15] This section draws upon Harshan Kumarasingham's recent comprehensive analysis of the clashes between Prime Minister Nehru and President Prasad. See Kumarasingham (n 8) chapter 3, 'The Indian Version of First among Equals: The Battle for Executive Ascendancy' 72–89.

that the office of the President had substantive content and substantial power. At the end of his first term as President in 1957, Nehru would have preferred to appoint S Radhakrishnan as President but Prasad prevailed yet again and served out a second term until 1962. At that time, Radhakrishnan, who was Nehru's chosen candidate, was elected India's second President. Some of the arguments used by Prasad in relation to the position of the President have been a recurring feature in Indian constitutional discourse.[16] Champions of a strong Presidency have not been dissuaded despite a series of decisions by the Supreme Court (examined in a subsequent section) on the issue.

The Nehru era also witnessed tensions between the executive and the judiciary, which were to become exacerbated under Prime Minister Indira Gandhi's tenure, which followed. However, Nehru was—for the most part—a constitutionalist and statesman and treated the judiciary with respect, using the legitimate power given to the legislature to overrule judicial rulings through a constitutional or statutory amendment. He set the tone for India's constitutional democracy and encouraged respect for constitutional culture and values more than anyone who has occupied the office of Prime Minister since. Even during the Nehruvian period of 'one-party dominance', the approach towards federalism was a sagacious one. As scholars have noted, there was a great deal of internal heterogeneity and respect for pluralism within the Congress party, especially at the State level, a process that Nehru encouraged.[17]

Even before his death in 1964, Nehru's authority had started to decline. In 1957 the Communist Party of India won control of the State government in Kerala, thereby breaching the Congress's hold over the States. Although Nehru led India to massive victories in the general elections, he never secured more than 50 per cent of the popular vote, indicating the sheer diversity of interests and allegiances in the vast

[16] For a discussion of a series of separate episodes where these questions became contentious, see generally, AG Noorani, *Constitutional Questions in India: The President, Parliament and the States* (New Delhi, Oxford University Press, 2006) 17–116.

[17] Sudipta Kaviraj, 'Government and Opposition: Fifty Years of Indian Independence' in Sudipta Kaviraj, *The Imaginary Institution of India* (New Delhi, Permanent Black, 2010) 235–36. This section also draws upon Partha Chatterjee, 'Introduction: A Political History of Independent India' in Partha Chatterjee (ed), *State and Politics in India* (New Delhi, Oxford University Press, 1997) 1–40.

country. The disastrous military loss to China in 1962 caused a massive dent to Nehru's influence.

C. Phase III: Congress Rule Weakened, Clashes with the Judiciary, Emergency (1964–77)

Upon Nehru's death in May 1964, Lal Bahadur Shastri served as India's second Prime Minister for two short years, until his own untimely death. Senior leaders of the Congress pushed Indira Gandhi to become India's third premier, acting upon the mistaken belief that she would be amenable to their guidance. The Congress suffered reverses in the fourth general elections in 1967 (being returned with a bare majority of 283/520 seats) and lost in eight State elections soon afterwards. In 1969 Indira Gandhi split the Congress party over disputes with the senior party leadership, named it after herself and won a convincing victory in the fifth general elections in 1971. Although her government was returned with an improved majority of 352/518 seats in the Lok Sabha, her takeover of the party structure signalled the beginning of the end of the democratic character that the Congress party had exhibited throughout the nationalist movement.

With a renewed mandate from the 1971 elections, an ebullient Prime Minister Gandhi aggressively pursued putative socialist policies and displayed an impatience for anyone who stood in her way. She was particularly strident about legitimate opposition parties, which she began to see as subversive and anti-national. This also led her to become more aggressive in her approach to the judiciary, with which she had been engaged in a battle for supremacy since 1967. A series of clashes over high-profile laws and cases (which will be covered in Chapters 4 and 7) led, ultimately, to her suspending the Constitution and plunging the country into an 'internal emergency' over two long years, between 1975 and 1977. The period was marked by grave acts of oppression. Over 30,000 persons were reportedly detained, largely for their political opposition to the regime. Freedom of press was severely curtailed and newspapers were subject to strict rules of censorship. Public assemblies were banned and freedom of speech of individuals was curtailed. During this period, when most opposition leaders were detained, the Indira Gandhi government amended the Constitution through the 42nd amendment, which drastically altered many of the founding constitutional ideals. The Emergency, as it has come to be known, has cast a long shadow over constitutional discourse and culture and is universally acknowledged as a low point in the nation's history, to be avoided in the future. There is some evidence that Indira Gandhi was troubled by the barrage of commentary attacking her dictatorial tendencies both within the nation and outside, and this may explain her sudden, unexpected decision to call for elections in 1977.

Prime Minister Gandhi's tenure was marked by a near-obsessive tendency towards centralisation—both within the Congress party's institutional structures and more broadly, in the federal and constitutional system as a whole. This reversed the Congress party's nearly century-old strategy of using the tools of negotiation, compromise and accommodation, and had disastrous results: it radically altered the pluralistic nature of the Congress party and the nature of regional party dynamics. This led to a surge in new regional parties that altered the political and constitutional set-up, and set in place the triggers for the end of the dominance of the Congress party.[18]

D. Phase IV: Crises and Weaknesses in the Political Order, Emergence of the 'Weak-Strong State' (1977–89)

In the sixth general elections held in 1977, the opposition parties came together under the umbrella of a new political entity called the Janata Party and garnered a majority of 345/553 seats in the Lok Sabha. Indira Gandhi's Congress (I) party was reduced to 189 seats, which was nevertheless an indication that the Congress still had traction among sections of the country's populace. India's first non-Congress Prime Minister, Morarji Desai, came to office with hopes of finally providing an alternative to the Congress party, which had been in power continuously for three decades since independence. However, Morarji Desai's coalition government was beset by petty squabbles between its various constituent parties, which had little in common apart from their desire to unseat the oppressive Indira Gandhi government of the Emergency. In its two-year existence, Prime Minister Desai's government did not achieve much in governance terms, but was able to push through the

[18] Kaviraj (n 17) 237–38.

important 44th amendment to the Constitution to offset much of the damage done through the 42nd amendment, and restore or modify parts of the original vision. The government also sought to bring some balance and lack of partisanship to constitutional institutions that had been corrupted by the partisan policies of the Indira Gandhi era, but its short lifespan prevented it from having a lasting impact. The Morarji Government was replaced briefly by the government of Prime Minister Charan Singh, which in turn lasted for six months.

In the seventh general elections held in 1980, Indira Gandhi came back to power after securing 353/529 seats in the Lok Sabha. Given that, only three years prior to the elections, she was being written off politically, this was a remarkable political rebirth. However, her large parliamentary majority could not obscure the reality that she no longer had the support required, especially in the States, to push forward governance schemes. Her handling of the Punjab imbroglio led, in part, to her assassination by a personal bodyguard in 1984. The Congress party had no leadership plan and her elder son, who had little political training, was pitched into the campaign for the eighth general elections that were held in 1984. These elections saw Rajiv Gandhi being elected Prime Minister with 404/514 seats in the Lok Sabha. Despite having been elected with the largest mandate in the history of independent India (though still short of 50 per cent of the total votes cast), Rajiv Gandhi's inexperience and a slew of difficult political issues saw him squander away the political advantage gained by his government. By the late 1980s, in the words of one scholar, 'India became increasingly democratic and increasingly difficult to govern'.[19] It was also evident that while the Central Indian State was appearing to gain in strength, its capacity to realise its will was weaker than before, leading to its description as a 'weak-strong state'.[20] Given this, the results of the ninth general elections in 1989, which reflected the fragmentation of the people's verdict, was not altogether surprising. Rajiv Gandhi's Congress, while still the largest single party with 197/545 seats, was not in a position to form the government. Instead, VP Singh, a former finance

[19] James Manor, 'Parties and the Party System' in Atul Kohli (ed), *India's Democracy: An Analysis of Changing State–Society Relations* (Princeton, NJ, Princeton University Press, 1988) 72.

[20] Lloyd Rudolph and Susanne Hoeber Rudolph, *In Pursuit of Lakshmi: The Political Economy of the Indian State* (Chicago, IL, University of Chicago Press, 1987).

minister in the Rajiv Gandhi Government, became Prime Minister at the head of an unstable coalition.

E. Phase V: The Coalition Era in Indian Politics (1989–2014)

The 1990s were a tumultuous and eventful decade in Indian politics and public life. Starting with the general elections in 1989, there were four more in the decade (in 1991, 1996, 1998 and 1999) making it a period of greater political instability than ever before.

Prime Minister VP Singh's minority government lasted only for a year, but his momentous decision to implement the Mandal Commission Report on reservations (or affirmative action) had a dramatic effect on the role of caste in Indian politics, which will continue to have an impact in the foreseeable future. The early 1990s also saw the Ram temple movement in Ayodhya, which led to a brand of right wing Hindu politics and the revitalisation of the political fortunes of the Bharatiya Janata Party (BJP). The BJP had been reduced to only two Lok Sabha seats in the 1984 elections but on the back of this religious revival movement was able to form minority governments in 1998 and 1999. The same decade witnessed a monumental shift in economic policy as India started abandoning its socialist policies and gradually embraced neoliberal market-based policies. Also, the successful enactment of the 73rd and 74th constitutional amendments resulted in a potentially revolutionary process of decentralisation that went far beyond the modest nod to decentralisation made in the Constituent Assembly (the motivations and problems with this are examined in Chapter 3).

The general elections of 1991 witnessed the return of the Congress party to power, with 244/545 Lok Sabha seats, which meant that it was a minority government dependent upon external support of other parties. Under Prime Minister Narasimha Rao, it survived a full term but in the general elections of 1996 the BJP emerged as the single largest party and was able to get support to count a total of 161/545 seats in the Lok Sabha. It formed the government but survived for only 13 days, to be replaced by a 13-party United Front government, which limped along under two Prime Ministers (Deve Gowda and IK Gujral) with the external support of the Congress party. When this government fell in 1998, fresh elections were held in 1999 (first in April and then in October) which finally resulted in a five-year term served out by a coalition called the National Democratic Alliance, with the BJP as its dominant party. In 2004 the Congress-led United Progressive Alliance coalition commanded a majority of seats in the Lok Sabha, even though the Congress itself could win only 145/543 seats. The BJP, as the second largest party, secured 138 seats. In 2009 the United Progressive Alliance managed to stave off the challenge of the BJP-led National Democratic Alliance once again to secure an overall majority of 262/543 seats. This time the Congress won 206 seats on its own, while the BJP secured only 116. What is striking is that the two largest parties in the nation won only 322/543 seats in the Lok Sabha. This gave rise to the conventional wisdom that Indian politics would be in a coalition government mode for some time to come.

Opinion is divided on whether the consequent political instability is necessarily a negative feature. As was becoming evident, the dominance of the Congress had begun to reveal negative patterns for the health of the nation and its constitutional system of checks and balances. Through the 1990s and 2000s, some scholars argued, Indian politics was exhibiting a new pattern of stable 'two-coalition' politics, albeit one in which shifts in the balance of power depended on the changing alliances of minority, mainly regionally based parties.[21] This has, as we shall see in Chapter 3, significant implications for the rise of the power of States in the Indian federal model.

That apart, some have argued that the Indian political landscape has experienced 'the second democratic upsurge' as certain historically subordinated communities from among the backward classes and the scheduled castes have become politically mobilised and empowered through the electoral process, even as their political leaders and political groups (such as the Dalit leader from the State of Uttar Pradesh, Mayawati and her Bahujan Samaj Party) are far from democratic in their own functioning.[22]

The changed socio-political equation has had dramatic consequences for the institutional dynamics and power relations of other

[21] See, eg, John Harriss, 'Political Change, Political Structure, and the Indian State since Independence' in Paul Brass (ed), *The Routledge Handbook of Politics in South Asia* (New Delhi, Routledge, 2013) 60.

[22] Yogendra Yadav, 'Reconfiguration in Indian Politics: State Assembly Elections 1993–5' (1996) 31 (2–3), *Economic and Political Weekly* 95–104.

constitutional institutions. During the period of governmental weakness and instability through the 1980s and the 1990s the Indian judiciary started becoming more activist, engaged in blatant exercises of policy making, and gradually expanded its own power in relation to the executive and legislature, a process which is analysed in Chapter 4. Lloyd and Susanne Rudolph have powerfully demonstrated that these changes in the political landscape have radically altered equations within the constitutional framework. In their analysis, since 1989 'the planned economy and the centralized state have gradually given way to a regulatory state more suited to coalition governments in a multiparty system, to economic decentralization, and to more independent and competitive federal states'.[23]

A number of other actors have flexed their constitutional muscle during the period since 1989: the office of the President once again became pivotal in the era of coalition governments. The long-dormant institution of the constitutionally empowered Election Commission became very active in the 1990s, as did the constitutionally created office of the Comptroller and Auditor General. The rise of these institutions and new regulatory institutions, which are technocratic rather than democratic, and their implications for the new equation of Indian constitutional democracy are examined in Chapter 5.

F. Phase VI: The BJP's Surprising Electoral Comeback in 2014: End of the Coalition Era?

Constitutional politics have a way of proving even seasoned commentators wrong. Just as there was a growing consensus that after 25 years of coalition politics they had become a mainstay of Indian democracy, along came the political phenomenon of Narendra Modi and the stunning electoral gains made by the BJP in the 16th general elections held in 2014. These elections were once again a contest between the

[23] Lloyd Rudolph and Susanne Rudolph, 'Redoing the Constitutional Design: From an Interventionist to a Regulatory State' in Atul Kohli (ed), *Success of India's Democracy* (New York, Cambridge University Press, 2001) 161.

BJP-led National Democratic Alliance and the Congress-led United Progressive Alliance, the latter having been in power continuously for a decade. Quite surprisingly, and owing to the Presidential-style campaign led by Narendra Modi, who had been a Chief Minister of a prominent State for three successive terms before entering the national arena, the BJP on its own strength secured a bare majority of 282/545 seats in the Lok Sabha, which meant that it could have formed the government on its own. The National Democratic Alliance's combined seat tally rose to 336 in the Lok Sabha, which gave it a solid majority. The Congress was routed, securing only 44 seats, while the rest of the United Progressive Alliance fared little better, securing a combined total of only 60 seats. However, it is significant that in terms of vote share, the BJP won only 31 per cent of the overall votes, while the Congress still secured 19.1 per cent of the overall votes cast. Together the two parties garnered barely 50 per cent of the overall vote. Since a number of regional parties also fared poorly, it seems that the Indian political landscape is heading for another period of transition and change.

What this has meant is that for the first time in a quarter-century, a government has come to power at the Central level with numbers that should enable it to drive policy comfortably. This is so especially when compared to the constrained coalition governments since 1989, which often had to move very cautiously to keep all their partners on board. At the time of writing, three years on, this promise has not come to be realised. The reasons for this are diverse, including the fact that the BJP has squandered its newly won political capital in pandering to its right wing fringe, pursuing questionable and anti-secular policies that have angered minorities and the more moderate Hindus. These issues, and their implications for the future of India's constitutional order, are examined at some length in the Conclusion to this book.

From a constitutional perspective, for the National Democratic Alliance government led by Prime Minister Modi a stumbling block has been the fact that, while it has a solid majority in the Lok Sabha, a number of its legislative initiatives could potentially be blocked in the Rajya Sabha where—due to the staggered elections for the upper house—the Congress still had favourable numbers (till mid-2017). Once again, this seems to be a case of constitutionally designed checks playing their intended balancing role in moderating executive–legislature relations.

V. THE CHANGING ROLE OF PARLIAMENT IN INDIAN CONSTITUTIONAL DEMOCRACY

The previous section focused on the way executive power has changed hands across the 67 years of the working of the Indian Constitution, and the manner in which party and electoral politics have shaped the ways in which the executive and legislature have been able to exercise power. In this brief section, I focus specifically on the changes that have been brought about to the Indian Parliament and its functioning across this span of time.

It is important to emphasise that over time the Indian Parliament has become more representative of the wider masses of India. At the time of independence, Parliament was dominated by politicians from the nationalist elite, many of whom were from the Congress party. While their nationalist credentials were impeccable, the Congress party drew its most important leaders from the ranks of upper caste, often landowning Hindus. As the Constitution has pursued its social revolution, the composition of Parliament has changed and it has now come to represent more fully the vast diversity of India's population. This has not, however, been a uniformly positive trend. In recent years, the number of persons with criminal records has also increased, as a reflection of the growing criminalisation of Indian politics more generally. This is accompanied by an equally distressing pattern: the rise of family/dynastic connections among legislative representatives. A recent analysis shows that in the 15th Lok Sabha (2009–14), as many as 28.6 per cent of MPs had a family connection to other politicians. This proportion was higher among the Congress party's MPs where it counted for 37.5 per cent. More worryingly, and suggesting that politics in India is becoming more hereditary rather than less, the figures showed that every single MP below the age of 30 in the 15th Lok Sabha had entered Parliament through a family connection.[24] This proportion was 65 per cent for MPs in the age range of 31–40, and 36.8 per cent for MPs between the ages of 41 and 50. Democracy activists have sought to counter this trend by forcing disclosure of candidates' records in advance of elections and by seeking to create awareness of these issues with voters. This has also resulted in judiciary-led legislation to

[24] Patrick French, *India: An Intimate Biography* (New Delhi, Allen Lane, 2011) 91–123.

control the injection of corrupt wealth and criminality in politics, but the struggle is an ongoing one. The increased representation of social classes has not been matched by a greater degree of representation of women and Muslims in Parliament. The 16th Lok Sabha (2014–present) has the lowest ever number of Muslim MPs and a fairly low proportion of women MPs. This explains why a legislative proposal to have 30 per cent quotas for women in Parliament has been on the agenda for the past two decades, even though feminists have hotly debated whether this will be a good measure for advancing women's interests more generally.

Prime Minister Nehru was a committed Parliamentarian and, believing that matters of policy should be debated in the Houses of Parliament, often took great care to attend Parliament to explain government policy and respond to questions from opposition members and fellow Congress MPs. Nevertheless, the scale of parliamentary majorities enjoyed by him meant that despite fierce debates (such as those which occurred over the enactment of the first amendment to the Constitution, which involved making changes to laws relating to the freedom of the press, reservations and land reforms), it was never in doubt that his government would carry the votes required. It is worth recalling that in his 17-year tenure as Prime Minister, Nehru faced only one 'no confidence' motion in the wake of the 1962 Indo-China war. Despite having to agree to fire his Minister of Foreign Affairs, Nehru was easily able to garner the numbers to have the motion dismissed. Later Prime Ministers were less committed to the fundamentals of parliamentary and constitutional democracy and were inclined to treat their parliamentary duties with much less regard, focusing instead on getting the required numbers for passing legislation and constitutional amendments. Prime Minister Indira Gandhi provided many examples of manipulation of Parliament by the executive, especially during the years leading to and during the period of Emergency.[25] Very few Prime Ministers since have taken their parliamentary duties—or indeed the institution of Parliament as a deliberative forum—seriously since then.

Faced with a situation where they were numerically weak, and could not hope to defeat government legislation, the opposition began to

[25] Vernon Hewitt and Shirin M Rai, 'Parliament' in Nirja Gopal Jayal and Pratap Bhanu Mehta (eds), *The Oxford Companion to Politics in India* (New Delhi, Oxford University Press: 2010) 28–42.

adopt extensive extra-parliamentary protests and disruptive behaviour to frustrate successive governments. Such forms of protest occur both within and outside Parliament, and rely on an extensive and vibrant print and television media to inform the wider public of their reasons. During the ninth Lok Sabha (1985–89), when the Congress government had the largest ever majority in Parliament, there were on average three walkouts per parliamentary session, usually following a ruling by the Speaker against the opposition.[26] Some scholars have noted that these protests have sometimes served wider purposes, such as forcing governments to hold parliamentary elections in situations of widespread social unrest. Such conduct has, however, continued into the era of coalition governments, when their use is questionable, given that no single party now enjoys the dominant role that the Congress did during the Nehru years.

The onset of coalition governments containing large numbers of smaller parties has made the task of piloting legislation through India's Parliament a difficult one. The habits of protest and disruption that Indian parliamentarians have become accustomed to have a severe effect on parliamentary business and the overall efficiency of the House. The 15th Lok Sabha (2009–14) was the worst performing ever, functioning for only 73 per cent of the scheduled time. Consequently, it passed fewer Bills than any previous Parliament. For example, during the three sessions of Parliament in 2012, the government had planned for 37, 32 and 39 bills to be passed respectively. Of these, only 10, 15 and 12 respectively were in fact passed.[27] This situation has become dire and has long-term consequences for the faith of the public in one of the most important institutions in a constitutional democracy.

The response of successive governments to this state of affairs has led to other problematic concerns for constitutionalists. As noted earlier, the executive in India is empowered, both at the Central and State level, to issue temporary legislation in the form of ordinances. Though designed to enable executive authorities to act in times when Parliament is not in session, these have now become the instrument of choice for

[26] ibid 35.

[27] MR Madhavan, 'Low Bill Power', *Indian Express*, 29 August 2012. Available online at <http://indianexpress.com/article/opinion/columns/low-bill-power/>.

governments which fear that their efforts at legislation will be stalled in Parliament. Consequently, there has been a discernible rise in the use of ordinances, which is troubling.[28]

Intra-institutionally speaking, the end of the era of Congress dominance, and the rise of coalition governments has meant that the role of the Speaker has become far more important. Coalition governments are vulnerable to adverse rulings by the Speaker and the office has attained great stature as a way of resolving disputes within Parliament.[29] Equally, the same trends have stimulated the role and functions of parliamentary committees, given their potential benefit to governments in managing broad coalitions. A number of new Committees have been constituted in recent years and they have come to wield greater power and authority within the House, which augurs well for norms of parliamentary democracy.[30]

All this indicates that the role and performance of the Indian Parliament has undergone a transformation across the seven decades it has been in existence. While many commentators bemoan the contemporary role of Parliament, which is not characterised by a respect for democratic deliberation or for attributes that can be identified with the aspirations of a liberal polity based on the bedrock values of public reason, other scholars have noted that the current trends in Parliament are a reflection of the churning that is underway in Indian society more generally. There is no denying that the institutional performance of Parliament displays many worrying tendencies. No constitutional democracy can survive if its principal institutions are in a state of disarray. Given the importance of a well-functioning Parliament and a responsible and efficient executive for a healthy constitutional order, it is imperative that these aspects improve in the near future.

[28] See, successive works by Shubhankar Dam which highlight several concerns about this trend, and also document the increase over time. Shubhankar Dam, *Presidential Legislation in India: The Law and Practice of Ordinances* (Cambridge, Cambridge University Press, 2014).

[29] Hewitt and Rai (n 25) 37–38.

[30] ibid 31–32.

VI. SIGNIFICANT JUDICIAL PRONOUNCEMENTS ON CONSTITUTIONAL PROVISIONS RELATING TO THE EXECUTIVE AND PARLIAMENT

The manner in which the judiciary has interacted with the executive and legislative wings of government is the focus of Chapter 4. In this section, I seek to cover some important rulings by the judiciary which sought to clarify the meanings of contested issues of executive and legislative power.

As mentioned earlier, a textual reading of the provisions relating to the executive power in the Indian Constitution can give rise to a potential for conflict between an indirectly elected President with substantial powers and the Council of Ministers and the Prime Minister on the other hand. President Prasad did, in fact, point to this tension and sought to use his constitutionally given powers to thwart particular policies of the Nehru government, though this never led to a direct confrontation. This issue also came to be litigated before the courts and the Supreme Court's rulings helped to clarify the existing legal position. In *Ram Jawaya Kapur v State of Punjab* (1955) publishers of school text books challenged the State's education policy crafted by the Council of Ministers on the ground that they did not have the authority to formulate policies that infringed their fundamental rights. The Supreme Court interpreted the relevant constitutional articles and asserted that the President in India is a formal constitutional head and 'real executive powers are vested in the Ministers or the cabinet' because 'they are collectively responsible to the legislature'.[31] The Court sought to authoritatively answer this question two decades later in *Samsher Singh v State of Punjab* (1974).[32] Here, two members of the lower judiciary in the State of Punjab challenged their dismissal on the ground that the Governor based the decision of dismissal on ministerial advice, but should have exercised the discretion involved in his own capacity. The Court categorically held that when the President or Governor exercises judgement, he is required to do so on the aid and advice of the Council of Ministers, and it is not a personal judgement. Though these decisions did not put an end to the ardour of champions of strong Presidential power in India, they did help settle the legal question involved.

[31] *Ram Jawaya Kapur v State of Punjab* AIR 1955 SC 549 at para 16.
[32] *Samsher Singh v State of Punjab* AIR 1974 SC 2192.

The Supreme Court has not, however, always spoken with such a clear voice. On the difficult question of whether the power of pardon under Article 72 enables the President to exercise a personal sense of discretion, the Supreme Court has rendered decisions which have wavered and offered conflicting answers. This may also have to do with the fact that many such cases involved the exercise of the death penalty option, which injects a greater degree of judicial subjectivity into the decisions as a result of the high stakes involved.[33]

The Supreme Court has also been approached to clarify disputes in relation to the provisions relating to the legislature. It has often had to rule on the technical aspects of interpreting the Constitution's specifications of the qualifications and disqualifications of members of Parliament. So, for instance, it has had to judicially interpret the bar against holding an 'office of profit' for someone to be eligible to be a Member of Parliament.[34] The injection of the anti-defection law in the Tenth Schedule of the Constitution has also required a number of judicial rulings to clear the legal position involved in what has turned out to be a complex and contradictory area of the law.[35]

The judiciary has also issued a series of rulings on interpreting the privileges, powers and immunities of legislators as specified in Articles 105 and 194. These questions became particularly contested because of a perceived tension between the privileges of Parliamentarians and the fundamental rights of ordinary citizens and journalists.[36]

[33] This line of cases is surveyed in Shubhankar Dam, 'The Executive' in Sujit Choudhry, Madhav Khosla and Pratap Bhanu Mehta (eds), *The Oxford Handbook of the Indian Constitution* (Oxford, Oxford University Press, 2016) 323.

[34] *Shibu Soren v Dayanand Sahay*, AIR 2001 SC 2583 (clarifying that the key question involved is whether the compensation receivable would bring the holder of the office under the influence of the executive).

[35] For a survey of decisions adverted to in this paragraph, see MR Madhavan, 'The Legislature: Composition, Qualifications and Disqualifications' in Sujit Choudhry, Madhav Khosla and Pratap Bhanu Mehta (eds), *The Oxford Handbook of the Indian Constitution* (Oxford, Oxford University Press, 2016) 270–89.

[36] For an analysis of the leading decisions involved, see Sidharth Chauhan, 'The Legislature: Privileges and Process' in Sujit Choudhry, Madhav Khosla and Pratap Bhanu Mehta (eds), *The Oxford Handbook of the Indian Constitution* (Oxford, Oxford University Press, 2016) 290–306.

VII. CONCLUSION

In this chapter, I have sought to provide an overview of the constitutional design of institutions that were to exercise executive and legislative power in India. I have also examined how the practice of the functioning of the executive and Parliament has unfolded across the seven decades of India's post-colonial governance. Some important themes to highlight are the continuance of the colonial model of Westminster government, the reasons for persisting with it, and the important ways in which 'Eastminster' was adapted and modified for operation in post-colonial India. This chapter has sought to provide a short overview of the evolution of the political and legal landscape in relation to executive and legislative power by focusing on the changes in government across the 16 general elections that India has experienced so far. This survey showcases some of the complexities involved in engaging with India's vast and populous parliamentary democracy. In identifying the aspects of the current order that are performing poorly, I have sought to identify the most pressing issues for those concerned with improving the health of India's executive and legislative institutions.

FURTHER READING

Granville Austin, *The Indian Constitution: Cornerstone of a Nation* (New Delhi, Oxford University Press, 1966).

Debtoru Chatterjee, *Presidential Discretion* (New Delhi, Oxford University Press, 2016).

Sujit Choudhry, Madhav Khosla and Pratap Bhanu Mehta (eds), *The Oxford Handbook of the Indian Constitution* (Oxford, Oxford University Press, 2016).

Shubhankar Dam, *Presidential Legislation in India: The Law and Practice of Ordinances* (Cambridge, Cambridge University Press, 2014).

Francine Frankel, *India's Political Economy, 1947–2004: The Gradual Revolution*, 2nd edn (New Delhi, Oxford University Press, 2005).

Sudipta Kaviraj, *The Imaginary Institution of India: Politics and Ideas* (New Delhi, Permanent Black, 2010).

Sudipta Kaviraj, *The Trajectories of the Indian State: Politics and Ideas* (New Delhi, Permanent Black, 2010).

Harshan Kumarasingham, *A Political Legacy of the British Empire: Power and the Parliamentary System in Postcolonial India and Sri Lanka* (London, IB Tauris, 2013).

MR Madhavan, 'Parliament' in Devesh Kapur, Pratap Bhanu Mehta and Milan Vaishnav (eds), *Rethinking Public Institutions in India* (New Delhi, Oxford University Press, 2017) 67–103.

AG Noorani, *Constitutional Questions in India: The President, Parliament and the States* (Oxford, Oxford University Press, 2006).

Lloyd Rudolph and Susanne Rudolph, *In Pursuit of Lakshmi: The Political Economy of the Indian State* (Chicago, University of Chicago Press, 1987).

Raghubir Singh and KNC Pillai (eds), *The Legislature and the Judiciary* (New Delhi, Orient Blackswan, 2011).

3

Federalism and Local Government

The colonial period and its influence on models of Indian federalism and local governance – The centralising bias in the Constituent Assembly's approach – Constitutional provisions relating to federalism and the evolution of Indian federalism over time – Constitutional provisions relating to local government and the evolution of local governance in India

I. INTRODUCTION

SOUTH ASIA HAS a long history of non-unitary, decentralised forms of governance dating back to ancient times. Some historians have asserted that pre-colonial empires had 'flexible, nuanced and overarching suzerainties' and the idea of unitary, indivisible sovereignty was a foreign import into Asian and African societies from post-enlightenment Europe.[1] The implication is that to address their many problems, including those relating to sharing of power between different levels of political authority, the societies of modern South Asia should revert to the concepts of shared and layered sovereignty known to the ancients. Scholars of federalism have, however, injected an element of realism into such calls by emphasising that for an arrangement to be termed 'federal' requires 'at least some demarcated jurisdictions for the exercise of meaningful governmental authority [between Central and regional authority] in a way that each is autonomous from the other'.[2] It is doubtful whether the arrangements for power sharing

[1] Sugata Bose and Ayesha Jalal, *Modern South Asia: History, Culture, Political Economy*, 3rd edn (New Delhi, Routledge, 2011) 207.

[2] Mahendra Prasad Singh, *Indian Federalism: An Introduction* (Delhi, National Book Trust, 2011) 20.

within the monarchical or feudal states which existed in pre-colonial India had such legally demarcated zones of authority: the power exercised by lower-level officials was contingent on pragmatic devolution by higher levels, which could be withdrawn rather abruptly and arbitrarily. There is a similar debate about institutions of local government in ancient India. That there were such institutions of local government is not in dispute, especially in relation to village panchayats (the traditional form of unelected councils by which villages in many parts of India were governed; these were almost exclusively staffed by upper caste males from economically and socially privileged backgrounds). What *has* been disputed is the relevance and importance of such institutions for post-colonial, post-independence India.

Federalism, as we know it in India today, was introduced towards the end of the colonial period and was originally designed to meet colonial interests. This is also true of local government institutions that today have constitutional status and form. Yet, between 1947 and 1949, the colonial forms of federalism and local government were moulded in significant ways to suit existing conditions in India by the framers of India's Constitution, and to address demands for democratic decentralisation from some nationalist figures. Since independence, shifts in political and socio-economic trends have further changed the relations involving federalism and democratic decentralisation in India. This chapter begins by covering the significant foundational moments in the evolution of India's federal and local governance systems. The colonial mechanisms of federalism became the template for some of the constitutional framework relating to these issues and thus need greater attention than in other contexts. This is followed by a close examination of the relevant textual provisions in the Indian Constitution, with a focus on the motivating logic and a brief discussion of how these provisions have evolved in post-colonial India across six decades. Politics in post-colonial India has shaped the way the constitutional scheme of federalism and decentralisation evolved and changed, and this evolution will form the focus of the penultimate section of this chapter.

The trajectories and narratives of federalism and local governance in India have different origins and inflection points, though there are also overlaps. Studying them together may seem contrived at times, but it is important to do so as this exercise reveals both complementary and contradictory trends in their evolution.

II. THE COLONIAL PERIOD AND ITS INFLUENCE ON LATER CONSTITUTIONAL DEVELOPMENTS RELATING TO FEDERALISM AND LOCAL GOVERNMENT

There has been considerable debate on properly characterising the nature of Indian federalism. Some of this stems from the unusual nature of Indian federalism, which departs in significant ways from the standard model of a federal state. It is important to understand that federalism in India emerged during the late-colonial era. As outlined in Chapter 1, in the early part of colonial rule, centralisation and unitary forms of control were administrative and political necessities. Later, improvements in means of communication greatly empowered the Central colonial authority, further hampering the development of local or regional authority. However, the colonial government had started introducing institutions of local government at least since 1882 (during the tenure of the erstwhile Viceroy of India, Lord Ripon). It is worth noting that even before the colonial government empowered provincial governments, it declared its intention, through the Ripon resolution, to institutionalise elected local governments, from municipal governments in urban areas to the block level (located administratively just above the village level and just below the district level) in rural areas. Within colonial regimes, this turn to decentralisation made sense as it enabled colonial authorities to co-opt local elites and ensure that no threats to colonial rule would emerge. This serves as a reminder that forms of government are not intrinsically morally worthy or superior and can be put to diverse uses, whether democratic, authoritarian or despotic.

As enumerated more fully in Chapter 1, demands towards self-government from the nascent nationalist movement, which became increasingly more strident and powerful across the first half of the twentieth century, led to gradual but significant constitutional changes, eventually leading to the emergence of basic forms of federalism and local government in the Government of India Acts of 1919 and 1935 ('Act of 1919' and 'Act of 1935' respectively).

It bears emphasis that the Indian federal experience is quite different from some of the classic federal situations (such as the US) as the individual units in India did not constitute a federal government by yielding up powers to it. The situation in India was quite the opposite. The regions which had been classified as 'Presidencies' under the East India Company's reign, came to be known as 'provinces' under the direct rule of the British government in India after 1858. From 1858 onwards, India was divided into two broad political units: the much larger British India (which accounted for 54 per cent of the territory and 70 per cent of the population, was administered directly by the British government, and was further divided into provinces) and the Princely States (which consisted of 600 odd separate and geographically widely disseminated units that were governed by local princes, kings and feudal lords, who were allowed limited internal autonomy in exchange for accepting British suzerainty). At the time of independence in 1947, British India consisted of 17 provinces, while the Princely States numbered close to 600. The latter were not nation states as we understand them, but sought to mimic some of the characteristics of a nation while strongly retaining the role of a hereditary monarch. They were regions in the Indian subcontinent which had not been conquered or annexed by the British, but were subject to subsidiary alliances. They had been formally granted internal autonomy while the colonial power exercised suzerainty over them and controlled external affairs. In practice, however, the British exercised considerable power over the Princely States, which were governed typically by hereditary monarchs whose appointments were influenced by the colonial authorities. As the movement for independence grew, the colonial authorities tried to advance the interests of the hereditary monarchs, often in the face of opposition from the nationalist movement, whose calls for democracy were targeted as much at the British as at the hereditary rulers.[3]

The Act of 1919 had introduced a system of 'dyarchy' for the provinces in British India, which involved devolving some powers onto the provincial level, even as most crucial powers were retained at the Central level by the colonial authorities. The Act of 1919 also made local self-government a subject under the control of provincial governments. This fell short of a properly federal system, attempts towards which were introduced as a result of the decision of the colonial government to accommodate the rulers of Indian Princely States at the round table conferences held between 1930 and 1932 in London.[4] In that sense,

[3] For more details on the Princely States, see generally Barbara Ramusack, *The Indian Princes and their States* (Cambridge, Cambridge University Press, 2004) 245–74 (focusing on federalism issues in particular).

[4] 'Relations Between the Union and the States' in B Shiva Rao (ed), *The Framing of India's Constitution: A Study* (Delhi, Universal Law Publishing Co, 1968, reprinted 2010) 592–95.

federalism was a gift bestowed upon Indian provinces and Princely States rather than the result of sustained demands by them. Indeed, as we shall see, there were few champions for 'states' rights' in the lead-up to, or within, the Constituent Assembly. The eventual model of federalism that was adopted in India has many features which would offend champions of the classic rights of provinces. To understand why this was the case, the historical and contextual circumstances that existed in India in the first half of the twentieth century have to be kept in mind.

Following the round table conferences, the Act of 1935 introduced some more elements of a federal model within colonial India. Arguably, the continuing influence of the Act of 1935 on the Constitution is strongest in the realm of federalism, as many of its signature elements were transposed, either directly or after slight modifications. The Act of 1935 drew considerably from Canadian and Australian federal models, which the British naturally looked to as precedents.[5] The Act applied to three types of units: the provinces, Princely States and what were termed as 'Chief Commissioner's Provinces'. The latter were directly administered by the Central authorities (these came to be termed 'Union Territories' in independent India). The Government of India Act 1935 sought to create a federal Union which would be obligatory for the provinces of British India, but could be voluntarily joined by the Princely States. Replacing the existing system of 'dyarchy', the Act proposed two levels of government in India, with the Governor-General and provincial Governors as well as ministries responsible to indirectly elected legislators at the Central and provincial levels. The jurisdiction and powers of the two levels of government were demarcated in three lists, setting out the subjects on which the federal legislature and the provinces could make law. The third of these lists, called the Concurrent List, enabled both levels of government to make law, but the federal government would have superior claims to its use. The list system, inspired by the Canadian and Australian Constitutions, made its entry into India through the Act of 1919, but was more fully developed in the Act of 1935, and became the basis for the distribution of powers in the Constitution of India. The provisions relating to distribution of revenues and federal finance in the Act of 1935 were, as we will see, also largely adopted by the Constitution of India.

[5] AB Keith, *A Constitutional History of India, 1600–1935* (New Delhi, Pacific Publication, 2010) 354–59.

The Act of 1935 also had provisions with respect to local government. The latter came under the control of provincial governments but no common legal structure or status was created for them. While they enabled Indian leaders to gain representative office and obtain experience in the practice of parliamentary processes, their powers, finances and functions were limited and controlled by provincial legislatures and Central authorities.[6]

Even as it devolved some power to the provinces, it is important to remember that the Act of 1935 was an instrument of colonial power. Consequently, it contained several mechanisms by which the Central authority could retain power and wrest back control. This is evident most clearly in the powers of the Governor-General to issue 'ordinances' and the 'emergency' provisions which enabled him to take over the governance of a particular province, particularly through the infamous section 93 procedure. The legacy of such provisions continues to haunt the constitutional democracy inaugurated in post-colonial India, which retained these provisions.

Ultimately, the Princely States opted not to join the federation, and the federal system envisaged by the Act of 1935 was only partially operationalised, in the British Indian provinces. However, the working of the Act of 1935 allowed the leaders of the Indian National Congress to experience 'responsible government' for the first time across a period of nearly two years, before they resigned en masse in October–November 1939 to protest at the unilateral decision of the British to involve British India in the Second World War. The fact that the only experience that the Congress politicians had of governance occurred within the framework of a centralised form of governmental structure might well have made them more inclined to the virtues of centralisation, since they had 'neither experienced nor participated in the working of a more traditional federal system like that of the United States or Australia'.[7] As we will see, however, the Indian nationalists had more substantive reasons for opting for a strongly federal model of government.

[6] KC Sivaramakrishnan, 'Local Government' in Sujit Choudhry, Madhav Khosla and Pratap Mehta (eds), *The Oxford Handbook of the Indian Constitution* (Oxford, Oxford University Press, 2016) 562.

[7] Granville Austin, *The Indian Constitution: Cornerstone of a Nation* (Oxford, Oxford University Press, 1966, reprinted in 2013) 235.

At the time of independence in 1947, British India consisted of 17 provinces, while the Princely States numbered nearly 600. These territorial units were completely altered in the post-independence era—both in terms of their physical boundaries and the nature of their populations due to extensive migration—when they became 'States' in the Republic of India. Of the 17 provinces from British India, 11 joined India, three joined Pakistan and the remaining three were partitioned between India and Pakistan. Of the Princely States, 552 joined India. 216 of these were merged into the former provinces; 275 were combined to form five new States, and the four largest units became States in India without substantial changes.[8]

III. UNDERSTANDING THE CENTRALISING BIAS WITHIN THE CONSTITUENT ASSEMBLY

> The members of the Constituent Assembly were not the representatives of separate states come together, as in the United States, to frame a constitution making them one nation. They were the members of a family who, for the first time in possession of their own house, must find a way to live together in it.[9]

By the time the framers of the Indian Constitution met in Delhi in 1947 to commence their monumental drafting work, several considerations had emerged to make the adoption of a centralised federal order nearly inevitable. As set out in greater detail in Chapter 1, shortly after the Assembly commenced work, the decision that British India was to be formally partitioned into the states of India and Pakistan was announced in June 1947, to take effect a mere two months later in August 1947. This led to violence on a horrific scale and the forced movement of nearly 15 million people, which in turn led to the influx of refugees in large numbers in both India and the newly created state of Pakistan. The prospect of communal tensions had in fact dominated the thinking of nationalist leaders since at least the 1920s. Several constitutional proposals advanced by the Indian National Congress had

[8] Francine R Frankel, *India's Political Economy 1947–2004*, 2nd edition (Oxford, Oxford University Press, 2005) 74.

[9] Austin (n 7) 239.

suggested federalism as an avenue for addressing communal tension, on the logic that allegiance to provincial autonomy would compromise unity. In the aftermath of Partition, the consensus view was that 'only a strong government could survive the communal frenzy preceding and accompanying Partition, accomplish the administrative tasks created by Partition and the transfer of power, and resettle the refugees'.[10]

There were other pragmatic reasons for preferring a centralised State: very few of the 552 Princely States had any effective governance systems, and most were hostile to the idea of co-operating with the newly formed government of India. In such a situation a strong government would be essential to meet the challenge posed by their existence. As already noted, the only experience that many of the new Indian leaders had of governance was under the centralised federal system created by the Act of 1935. That experience further convinced many within the Indian National Congress that the only way to secure the primary goals of the nationalist movement (of improving the quality of life of ordinary Indians, many of whom suffered from dire poverty, and of increasing agricultural and industrial productivity) was through a powerful Central authority. An independent factor which favoured centralisation was the unstable financial position of the new Indian state, which confronted a climate of economic uncertainty and whose finances were already being stretched by a range of hostile circumstances.

These overall circumstances also had a profound impact on demands for local government within the Assembly, where a sizable number of members strongly argued that the traditional village panchayat should be recognised as the basic unit of provincial government and should be financially empowered. This view received strong support from the Gandhians in the Assembly as Gandhi had favoured a state constituted by independent and self-sufficient village republics. The opponents of this view were led by BR Ambedkar, who viewed the traditional Indian village as the chief source of exploitation of the communities referred to as Untouchables. Eventually a compromise was worked out: Article 40, housed in the judicially unenforceable Directive Principles of State Policy, exhorted the Indian State to make efforts to organise village panchayats. This provision completely ignored urban local government

[10] ibid 236.

institutions and was viewed as an ineffective guarantee by itself. More significantly, the Assembly bestowed legislative power over local government on State governments rather than the Central government, which was to have long-term consequences for the ability to decentralise power to local government institutions over time.

All this did not, however, mean that the framers in the Assembly failed to appreciate the need for a federal and decentralised as opposed to an entirely unitary State. The experience of governing under the Act of 1935 had given rise to the phenomenon of the 'provincial politician' and some of them had assumed significant power within the Indian National Congress, becoming champions of a limited form of provincial autonomy (though still a far cry from their predecessors in other federal systems). To understand the special nature of federalism and local government in India, we now turn to the actual provisions and structures set up in the text of the Constitution.

IV. THE STRUCTURE AND CONTENT OF PROVISIONS IN THE INDIAN CONSTITUTION ON FEDERALISM AND THEIR EVOLUTION OVER TIME

As noted earlier, the Constitution of India divides and confers governmental power across several planes. Institutionally speaking, these planes have overlapping but also distinct dimensions. At the horizontal level, as we saw in Chapter 2, governmental power is divided between the executive (the President, the Prime Minister and the Council of Ministers), the legislature (the Union Parliament, consisting of a directly elected Lok Sabha and an indirectly elected Rajya Sabha), and the judiciary (a unitary judiciary with the Supreme Court of India at its head). The vertical division of power, which is our concern when considering federalism and decentralisation, is between the Union and the States. The States were initially divided into four categories (Part A States being the former provinces, Part B States being the former Princely States, Part C States being the former Chief Commissioners' Provinces and 'Andaman and Nicobar' being the sole Part D State). However, after the reorganisation of States in 1956, an event which requires separate focus later, the two categories are now known as States and Union Territories. At the time of writing, there are 29 States and seven Union Territories in India. In 1992, through the enactment of the 73rd and the 74th constitutional amendments, a third tier of governance was added in the vertical plane through the introduction of sub-State level, village and municipal-based political institutions. An analysis of this important set of changes in a separate section will show that while decentralisation has been introduced at the *political* level, the failure to simultaneously bring about *administrative* and *fiscal* decentralisation has hampered the effectiveness of these changes. There is also a set of institutions—such as the Finance Commission, the Inter-State Council, the Inter-State Tribunals, the National Development Council and the Planning Commission (replaced by the *Niti Ayog* in mid-2014)—which serve as bridging mechanisms, enabling *transversal* as well as horizontal power sharing between the various planes identified above.[11]

In the following sub-sections, we focus on some crucial dimensions of textual aspects of federalism in India. The narrative also seeks to track the changes that have been made to the original provisions over time and to briefly explain the broader context that may have motivated such changes. At times, the changing context has to do with the narrative of the evolution of the political landscape of India that was briefly summarised in Chapter 2. That narrative will be referred to incidentally in explaining the specific trajectory of provisions of federalism and local government.

A. The Federal Power to Rearrange and Create New States: Articles 2–4

Focusing more squarely on the provisions directly relating to federal relations, Articles 2–4 of the Constitution are among the unusual features of Indian federalism. These provisions vest in the Parliament the power to create new States or to alter the area of an existing State, doing away with the traditional sanctity accorded to the territorial boundaries of constituent units within federations. Although Article 3 imposes a requirement that the affected States be 'consulted', Parliament is not bound to consider the view of the States affected and

[11] Subrata K Mitra and Malte Pehl, 'Federalism' in Niraja Gopal Jayal and Pratap Bhanu Mehta (eds), *The Oxford Companion to Politics in India* (Oxford, Oxford University Press, 2010) 46–47.

the change in territory can be effected by a mere parliamentary law, without having to pursue a constitutional amendment. This has resulted in changes in the nomenclature and form of States at regular intervals in India. The original motivation for these provisions appears to have been to ensure that considerations of national unity were given priority over claims for provincial autonomy and identity. At least some of the framers appear to have been concerned that without such provisions, the demands for linguistic provinces (which had been increasing rapidly since August 1946) would increase and overtake the nation-building efforts of the new government.[12] The influential members of the Assembly managed to resist such efforts within the Constituent Assembly, but these demands continued to escalate into the 1950s during the post-independence phase. In 1953, over his initial objections, Prime Minister Nehru had to accept the formation of the new State of Andhra Pradesh or face the prospect of violent agitation among the Telegu people. Once the dam had been breached, the demand for linguistic reorganisation grew stronger and in 1956 Parliament enacted a law to enable the creation and rearrangement of several States along linguistic lines. Following this, the units within India were reclassified, resulting in 14 States and six Union Territories. At the time of writing, that has increased to 29 States and seven Union Territories. The steady increase in the number of States has been a consequence of shifting political developments across the vast nation. Following Nehru's logic, there was a sense in 1956 that the movement for linguistic States would lead to the Balkanisation of India. Over time, however, scholars have come to recognise that the phenomenon of linguistic reorganisation has consolidated rather than diminished unity in India, by acting as a 'constructive channel for provincial pride'[13] and by facilitating multiple identities among the vast numbers of people who reside within the Indian nation.

Demands for new States have, somewhat unusually, 'become an everyday feature of the political marketplaces' in India.[14] So far, there

[12] Austin (n 7) 294–302.

[13] Ramachandra Guha, *India after Gandhi* (London, Macmillan, 2007) 180–200 at 200. See also Domenico Amirante, 'Nation-building through Constitutionalism: Lessons from the Indian Experience' (2012) 42 *Hong Kong Law Journal* 23, 34–35.

[14] Louise Tillin, *Remapping India: New States and Their Political Origins* (New Delhi, Oxford University Press, 2013) 1. Tillin sets out the following major dates as

have been five major revisions to State boundaries in India since 1947, even as other smaller changes have occurred with regularity. These have included: (i) the merging of Princely States and former British provisions at the time of independence between 1947 and 1950; (ii) the creation of 'linguistic' States in the 1950s and 1960s; (iii) the formation of autonomous units for minority communities in the State of Assam in north-east India between the 1960s and 1980s; (iv) the reorganisation and creation of the three new States of Chattisgarh, Jharkhand and Uttarakhand within the predominantly Hindi-speaking region of north and central India in 2000; and (v) the carving out of the new State of Telengana out of the existing State of Andhra Pradesh in 2014.

B. The Distribution of Legislative Power

Part XI of the Constitution of India, comprising Articles 245–300A, is entitled 'Relations between the Union and States'. It consists of two chapters that deal respectively with 'Legislative relations' and 'Administrative relations'. Despite the implicit suggestions in the title, provisions affecting federal–State relations, and the distribution of powers between them, are scattered throughout the text of the Constitution. Articles 245 and 246, read with the Seventh Schedule to the Constitution, lay down the scope of the legislative powers of the Union and the States within the territories over which they have exclusive power. The subjects over which the Union legislature has exclusive power are set out in List I (or the 'Union List') of the Seventh Schedule. The Union List contains 97 entries including important subjects such as 'Defence of India' (Entry 1), 'Foreign

representing major moments in the reorganisation of states in India: 1950 (creation of Part A, B and C states); 1953 (creation of Andhra); 1956 (creation of Andhra Pradesh, Assam, Bihar, Bombay, Delhi (UT), Himachal Pradesh (UT), Jammu and Kashmir, Kerala, Madhya Pradesh, Madras, Manipur (UT), Mysore, Orissa, Punjab, Rajasthan, Uttar Pradesh, Tripura (UT) and West Bengal); 1960 (Bombay divided into Gujarat and Maharashtra); 1962 (Goa, Daman and Diu); 1963 (Nagaland); 1966 (Punjab divided into Punjab and Haryana); 1971 (Himachal Pradesh made into a state); 1972 (Meghalaya created from Assam, Arunachal Pradesh (UT), Mizoram (UT), Manipur and Tripura given statehood); 1975 (Sikkim); 1987 (Arunachal Pradesh, Mizoram and Goa given statehood); 2000 (creating Chattisgarh, Jharkhand and Uttarakhand); ibid 209–10. To this can be added 2014 (Telengana), an event that occurred after the publication of Tillin's book.

affairs' (Entry 10), 'Banking' (Entry 45), 'Insurance' (Entry 47), 'Taxes on income other than agricultural income' (Entry 82) and 'Offences against laws with respect to any of the matters in this list' (Entry 93). List II (or 'The State List') comprises 66 entries over which the States have exclusive power to make laws, and consists of subjects such as 'Police' (Entry 2), 'Public health and sanitation' (Entry 6), 'Agriculture' (Entry 14) and 'Betting and Gambling' (Entry 34). List III (or 'The Concurrent List') sets out 47 subjects on which both the Union and the State legislatures can pass laws. The subjects include 'Criminal law' (Entry 1), 'Marriage and divorce' (Entry 5) and 'Economic and social planning' (Entry 20).

Judging by the quantity and quality of the entries, it is clear that the Union legislature is the dominant actor in this context. This impression is confirmed by a reading of Article 248, which declares that residuary power of legislation vests in the Union Parliament, a departure from the norm in several federal States where residuary powers vest in the State units. Several other provisions in the first chapter outline how the basic distribution of power can be altered to the advantage of the Union through action by the Council of States and the Union Executive. During the lead-up to the Constituent Assembly, there was considerable debate among Indian nationalists over the issue of residuary powers, which also took on a communal dimension. Hindu groups generally asked for residuary power to vest in the federal government whereas Muslim groups, fearing that this would lead to less protection for minorities, wanted residuary power to vest in the provinces. The Indian National Congress had taken contrasting stances on this issue but by the time this came up for decision in the Constituent Assembly, the state of Pakistan had been created and the Assembly decided to vest such powers in the Union.

Two broad reasons were asserted for the dominance of the Union Parliament on the issue of distribution of legislative powers.[15] The first was that of constitutional flexibility. BR Ambedkar expressly drew a contrast with rigid federal Constitutions such as that of Australia, which, according to him, suffered from providing only three matters where the Australian Commonwealth had exclusive legislative authority. Ambedkar believed that giving the Indian Parliament greater powers in this respect would 'lead to the greatest possible elasticity in its

[15] Austin (n 7) 198–99.

federalism'.[16] The second reason follows from a rationale noted earlier: the desire of the framers to enable the Union to meet the pressing economic needs of the people and to withstand the pressures of economic uncertainty, national security concerns and related factors. Internal governmental documents from the time reveal the preoccupation of the founding generation with such matters and their conviction that only a strong central authority could secure these goals.

For the purposes of local government institutions it is significant, as noted earlier, that legislative power over them vests with the State governments, under Entry 5 of List II. This was sought to be altered through the introduction of local government institutions via the 73rd and 74th constitutional amendments in 1992, but as we shall see in a subsequent section, the presence of Entry 5 in List II appears to have had a restraining effect, with negative consequences for the administrative and financial powers of local government institutions.

Over time, the Indian judiciary has played a major role in resolving disputes over interpreting Articles 245 and 246. Judges have evolved a number of doctrines, often borrowing from the prior rulings of Canadian and Australian courts, to find creative ways of doing so.[17] The general view of scholars is that the judiciary has, in doing so, 'clarified and harmonized many aspects of centre–State relations'.[18] Later we will examine how the Supreme Court has performed crucial roles in safeguarding the federal character of the Indian Constitution in specific areas.

C. Executive and Emergency Powers in Relation to Federalism

The pronounced tilt towards the Union is strongly evident in these provisions, several of which were either lifted directly from or inspired by

[16] Constituent Assembly Debates (CAD) VII 1, 35–36.

[17] For details of some of these innovative court actions, see Madhav Khosla, *The Indian Constitution* (New Delhi, Oxford University Press, 2012) 48–66. Also see Sudhir Krishnaswamy, 'Constitutional Federalism in the Indian Supreme Court' in Mark Tushnet and Madhav Khosla (eds), *Unstable Constitutionalism: Law and Politics in South Asia* (Cambridge, Cambridge University Press, 2015) 355–80.

[18] Ravi P Bhatia, 'Federalism in India and the Supreme Court Rulings' in BD Dua and MP Singh, *Indian Federalism in the New Millennium* (New Delhi, Manohar, 2003) 231.

their analogues in the Act of 1935. Article 256, which has rarely been invoked in practice, stipulates that every State should exercise its executive power to ensure compliance with parliamentary laws. It further empowers the Union executive to issue directions to ensure such compliance. Many of the provisions in Chapter II of Part XI (specifically Articles 256–261) seek to empower the Union executive in respect of diverse situations. One of the most controversial provisions in the context of federal–State relations is Article 356. This provision empowers the President of India (who acts on the advice of the Union Cabinet) to declare that a situation has arisen in which the government of a State cannot be carried out in accordance with the provisions of the Constitution. To reach this decision, the President must have received a report issued by the Governor of a State (who is an unelected, political appointee very often beholden to the ruling party at the Union). This then enables the President to assume to himself the powers of the State government, giving rise to the popular understanding that the provision authorises 'President's Rule'.

As already noted, this provision bears resemblance to Section 93 of the Act of 1935 and was criticised in the Constituent Assembly for continuing the colonial abuse of executive authority at the expense of legislative power. Defenders of this provision in the Assembly included Alladi Krishnaswamy Aiyyar and BR Ambedkar. Ayyar once again alluded to the prevailing mindset among the elite echelons of the Congress Party: 'the grave and difficult times facing the nation'.[19] There were no doubt significant troubles confronting the nation at the time, including 'the lawlessness and terrorism in Bengal, the continuing activities of the Communists in Telangana, as well as the uncertain agricultural and financial situation'.[20] Ambedkar, however, saw the force of the argument and the very real potential for abuse. He argued that the provision was a measure of last resort in times of severe governmental crisis. However, he did not take the criticism on board beyond agreeing with the hope expressed by another member that the Union would ensure that the legislature was dissolved and fresh elections called for, thereby giving the province a second chance to manage its own affairs before the Union intervened.

[19] CAD IX 4, 151.
[20] Austin (n 7) 267.

This hope was, however, not realised in actual practice, as frequent invocation of the provision in later years demonstrated. On an average, President's Rule under Article 356 was declared 1.5 times per year during the years between 1951 and 1966, 3.1 times between 1967 and 1988, and 2.3 times between 1989 and 1997.[21] The lower rate of invocation of this provision since the early 1990s can be attributed to the proactive role taken by the Supreme Court in the cases of *S.R. Bommai v Union of India* (1994)[22] and *Rameshwar Prasad v Union of India* (2006).[23] In both cases, the Supreme Court showed that it was willing to adopt creative interpretations of the provisions involved to impose checks and balances on their use, including conducting a basic review of the grounds on which the President exercised his power. This, more than any change in the actual text of the provision and coupled with the changing political context in India which witnessed coalition governments from the early 1990s onwards, seems to have stemmed the abuse of Article 356. In the most recent past, since the ascension to power of the Modi Government in May 2014, there has been renewed invocation of President's Rule in the States of Arunachal Pradesh (June–August 2015) and Uttarakhand (April 2016). It is too early to tell whether this signals yet another chapter in the tortuous saga of Article 356; a lot will depend on how the judiciary reacts to the renewed manipulation of the provision.

D. Fiscal Federalism: The Distribution of Revenues and Finances Between the Union and the States

One of the requirements of a classic federal Constitution is that 'both general and regional governments must each have under their own independent control financial resources sufficient to perform their exclusive functions'.[24] The Indian case fits this classic notion of federalism rather poorly. Once again, it is a contextual understanding

[21] Mitra and Pehl (n 11) 51.

[22] *S.R. Bommai v Union of India*, AIR 1994 SC 1918.

[23] *Rameshwar Prasad v Union of India*, AIR 2006 SC 980.

[24] KC Wheare, *Federal Government*, 4th edn (London, Oxford University Press, 1963) 97.

of the existing historical circumstances that enables an understanding of the reasons for this particular departure from the norm. Austin invokes the familiarity of the leaders of the Indian National Congress with the working of the Act of 1935 as a reason, since most of the constitutional provisions in relation to finance are closely modelled on that statute. This, according to Austin, has resulted in a situation 'making the union government the banker and collecting agent for the state governments'.[25] Another factor worth recalling is that the provinces had a relatively low bargaining status: no provincial delegation could quit the Assembly and this had to be borne in mind while negotiating for claims on behalf of the provinces in the Constitution. A significant factor that contributed to this mindset was the extremely unstable and uncertain financial situation confronting the newly formed nation. All of this reinforced the view that finances should be tightly regulated and carefully controlled, preferably through a centralised system. There was also a consensus among the decision makers in the Assembly that the primary consideration for distribution of revenues should be based on the 'need' of provinces. This was against the reality (then and now) that the provinces in India vary greatly in their access to resources and wealth, resulting in some being very rich while many others are poor and in need of support for providing social welfare and development related services.

The response of the Assembly was to adopt the following arrangement: certain basic taxes and revenue from them were to be left within the legislative jurisdiction of the provinces but the most lucrative tax heads were to be levied and collected by the Union and distributed among the provinces according to their need.[26] The result of such a logic was an increase in the authority of the Union, which also became the arbiter of which province was deservedly needy and how much proportion of revenues it was entitled to, over or below the entitlement of other provinces. Recognising that this important power was a great one, and hence capable of being abused, the framers sought to empower the Finance Commission to play the role of guardian. We now turn to the actual provisions in the Constitution which reflect the final decisions of the Assembly on issues of distribution of revenues and finance summarised above.

[25] Austin (n 7) 275.
[26] ibid 276.

Part XII of the Constitution is entitled 'Finance, Property, Contracts and Suits' and comprises Articles 264–300A. A section of this Part, consisting of Articles 268–281, is entitled 'Distribution of Revenues between the Union and States'. Article 280 provides for the creation of a Finance Commission, which, as noted above, has a significant role to play in the distribution of revenues because the Constitution only outlines how certain revenues are to be levied and collected but does not prescribe how the proceeds are to be distributed. The Finance Commission is bestowed with the important power to decide how to make adjustments in the distribution of revenues and thus affect the balance of the federal system. As noted above, the provisions in this section of the Constitution authorise the allocation of the more lucrative sources of revenue such as import or export duties, non-agricultural income tax and corporate taxes to the Union government. The Union is also empowered, as we have seen, to levy residual tax powers.

The revenues of the States arise from four principal sources: (i) tax and expenditure derived from subjects set out in the State List of the Seventh Schedule; (ii) transfers allocated by the Finance Commission (Article 275); (iii) transfers from the Planning Commission (an extra-constitutional body set up by Prime Minister Nehru which came to assume significant powers in the Nehruvian era but has since 2014 been demoted to one of lesser status); and (iv) transfers from central ministry budgets to the States. The transfers in the latter category assume the form of grants and loans to the States.[27]

Although States could potentially levy taxes on a host of subjects in the State List, in practice only the tax on sale of goods has turned out to be significant for State revenues.[28] This is also because, under pressure of populism, many States have either done away with or drastically reduced the taxation on land and income from agriculture. This has resulted in a drastic reduction of the capacity of States to finance both revenue and capital expenditure from their own resources: in 2000–01, only 42 per cent of the States' total expenditure was covered by their own revenue receipts.[29]

[27] Mitra and Pehl (n 11) 52.

[28] Nirvikar Singh, 'Fiscal Federalism' in Sujit Choudhry, Madhav Khosla and Pratap Mehta (eds), *The Oxford Handbook of the Indian Constitution* (Oxford, Oxford University Press, 2016) 4.

[29] Nirvikar Singh, 'India's System of Intergovernmental Fiscal Relations', Working Paper, Santa Cruz Department of Economics, University of California, 2004.

The Finance Commission sought to remedy this situation by allocating resources based on changing criteria. From 1950 to 1995 all the Finance Commissions worked on the original criterion of 'need' to make recommendations for distribution of revenues, which were invariably followed without question. Starting from the Tenth Finance Commission (1995–2000), the earlier trend witnessed a change, arguably as a result of policies of liberalisation that were introduced into the Indian economy in the early 1990s. This is evident also in the attempt of the Thirteenth Finance Commission (2010–15) to assign greater weight to economic performance of States over the older criteria of population and backwardness.[30] The introduction of a General Sales Tax through the 101st constitutional amendment (2016) is viewed as a significant change. It bears the promise of further altering the evolving shape of fiscal federalism in contemporary India.

The original constitutional provisions relating to distribution of revenues have undergone several changes, either because of express constitutional amendments or due to changes brought about in the interpretation of the provisions by the courts.[31] As we will see, changes in the political landscape of post-independence India have sometimes had a profound effect on federal–State relations in other contexts. Overall, in the assessment of a leading scholar, 'the Constitution of India has provided a durable and flexible, if imperfect, framework for India's fiscal federal arrangements'.[32]

E. Provisions Exemplifying Asymmetric Federalism in India

One of the features of a classic federal state is that it treats its constituent units equally and provides some guarantee that they will not be treated unequally, and hence, unfairly in relation to each other. By this logic, federalism necessarily has to be symmetrical. Indeed, the scholar who coined the term 'asymmetrical federalism' gave it a negative connotation, focusing on its 'secession potential'.[33] In more recent work, other scholars have given it a positive normative connotation by considering

[30] Singh (n 2) 166–67.
[31] ibid.
[32] ibid.
[33] Charles Tarlton, 'Symmetry and Asymmetry as Elements of Federalism: A Theoretical Speculation' (1965) 27(4) *Journal of Politics* 861–74.

polities that subscribe to this concept as those which 'in order to "hold together" their great diversity in one democratic system, had to embed in the Constitution special cultural and historical prerogatives for some of the member units, prerogatives that respond to their somewhat different linguistic or cultural aspirations, demands, and historical identities'.[34] Not surprisingly, the principal focus of these scholars is on Indian federalism which, they assert, was an early exemplar of the 'asymmetric federalism' model.

India's federal model is rife with asymmetries. As we have noted, the original classification of States was based on their different pedigree and needs. Even today, the States and Union Territories are treated differently and there are further differences between the Union Territories themselves and the National Capital Territory of Delhi, which enjoys a unique status. Besides these, there are three major types of asymmetry in Indian federalism, First, Article 370 provides an example of asymmetric federalism because it grants the State of Jammu and Kashmir, which is the only State to have its own Constitution, autonomy in respects that other States in India are not entitled to (at least in theory).[35] The second major example of asymmetric federalism in India is the special measures for 'Scheduled Tribes' set out in the Fifth and Sixth Schedules to the Constitution. The Fifth Schedule applies to majority tribal districts outside of the north-east States, and enables the Union government, acting through the Governor, to intervene to aid the socio-economic development of tribal populations. Each State covered by the Fifth Schedule is to establish a Tribal Advisory Council and the Governor is empowered to declare that particular parliamentary or State legislative enactments are not to apply to Scheduled Areas. The Sixth Schedule applies to States in the north-east of India and creates entities referred

[34] Alfred Stepan, Juan Linz and Yogendra Yadav, *Crafting State Nations* (Baltimore, MD, John Hopkins University Press, 2010) 5. See also the discussion of asymmetric federalism in Khosla (n 17) 74–86.

[35] As Louise Tillin notes, 'the extension of very numerous constitutional provisions to Jammu and Kashmir via presidential orders has reduced the extent to which Article 370 has functioned as a form of ethnic conflict management'. See, Louise Tillin, 'Asymmetric Federalism' in Sujit Choudhry, Madhav Khosla and Pratap Mehta (eds), *The Oxford Handbook of the Indian Constitution* (Oxford, Oxford University Press, 2016) 545–47.

to as 'Autonomous District Councils' (ADCs), which are given more extensive powers of self-governance and have been established in the States of Assam, Meghalaya, Tripura and Mizoram. The third category of asymmetric treatment is to be found in the special provisions for other States that are captured in the 11 provisions that constitute Articles 371–371J.[36] These consist of special arrangements for new States that have been created or admitted since independence as a result of two types of processes: the reorganisation of State boundaries, which gave rise to concerns about intra-State equity in newly merged regions, and the resolution of ethnic conflicts in the north-east States. As noted earlier, the Indian Union's willingness to make such special concessions to individual federal units has been praised by scholars as contributing to the integration of States that have at times experienced secessionist movements, and for facilitating plural identities and avoiding the perils of the creation of uniform national identities.[37]

At the same time, other scholars have doubted how committed the Indian State is to the asymmetric model, whether it alone can explain the relative success of the Indian federation, and whether the States that are the ostensible beneficiaries of asymmetric provisions are actually benefiting from them.[38] It has been noted, for instance, that asymmetric options were not considered in dealing with the tensions with two of India's major States—Tamil Nadu (1950s–1960s) and Punjab (1980s).[39] The debate over whether India's asymmetric features enhance or curb its unique model of federalism is thus an open and continuing one.

[36] These provisions deal respectively with special provisions for the states of Maharashtra and Gujarat, Nagaland, Assam, Manipur, Andhra Pradesh, Sikkim, Mizoram, Arunachal Pradesh, Goa and Karnataka.

[37] Stepan et al (n 34) 5. See also Domenico Amirante, 'Nation Building through Constitutionalism: Lessons from Indian Constitutionalism' (2012) 42 *Hong Kong Law Journal* 23–42.

[38] Louise Tillin, 'United in Diversity, Asymmetry in Indian Federalism' (2007) 37(1) *Publius: the Journal of Federalism* 45–67; Khosla (n 17) 85–86 (questioning whether Jammu and Kashmir and the north-east states have benefited from the asymmetric provisions carved out for them).

[39] Tillin (n 38) 47.

F. Assessing the Evolution of the Federal Model in India Across Its Post-independence Years

Bargains about federalism are deeply intertwined with contemporaneous socio-political issues. If India's economic and political situation in 1947 had been more stable, perhaps the need for ensuring national unity and focusing on a top-down model of development would have been less pressing and the Constitution's provisions relating to federalism would have evolved differently.

Scholars of federalism in India generally agree that the post-independence evolution of federalism in India has similarly been affected by socio-political and economic changes across the decades since independence. In this section I seek to cover some of this discussion, to provide a sense of these changes and their momentous consequences.

Lloyd and Susan Rudolph have argued that federalism in post-independence India has transformed from 'a relatively centralised "old" to a relatively decentralised "new" federalism'.[40] According to this analysis, the period of four decades from 1950 to 1990 can be characterised as exemplifying the 'old' federalism model, while the period from 1990 onwards is representative of the 'new' model. For the Rudolphs, the following features were prominent in the 'old' model: (i) a planned economy which was characterised by Prime Minister Nehru's desire to industrialise India through a process of central planning for which the extra-constitutional Planning Commission was created; (ii) the existence of a one-party dominant system which enabled the Indian National Congress to counter the constitutional divisions of functions across many levels; (iii) a model of fiscal federalism where the Union government and Finance Commission, which took cues from the Union government, dictated terms to the States with hardly any resistance. By contrast, the 'new' federal model that began to emerge from 1989 onwards had the following characteristics: (i) the replacement of the planned economy with a market economy, which saw a diminishing role for centralised institutions such as the

[40] Lloyd I Rudolph and Susanne Hoeber Rudolph, 'The Old and the New Federalism in Independent India' in Paul Brass (ed), *The Routledge Handbook of South Asian Politics* (London, Routledge, 2010) 147–61.

Planning Commission, replaced instead by a growing role for State Chief Ministers and entrepreneurs; (ii) the substitution of a one-party dominant system with that of a multiparty system, where regional parties began to play a key role in the formation of coalition governments at the centre and in the making of policy decisions; and consequently, (iii) the transformation of the model of fiscal federalism, which in turn witnessed State Chief Ministers pushing back against traditional directives issued by the Finance Commission and demanding market-based measures to determine allocation of revenues and funds.[41]

It is clear that India's complex model of federalism will continue to evolve to meet the demands of its ever-changing political landscape. The attempt here has been to provide a brief overview of its overall features and to outline a narrative of their evolution up to the present time.

V. THE STRUCTURE AND CONTENT OF PROVISIONS IN THE INDIAN CONSTITUTION ON LOCAL GOVERNMENT AND THEIR EVOLUTION OVER TIME

A. Background and Post-independence History of Local Government Initiatives

The story of how local government institutions found constitutional recognition nearly four-and-a-half decades after they were given short shrift at the time of the founding of the republic is a long and fascinating one, with complex political motivations guiding different actors at different points of time.

As noted earlier, the framers of the Constitution did not make a binding commitment in relation to issues of local government beyond

[41] See also the analysis of Mitra and Pehl, who consider the evolution of federalism in post-colonial India across three phases: Phase I (lasting from 1950 to 1965) characterised by Prime Minister Nehru's statesmanlike approach to federal issues; Phase II (lasting from 1967 to 1989), which initially saw the decline of the Congress, and which led Prime Minister Indira Gandhi to adopt radical measures to shore up her centralised form of leadership; and Phase III (1989–present), which is characterised by coalition governments at the centre and the rise of regional parties. Mitra and Pehl, like the Rudolphs, also consider the impact of policies of liberalisation since the 1990s. Mitra and Pehl (n 11) 45–46.

the vague allusion in Article 40 to the ideal of village panchayats. However, this did not mean that ideas of what a leading scholar has termed 'democratic decentralisation' did not find favour with leaders and elites within the political system.[42] So, even while Prime Minister Nehru was committed to the centralised State that he felt was essential for creating the levels of economic development that had been denied to India under colonial rule, he also championed institutions of local governance and community development.[43] Equally committed were Gandhians such as Vinobha Bhave and Jayaprakash Narayan, who kept up the aspiration for a village republic by making demands for local governance in both rural and urban areas. Through 1947 to the mid-1960s, various efforts were made to enhance local government initiatives, including the launching of the Community Development Programme in 1952.[44]

The aspirations for local government were kept alive through and in a number of government committee reports authored by various significant figures over a period of time. In 1957 the Balwantrai Mehta Committee was established as the Community Development Programmes were perceived, after having been in existence for five years, to be ineffective. The Mehta Committee recommended several measures to strengthen local government initiatives, especially in rural areas. Similarly, the K Santhanam Committee in 1963 and the Ashok Mehta Committee in 1977 also made significant recommendations urging the adoption of local government institutions.

In part as a result of these and other initiatives, local governments had been established in most parts of India by the early to mid-1960s: these included 60,000 village panchayats, 7,500 panchayat samitis (or panchayat Societies), and 330 Zilla Parishads (or District Boards). The situation with respect to urban local bodies was less impressive, in part because most municipalities across the country were vulnerable to supersession by State governments. A mere decade later, the situation had transformed: under Prime Minister Indira Gandhi, who was

[42] James Manor, 'Local Governance' in Niraja Gopal Jayal and Pratap Bhanu Mehta (eds), *The Oxford Companion to Politics in India* (Oxford, Oxford University Press, 2010) 62.

[43] Rani D Mullen, *Decentralization, Local Governance, and Social Wellbeing in India* (London, Routledge, 2010) 28.

[44] Manor (n 42) 63.

among the most centralising of India's several Prime Ministers, local governance initiatives came to a near standstill.

The situation changed again when the first non-Congress government came to power at the central level in 1977, following the defeat of the Indira Gandhi government in the elections held in the aftermath of the Emergency. The Janata Government was in favour of local government structures: one scholar has speculated that this was motivated also by the Janata Party's need to break the political patronage network of the Congress Party, which had entrenched itself after nearly a quarter of a century in power at the centre.[45] A similar political logic may have motivated two other initiatives, also by opposition party governments, to promote local government initiatives at the State level in two major States. The first was by the government of the Communist Party of India (Marxist) in West Bengal, which came to power in 1977 and sought to revive legislation regarding local government institutions. The second was the efforts at local government taken by the Ramakrishna Hegde government in Karnataka after 1983.[46]

Local government reform measures found crucial support among civil society activists as well. By the early 1990s it had become clear that a half century of 'pro-poor' social and economic policies, all of which had adopted a top-down planning model, had not had much effect on the ground. Many civil society and social movement actors were convinced that going beyond these policies, it was necessary that a system which enabled the delivery of social services on the ground and ensures accountability for public programmes at the local level, was introduced. Many such groups thus began backing the idea of local government institutions both at the rural and urban level.[47]

Ultimately, however, it was only when the Congress government under Prime Minister Rajiv Gandhi became committed to the need for local government reform that a central Bill was sought to be passed in 1988. It failed to pass in the Rajya Sabha, in part because the opposition parties perceived the initiative as an attempt to make a direct connection between the central and local governments, bypassing the State governments, many of which were ruled by non-Congress governments.

[45] Mullen (n 43) 29.
[46] Manor (n 42) 64.
[47] Mullen (n 43) 21–22.

By the early 1990s, however, there was a recognition among all political parties that the nature of the old politics had changed and pushing for local government initiatives would benefit various political alignments. The demise of the hegemony of the Congress Party meant that a host of new parties had emerged, several of which had regional, linguistic and caste-based constituencies, which would stand to benefit from stronger attempts at entrenching local government institutions with greater representation for women and lower caste and underprivileged groups. At the same time, the changed scenario also presented opportunities for the Congress Party to reinvent itself and begin a new phase of dominance. It is this political dynamic that explains the relative ease with which the 73rd and 74th constitutional amendments passed in both houses of Parliament in 1992, whereas only four years previously they had been the subject of a pitched battle.

B. The Text, Structure and Content of the Provisions Relating to Local Government

The 73rd and 74th amendments introduced two new Parts into the Constitution: Part IX (entitled 'The Panchayats' and consisting of 16 provisions numbered as Articles 243–243O) and Part IXA (entitled 'The Municipalities' and consisting of 18 provisions numbered as Articles 243P–243ZG). These provisions mandate the creation of rural and urban local government institutions. The former include panchayats at three levels: the village (called 'Gram Sabhas'), the 'intermediate' and the 'district'. Municipalities are of three kinds: Nagar Panchayats for areas transitioning from rural to urban; Municipal Councils for smaller urban areas; and Municipal Corporations for larger urban areas.

It must be emphasised that the new constitutional provisions do not by themselves mandate the implementation of local self-government. Instead, while authorising the creation of local self-governing bodies, they leave the question of delegating powers and functions to these bodies to the State legislatures. This aspect has been criticised for weakening these institutions. However, it is arguable that this is a necessary measure to ensure that the legitimate role of State legislatures in making local government institutions become operational is recognised. Otherwise, the argument goes, these local government bodies would be perceived as measures by which the central government could seek to bypass and undermine State governments. The 73rd and 74th constitutional amendments also introduced two new schedules to the Constitution: the Eleventh Schedule, listing 29 entries on which village panchayats can be empowered to make laws upon by the relevant State legislature, and the Twelfth Schedule, which similarly lists 18 entries upon which municipalities can be given legislative power by the relevant State legislature. These entries touch upon issues such as education, health, child welfare, farm and non-farm activities, and infrastructure for development-related activities.

One of the most significant changes that these provisions introduced was the constitutional recognition of elected local body representatives, adult franchise for this process and the introduction of legislative quotas or reservations for women and lower caste groups. It is clear that these provisions are creating a democratic revolution: there are now over 3 million elected representatives in panchayats and municipalities. Over 1 million of these are women, while Dalits and tribals are also represented as per their proportion in the population.[48]

The constitutional provisions also envisage the creation of State Finance Commissions, mirroring the Finance Commission at the centre, to review the finances of panchayats and municipalities, and to decide on State funds to the different layers of local government bodies.

C. Assessing the Impact of the Introduction of Local Government Institutions

One of the major paradoxes of Indian democracy as it has evolved in relation to issues of federalism and local government is that the very same State governments that have been extremely vocal in demanding more powers, finances and authority for State governments in the context of India's evolving federal model are also the ones who have become the principal obstacles for empowering local government institutions established by Parts IX and IXA of the Constitution. Such institutions of local government rely heavily upon State governments

[48] Kuldeep Mathur, *Panchayati Raj* (New Delhi, Oxford University Press, 2013) 134.

to empower them both administratively and fiscally, as the constitutional provisions only ensure their political existence and sustenance through regular elections. Across the nearly quarter century that these provisions have been in existence, very few State governments have demonstrated the necessary political will to fully implement these constitutional provisions. In many situations, panchayats and municipalities are seen as additions to and not as replacements of the existing administrative structures. Thus, many local government institutions have become mere agencies to implement centrally sponsored schemes. The reluctance of State governments to implement the terms of the Eleventh and Twelfth Schedules has led some scholars to note that 'state governments are more zealous for transfer of powers from the centre to the states than for [further] devolution'.[49] This had led a motivating figure behind the 73rd and 74th amendments to conclude that they were 'failed attempts to widen and deepen federalism'.[50]

Yet other scholars have, however, noted that despite this reality, the fact remains that many positives have emerged. There is no question that there has been a democratic upsurge and that the elected representatives in Gram Sabhas and municipalities are making a difference to the political culture at the grassroots and are making their presence felt. Other scholars report that despite having few autonomous powers in relation to finance, 'fiscal decentralization, in terms of local government having increased funds at their disposal, has clearly occurred over the past two decades in India'.[51] Also, the local government bodies are now able to give 'voice and representation to poorer and generally more vulnerable groups, thereby instituting a system of affirmative action that is intended to improve the welfare of more vulnerable groups over the long term'.[52]

VI. CONCLUSION

This chapter has focused greatly on the colonial period and the framing of the relevant constitutional provisions in the Constituent Assembly

[49] Singh (n 2) 179.
[50] Sivaramakrishnan (n 6) 578.
[51] Mullen (n 43) 38.
[52] ibid 51.

for the reason that those factors continue to dominate how issues of federalism and local government are perceived and negotiated in contemporary India. This is not to suggest, however, that that biography will be determinative of the evolution of federalism and local government in India in the future. As briefly noted, considerable changes have been afoot in recent years. What is interesting about these changes is that very few of them involve actual changes to the textual provisions in relation to federalism and local government in the Indian Constitution. It should be noted that one consequence of the 'basic structure' doctrine formulated by the Supreme Court of India—which we will examine closely in Chapter 7—is that the federal nature of the Indian Constitution cannot be amended away by Parliament as it has been adjudicated to be part of the 'basic structure' of the Constitution of India.

Nevertheless, it is important to remember that Constitutions change not only through formal amendments; at times they change informally in response to shifts in economic and political trends. Such changes, even though they do not result in textual changes, can lead to a complete transformation of the concepts and institutions involved. Some contemporary scholars have asserted the belief that federalism in India has been in a state of flux in recent years. This is particularly so in relation to issues of fiscal federalism and the growing tensions between rich and powerful States which no longer accept the traditional rules for distributing revenues under the model set out in the Constitution. An aspect that is increasingly viewed as failing is the mechanisms for coordinating actions and interests among the States and for their disputes with each other, on the one hand, and the Union on the other.

Similarly, despite the limitations of the textual provisions relating to local government in India, it is clear that they have unleashed new forces of democratic decentralisation which cannot be contained by old mechanisms. The numerous elected representatives are slowly but surely making claims to their due administrative and fiscal powers, which will eventually develop to complement the political power that they already possess under the constitutional amendments enacted in 1992.

It is thus clear that India's models of federalism and local government will continue to witness change and evolution in the foreseeable future. There is also no doubt that the manner in which they have evolved over the post-independence phase of India's history has led to a considerable deepening of its constitutional democracy.

FURTHER READING

Granville Austin, *The Indian Constitution: Cornerstone of a Nation* (New Delhi, Oxford University Press, 1966).

Granville Austin, *Working a Democratic Constitution: A History of the Indian Experience* (New Delhi, Oxford University Press, 2000).

Niraja Gopal Jayal, Amit Prakash and Pradeep Sharma (eds), *Local Governance in India* (New Delhi, Oxford University Press, 2007).

Sudhir Krishnaswamy, 'Constitutional Federalism in the Indian Supreme Court' in Mark Tushnet and Madhav Khosla (eds), *Unstable Constitutionalism: Law and Politics in South Asia* (Cambridge, Cambridge University Press, 2015) 355–80.

James Manor, 'Local Governance' in Niraja Jayal and Pratap Mehta (eds), *The Oxford Companion to Politics in India* (New Delhi, Oxford University Press, 2010) 61–79.

Kuldip Mathur, *Panchayati Raj*, Oxford India Short Introductions (New Delhi, Oxford University Press, 2013).

Subrata K Mitra and Malte Pehl, 'Federalism' in Niraja Jayal and Pratap Mehta (eds), *The Oxford Companion to Politics in India* (New Delhi, Oxford University Press, 2010) 43–60.

Anirudh Prasad, *Centre–State Relations in India: Constitutional Provisions, Judicial Review, Recent Trends* (New Delhi, Deep and Deep Publications, 1995).

MP Singh, 'The Federal Scheme' in Sujit Choudhry, Madhav Khosla and Pratap Mehta (eds), *The Oxford Handbook of the Indian Constitution* (Oxford, Oxford University Press, 2016) 451–65.

Nirvikar Singh, 'Fiscal Federalism' in Sujit Choudhry, Madhav Khosla and Pratap Mehta (eds), *The Oxford Handbook of the Indian Constitution* (Oxford, Oxford University Press, 2016) 521–39.

K Sivaramakrishnan, 'Local Government' in Sujit Choudhry, Madhav Khosla and Pratap Mehta (eds), *The Oxford Handbook of the Indian Constitution* (Oxford, Oxford University Press, 2016) 560–80.

4

Fundamental Rights, Directive Principles and the Judiciary

Constitutional history and text of relevant provisions – Evolution of institutional role of the Indian Supreme Court over five phases – The crisis of backlog and delay

I. INTRODUCTION

THIS CHAPTER FOCUSES on constitutional provisions that address three vital issues: (i) the Fundamental Rights, (ii) the Directive Principles and (iii) the model of a unitary judiciary established by the Constitution of India. The most important role of the Indian judiciary, arguably, is to safeguard, advance and secure the Fundamental Rights guaranteed by the Constitution. However, as will become clear, the framers of the Indian Constitution had several other roles in mind for the judiciary, including being a final court of appeal for all legal issues emanating across the nation, and serving as the referee for maintaining harmonious relations between the Union and the States in India's complex model of federalism. This latter role of the judiciary was briefly summarised in Chapter 3 while dealing with India's model of federalism and local government. That chapter also covered the role of the judiciary in shaping federal relations across six decades of the working of the Constitution.

This chapter therefore focuses on the institutional character and role of the judiciary, which has evolved over time as it has sought to advance and adapt to the demands of safeguarding the Fundamental Rights and Directive Principles. This then is the justification for treating these important but seemingly disparate issues within the same framework. This chapter will seek to argue that while the changing role of the Indian judiciary has much to do with wider changes in the socio-political landscape of the Indian polity, it is also linked to the way judges have changed their interpretive approach to the Rights and Principles over time. The chapter focuses on the well-acknowledged fact that the Indian judiciary has played a vital role in sustaining its constitutional democracy. This fact is even more striking when the Indian experience is compared to that of its judicial counterparts in the immediate South Asian context, where judiciaries have struggled to establish themselves and maintain their independent existence in countries such as Pakistan, Bangladesh, Sri Lanka and Nepal. While this fact is well known, credit for it is usually given to the vision and leadership of judges in India and to wise political leaders who conceded space to judges at crucial times. Less credit is given to the vision of the framers of India's Constitution, who laboured mightily to debate the conditions that would help entrench an independent and democracy-enhancing judiciary in India.

This chapter is divided into four sections. Following this introductory section, Section II deals with the provisions of the Constitution and seeks to analyse the textual scaffolding to draw conclusions about the motivations of categorisations and to infer what has been included, what has been left out, and what may have caused such inclusions and exclusions. This section focuses on the extensive textual provisions relating to the Fundamental Rights, the Directive Principles and the judiciary. It is important to do so because the Indian Constitution was unprecedented at the time of its creation—though it may not be so now—in the level of detail it contains on these issues. This, among other things, exhibits the conviction of the framers that the matters at stake were pivotal to the successful working of the Constitution as a whole. While much has been made of the essential continuities between the colonial legal structure and the post-constitutional order, it is the content of this chapter that makes the novel contributions of the framers of the Indian Constitution stand out. As will become clear, the colonial regime for the most part rejected the discourse of rights and entitlements on the part of the subject population. The colonial judiciary, on the other hand, saw itself more as a subordinate ally of the regime than as an instrument to check the excesses of the other wings of government or as a guardian of the values of the people. The provisions we focus upon also provide an insight into what the framers felt was critical for the audacious Indian constitutional experiment to succeed.

Section III focuses on the relevant constitutional history for these provisions. Here we depart from the norm in this book, where this typically takes up considerable space. The reason is that some of the history for these provisions has been covered quite extensively in Chapter 2. Section III covers the experience of the colonial judiciary to provide context for the changes that were made to that system by the Constitution. As in other chapters, the latter half of this chapter too will focus upon the developments that occurred in the six decades of the working of the Constitution. However, more than in other chapters, the emphasis will also be on assessing the significance of the original constitutional provisions, which marked quite radical departures from pre-existing practices and could be said to have contributed greatly to the robust rights discourse that the increasingly powerful judiciary could deploy to enhance its own powers and jurisdiction.

Section IV focuses on the role of the Supreme Court of India in interpreting the rights provisions from independence until the present time, seeking to identify broad trends across the six-and-a-half decades that the Constitution has been in force. This will necessarily have to be a summary—and selective—survey since both the volume and range of cases is large. This section will also focus, relatedly, on the consequences of such trends for the understanding of the Fundamental Rights and Directive Principles. The claim is that these developments were inextricably intertwined and cannot be understood in isolation from each other. Section V focuses on the extremely distressing levels of backlog and pendency in the Indian judicial system, which are greatly impeding its ability to function at a reasonably acceptable level. This failing too, as it turns out, is something that can be ascribed to constitutional design.

II. RELEVANT CONSTITUTIONAL PROVISIONS: TEXTUAL CATEGORISATION AND ANALYSIS

This section provides a brief overview of the textual provisions relating to rights, principles and the judiciary. While Bills of Rights were not drawn up from scratch by the framers of the Indian Constitution (indeed, they expressly drew inspiration from earlier efforts and sought openly to emulate them), their efforts at identifying particularities were innovatively extensive. It is for this reason that their efforts came to be studied closely by Constitution makers who sought inspiration for their own Constitutions across the next half-century, extending from countries in Southeast Asia to Southern Africa.

A. Fundamental Rights

The 'Fundamental Rights' guaranteed to Indians are outlined in Part III of the Constitution of India, which consists of 23 provisions (Articles 12–35). The rights guaranteed by this Part are classified under eight sub-headings. Six of these sub-headings guarantee the following categories of rights: the right to equality (Articles 14–18); the right to freedom (Articles 19–23); the right against exploitation (Articles 23–24); the right to freedom of religion (Articles 25–28); cultural and educational rights (Articles 29–30); and the right to constitutional remedies (Article 32). The remaining two categories include a 'General' section and another that seeks to save certain laws. The General section includes a definitions clause (Article 12) and a significant provision (Article 13) which declares that any laws made in contravention of the rights provisions will be void. This provision, *by implication*, vests in the judiciary the power to strike down parliamentary laws. This, then, is the source of the important power of judicial review over legislative and administrative action that is vested in the Indian judiciary. India's judiciary is regarded as one of the most powerful in the world today but it is generally assumed—wrongly—that the Constitution of India expressly vests the power of judicial review over legislation in the courts. As we will see over the course of this chapter, the Constitution, in its text, does vest important powers in the courts. However, these have been significantly expanded by the courts, largely through a process of judicial interpretation.

The rights guaranteeing equality consist of a general guarantee of equality and equal protection of the laws (Article 14) followed by a prohibition of discrimination on specified grounds (Article 15) and a provision that guarantees equality of opportunity in matters of public employment (Article 16). The framers' intention to act against the legacies of the caste system is most visible in the text of Article 17, which formally abolishes the caste practice of 'Untouchability' while also making it a criminal offence. Article 18 manifests a particularised concern about equality—seeking to reverse the colonial practice of co-opting elites by conferring hereditary titles—by prohibiting the conferral of titles by the post-colonial State.

Articles 19–23 guarantee several facets of freedoms to Indians. The most elaborate of the provisions is Article 19 which, through sub-clauses (a) to (g) of its first clause, guarantees the freedoms of speech and expression, peaceful assembly, association, movement and residence throughout the territory of India, and the freedom to practise any profession or carry on any occupation, trade or business. Originally, Article 19(1)(f) guaranteed a right to property, which was, as we shall see, the subject of a heated contest between the legislature and the judiciary and was ultimately amended out of Part III and inserted as Article 300A, making it a non-fundamental yet a constitutional and legal right. What is striking about the text of Article 19 is its framing and style. Clause 1 lists out the right or freedom guaranteed, before each of the remaining clauses goes on to list the grounds on which the particular right can be restricted through a Parliamentary law. On its face, this suggests that the restrictions can potentially overwhelm the right granted. However, as Ambedkar noted on the floor of the Constituent Assembly, the intention was quite the opposite—the motivation for listing out all the restrictive grounds was to ensure that no other ground could be conjured up by the legislature, thereby outlining a classically 'liberal' view on the part of the framers. That said, the grounds on which each individual freedom guaranteed by Article 19(1) can be restricted varies, often with few clues to the motivating logic. So, for instance, 'morality' is a valid ground for Parliament to restrict the freedoms of speech and the freedom to form associations (under Clauses 2 and 4 of Article 19), but is not a valid ground for restricting the right to assembly (under Clause 3 of Article 19).

Articles 20–22 deal with freedoms which become especially relevant in the context of situations such as criminal proceedings when issues of life and liberty come to the fore. Article 21, in its text, is a guarantee that a person can be deprived of life or liberty only after following a procedure established by law. This seemingly simple provision has played a disproportionately significant role in the flowering of constitutional rights in India, including, as we shall presently see, in providing the link between the Fundamental Rights and Directive Principles. Article 21A, which was introduced in 2002, establishes a Fundamental

Right to education for children between the ages of 6 and 14. Article 20's three clauses enshrine guarantees against retrospective application of criminal laws, while also prohibiting self-incrimination and double jeopardy. Article 22 outlines protections against arrest and preventive detention and includes guarantees such as the requirement of producing an arrested person before a magistrate within 24 hours (Clause 2). What is striking about Clauses 4–7, which deal with preventive detention, is that while seeking to provide protective guarantees to those who are preventively detained, the provisions also empower the preventive detention system by enabling restrictions on detainees which would otherwise be illegal. This seemingly paradoxical situation exemplifies the complex relationship between repressive emergency laws that were initially imposed by colonial authorities but were continued in the post-independence Constitution, often with the justification that they were necessary for safeguarding constitutional freedoms and democratic forms of government. Article 23 prohibits the traffic in human beings and other forms of forced labour while Article 24 prohibits the employment of children below the age of 14 in hazardous work. Articles 25–28 deal with the freedom of religion, while Articles 29–30 relate to cultural and educational rights. These last two sets of rights are examined more closely in Chapter 6, which deals with the models of multiculturalism and secularism in India. Article 32 stipulates that the right to move courts for the enforcement of Fundamental Rights is itself guaranteed and cannot ordinarily be suspended.

A textual analysis indicates that these provisions, where they were not created to respond to indigenous concerns, were inspired in part by the Bills of Rights in the US and French Constitutions, and by the Universal Declaration of Human Rights. In their terms, however, many of the Indian rights provisions tend to be more elaborate than those that inspired them. In this, they anticipated the later trend of providing elaborate descriptions of rights provisions and the conditions under which restrictions can legitimately be imposed upon them by constitutional authorities.

B. Directive Principles

Part IV of the Constitution bears the title 'Directive Principles of State Policy' and consists of 15 provisions (Articles 36–51). Tellingly, these

Principles have not been further divided into sub-categories, perhaps because of the difficulty involved as they contain many different types of provisions. While the rights provisions are, in keeping with general trends elsewhere, often abstract, the Principles tend to focus both on general and very particular issues.

The first provision, Article 36, states that the definition of 'State' applicable to Fundamental Rights will also apply to the Directive Principles, which has important implications that the courts later elaborated upon. Article 37 is significant as it first stipulates that the Principles 'shall not be enforceable by any court' before providing that they 'are nevertheless fundamental in the governance of the country'. It also imposes a duty on the State 'to apply these principles in making laws'. Later in this chapter, we shall see how courts have interpreted the seemingly contradictory motivations of this provision. Articles 38 and 39 can be seen as evidence of the claim of the English constitutional jurist Ivor Jennings that 'the ghosts of [the British socialists] Sidney and Beatrice Webb stalk through the pages of the [Indian constitutional] text'.[1] Article 38 exhorts the State to create a social order where the welfare of the people is promoted and all institutions of national life are infused with an overarching ideal of justice. Clause 2 of the provision more specifically targets inequality and urges the State to minimise income inequality and eliminate inequalities of status, facilities and opportunities. The six clauses of Article 39 focus on both general goals ('the ownership and control of the material resources of the community are so distributed as to secure the common good') and more specific ones (the right to livelihood, equal pay for equal work, the health and strength of workers, the basic rights of children to be protected from exploitation).

A number of provisions focus on specific aspirational goals: Article 39A, which was inserted through a constitutional amendment, exhorts the State to secure free legal aid to citizens; Articles 41, 42, 43 and 43A urge the State to achieve aspects of the right to work; Article 46 commends the adoption of policies to attend to the specific needs of Scheduled Castes and Scheduled Tribes; Article 47 enjoins the State to improve public health and raise levels of nutrition and standard

[1] Ivor Jennings, *Some Characteristics of the Indian Constitution* (Madras, Oxford University Press, 1953) 35.

of living; Article 43B seeks the promotion of co-operative societies; Article 48A recommends measures to protect the environment, forest and wildlife of the country; Article 49 seeks the protection of monuments and places of historic and artistic interest; Article 50 urges the separation of the judiciary from the executive; and Article 51 seeks the promotion of international peace and security also through fostering respect for international law and treaty obligations.

Some other Principles were initially put into the text as compromises or as gestures of appeasement but have gained importance over time through later developments. So, Article 45, which initially recommended a focus on the education of children below the age of 14, was one of the causal factors that led eventually to a fully-fledged Fundamental Right (the current Article 21A). The same constitutional amendment amended Article 45 to now urge the State to provide early child care and education for children below the age of six as they are not covered by the newly established Fundamental Right. Similarly, Article 40 urged the State to establish village panchayats (the traditional form of governance in Indian villages) and was placed in the Principles to appease the Gandhians in the Assembly. Four-and-a-half decades after independence, the Constitution was amended, as we saw in Chapter 3, to introduce a third tier of governance institutions at the village and municipal levels. Article 48, which somewhat incongruously urges the State to focus on animal husbandry and to prevent cow slaughter, was originally inserted to appease Constituent Assembly members of a Hindu nationalist persuasion who had a specific commitment to cow protection. With the election of successive BJP governments in several State legislatures and the Union legislature in 2014 this provision became the inspiration for several laws aimed at banning cow slaughter across the nation. As we shall see, the judiciary too has invoked the Principles to give them meaning and a fuller existence than the language of Article 37 would have suggested was possible.

The Directive Principles were originally inspired by the much smaller catalogue in the 1937 Constitution of the Irish Republic, but as with the rights provisions, became more extensive and more reflective of indigenous concerns by the time they were finalised. Although thought to be irrelevant, even by some of the framers, they have acquired a meaningful existence in their own right.

Having focused on what is included in the Rights and Principles, a few words about what was *not* included. A surprising omission from the chapter on Fundamental Rights is the category of citizenship rights, which were matters of deep concern in the aftermath of Partition. Provisions dealing with citizenship are in fact included in the Constitution, and appear in Part II, before the Fundamental Rights in Part III. However, the six provisions that deal with citizenship (Articles 5–11) are quite narrow in scope and have not been able to anticipate the many issues of citizenship that have arisen in later years. The fact that citizenship is not recognised as a Fundamental Right also has implications for the manner in which citizenship rights are pursued and taken account of by the State. A similar problem exists in relation to the right to vote, which, like the right to citizenship, is a constitutional right (recognised, as we will see in Chapter 6, in Article 326), but is not a Fundamental Right. Then there is the case of the right to privacy, which is not mentioned in the text at all, a surprising omission given the extensive use of surveillance and search and seizure measures by the colonial state. All this is to note that the vision of the framers of the Indian Constitution, while salutary in many respects, was not close to perfection as is sometimes asserted by over-enthusiastic votaries of the Indian Constitution.

C. The Judiciary

Although the Indian Constitution envisages a federal system of government generally, it created a unitary judiciary with three levels of courts, all of which work under the aegis of a powerful Supreme Court at the apex of the system. The rationale behind the provisions will be examined in the next section, but to understand the content and level of detail that follows in this section, it is worth noting Ambedkar's overall conception of the judiciary: 'one single integrated judiciary having jurisdiction and providing remedies in all cases arising under the constitutional law, the civil law or the criminal law'.[2] This, according to Ambedkar, was 'essential to maintain the unity of the country'.[3] Once again, the temporal concerns of the period surrounding the framing of the Constitution vitally affected the way the role and function of crucial institutions of government would be conceived by the makers of the Indian Constitution.

[2] CAD IX 21, 787.
[3] CAD VII 1, 37.

Chapter IV of Part V of the Constitution is entitled 'the Union Judiciary' and consists of 23 provisions (Articles 124–147). Another 23 provisions relating to the High Courts and the subordinate courts are set out in Chapters V (consisting of Articles 214–232) and VI (consisting of Articles 233–237) under Part VI of the Constitution, which deals with 'The States'.

The provisions on the Union judiciary deal with the following issues: the establishment of the Supreme Court, including the location of its seat in New Delhi (Articles 124, 130); its powers and jurisdiction in relation to its functioning (Articles 129, 131–144); the salaries and perquisites of judges of the Supreme Court (Article 125); the age, qualifications and process of appointment and removal of Supreme Court judges (Articles 124, 126–128) and the vesting of unique powers in the Supreme Court to make rules for its own operation and to appoint its own staff and officers (Articles 145–146).

A focus on the Supreme Court of India is important also because it is at the apex of the integrated judiciary in India. It is important to emphasise that the Indian Supreme Court performs several roles:

(i) that of a constitutional court (which in the Indian context involves cases where federalism disputes arise between the States and the Union under Article 131, constitutional cases where Fundamental Rights violations are alleged under Article 13(1) read with Article 32, or laws are challenged for lack of legislative competence under Articles 245 and 246, or cases under Article 132 where a High Court certifies that a case involves 'a substantial question of law as to the interpretation of the Constitution');
(ii) that of a court of final appeal in a range of constitutional, civil and criminal cases (this is a jurisdiction created by Articles 132–135 and provides an appeal by right in criminal cases involving capital punishment, imprisonment for life or for more than 10 years);
(iii) that of a court which can accept appeals by 'special leave' (a jurisdiction created by Article 136, which enables the Supreme Court, rather extravagantly, to grant appeals from 'any judgment, decree, determination, sentence or order in any cause or matter' issued by 'any court or tribunal' within India);
(iv) and that of a court which has inherent powers that allow it to do 'complete justice' and to review its own judgments (this jurisdiction flows from Articles 137 and 142 of the Constitution).

This scheme clearly establishes that the Supreme Court of India has extensive powers and jurisdiction, giving credence to the claim of one of the framers of the Constitution that 'it has wider jurisdiction than any superior court in any part of the world'.[4] This was certainly true in 1950, and remains true even today. As we will see in the next section, not all the framers believed this to be sensible; some warned that this would lead to a 'flood' of cases before the Supreme Court.[5] An empirical study conducted in 2011 showed that of the total workload of the Supreme Court, 84.6 per cent were special leave appeals under Article 136, and 3.1 per cent were other kinds of appeals. This means that less than 3 per cent of the cases heard by the Supreme Court in recent years have been constitutional cases, properly so called.[6] This aspect of the type and number of cases being adjudicated by the Supreme Court and the Indian judiciary as a whole will be the focus of Section V of this chapter.

The Indian Supreme Court currently has 31 judges, who sit in benches of two and three, resulting in a situation where on a single day, the Court may have 12–13 parallel benches sitting and hearing cases simultaneously. This is clearly quite different from an apex court which consists of judges sitting *en banc*. The Indian situation results in quite a complex situation with severe coordination problems, manifested in multiple judgments of two–three-judge benches which conflict with each other, requiring larger benches of the Court to resolve such contradictions. This also makes it difficult for the Supreme Court to have a coherent jurisprudence which is clearly set out and articulated over time. This is to be borne in mind as we seek to find coherence in the decisional output of a system that seems designed to create ambiguity, instability and incoherence.[7]

The provisions relating to the High Courts follow a similar pattern to that of the Supreme Court. Article 214 states that there shall be a High

[4] Alladi Krishnaswamy Ayyar, CAD VIII 596.

[5] Shibban Lal Saxena, CAD VIII 620.

[6] Nick Robinson, 'A Quantitative Analysis of the Indian Supreme Court's Workload' (December 2013), available online at <https://ssrn.com/abstract=2189181> or <http://dx.doi.org/10.2139/ssrn.2189181>.

[7] See further, Nick Robinson, 'Structure Matters: The Impact of Court Structure on the Indian and US Supreme Courts' (2012) 61 *American Journal of Comparative Law* 101–38.

Court for each State, but Article 231 specifies that two or more States may share a High Court (which is the case at present with 29 States having to share the 24 existing High Courts). Article 226 empowers the High Courts to issue writs to enforce the rights guaranteed under Part III of the Constitution. This is an important power which clarifies that though the High Courts are subordinate to the Supreme Court in hierarchy, they are independently equipped to act as guardians of the Fundamental Rights. Article 227 clearly establishes that a High Court will have powers of superintendence over 'all courts and tribunals' within its territorial jurisdiction. The provision further clarifies that this includes the power to make rules for the practice and procedure of these courts. Article 229 provides that High Courts will have powers to appoint their own staff as well as to make rules for their own functioning. The provisions relating to the subordinate judiciary under Chapter VI of Part VI of the Constitution make clear that the High Courts have the power to be consulted in the appointment of district judges (Article 233) and that control over the subordinate courts will vest in the High Courts (Article 235).

These sets of provisions stipulate a clear hierarchy between and among the three levels of the judiciary and also enable the judiciary to have control over appointments to its own staff and rule-making authority, thereby granting a high degree of functional autonomy to the courts.

Another set of provisions seeks to further entrench the independence of the judiciary from other wings of government. These include the provisions which lay down the salaries and service conditions of judges of the Supreme and High Courts in the text of the Constitution, in order to immunise them from easy amendment (Articles 125 and 221). Similarly, the procedure for appointments to both the High Courts and the Supreme Court is designed in a way to ensure that the inputs of the respective Chief Justices is taken into account. Although they are formally made by the President, appointments to the Supreme Court were to be made after consulting the Chief Justice of India and to the High Courts after consulting the Chief Justice of the respective High Court. As we will see, this issue became much more prominent in the years after independence, and especially in the years since the early 1990s. The mechanism developed by the framers for appointment of judges sought to involve the judiciary in the process but it seems clear that their intention was to give primary authority in respect of this important task to the executive wing of government at the Central and State levels.

Superior court judges in India can be removed only after an address in Parliament and after a supermajority of the voting members in Parliament approve (Articles 124 and 218). This is, both in theory and practice, a high requirement. Not surprisingly, despite attempts that were initiated against some individuals, no superior court judge has been successfully impeached in independent India to date.

The final strategy of the framers to make the judiciary truly independent was to impart to the provisions regulating the higher judiciary a superior status for purposes of constitutional amendment. Clause (2) of Article 368 lists a handful of provisions, including those relating to the judiciary, with the requirement that in order to successfully amend them, the amendment proposal must not only pass successfully in Parliament, but must also be endorsed by at least half of the State legislatures. By these sophisticated and intertwining methods, the framers of the Indian Constitution successfully devised ways of ensuring that the judiciary has a degree of independence that cannot easily be tampered with.

III. THE CONSTITUTIONAL HISTORY OF PROVISIONS RELATING TO FUNDAMENTAL RIGHTS, DIRECTIVE PRINCIPLES AND THE JUDICIARY

A. The Separation of Fundamental Rights and Directive Principles

It is worth noting that the colonial government, in tune with British political thought about rights more generally even within Britain, remained reluctant to bestow rights upon Indians. One scholar has recently characterised the approach of British colonial authorities to demands for rights provisions raised in the various colonies in the following terms:

> [A] bill of rights was ineffective at protecting rights, it limited the actions of the colonial administration, it hamstrung Parliament, it invited litigation, it required skilled judges to interpret, it politicized the judiciary, it was almost

> impossible to draft effectively, and perhaps most importantly, it was not the British way to protect rights.[8]

This attitude helps explain why the colonial authorities steadfastly rejected appeals by the Indian nationalist movement for a Bill of Rights from the time they were first made in 1895, all the way up to the grant of independence.[9]

For our purposes, it is significant that there was a shift in the thinking of the nationalist movement about the nature of rights over time. It is certainly striking that the distinction between Fundamental Rights and Directive Principles was made, for the first time, in the deliberations within the Constituent Assembly. In the half-century-long history of the evolution-of-rights documents crafted by the nationalist movement, as we saw in Chapter 1, there was an equal emphasis on the civil and political rights as well as the socio-economic rights that owed their origin respectively to the liberal and socialist wings of the Indian National Congress. During the drafting process in the Assembly, however, the lawyers BN Rau and Alladi Krishnaswami Aiyar argued that many of the social and economic rights or positive rights were not amenable to judicial review in the same way as were the classic civil and political rights. Since some members had already objected to the presence of mere 'moral precepts' in the text of the Constitution, the suggestion was that making the socio-economic rights non-justiciable would justify their presence in a separate section of the Constitution.[10] Other members such as the Gandhians in the Assembly and the powerful troika of KM Munshi, KT Shah and Ambedkar strongly urged for the inclusion of strong socio-economic rights as Fundamental Rights. They were opposed to such rights being housed in a separate section,

[8] Charles OH Parkinson, 'British Constitutional Thought and the Emergence of Bills of Rights in Britain's Overseas Territories in Asia at Decolonization' in H Kumarasingham (ed), *Constitution-making in Asia* (London, Routledge, 2016) 36.

[9] Parkinson notes that the Government of India Act 1935, in sections 275, 298(1) and 299, guaranteed some property rights and provided some protections against discrimination based on religion, sex, place of birth or colour for the purposes of public sector employment, property rights and access to a profession. While this is true, the limited and context-specific nature of these 'rights' should be emphasised.

[10] B Shiva Rao, (ed.), *The Framing of India's Constitution: Select Documents,* Vols I–V (New Delhi, Universal Law Publishing, 1967, reprint 2010) vol 5, 322.

which they noted would undermine the importance of socio-economic rights. Eventually, however, the view of Rau and Aiyar prevailed, and Ambedkar himself defended the decision to separate the justiciable Fundamental Rights from the non-justiciable Directive Principles.[11]

B. The Judiciary

As should be clear from a perusal of the length and detail of the bare provisions relating to the judiciary, the framers of the Constitution spent considerable time and effort in crafting them. However, unlike in the case of the rights provisions, they were not working from a blank canvas in terms of existing arrangements. The period of British presence in India had witnessed the establishment of an elaborate system of courts from the time of the East India Company. So, for instance, the Mayor's Court was established outside Bombay in 1728. While the Company administered India, there were two sets of courts: one administered by the British Crown, and another by the East India Company.[12] In 1861, after the formal end of Company rule in India, the British Parliament enacted the Indian High Courts Act, which authorised the Crown to set up High Courts of Judicature in the 'Presidency towns' of Calcutta, Madras and Bombay. By the time independence was achieved, this system of courts had been in place for nearly a century.

This situation presents a paradox which needs some explication. The nationalist movement often used the oppressive measures brought about by colonial laws to make its case for, initially, the need for reform in the colonial structures of power, and eventually, the need to reject colonial rule altogether. The sedition trials that the British initiated against important nationalist leaders across nearly 30 years (Jogendra Chandra Bose in 1891, Bal Gangadhar Tilak in 1897, Annie Besant in 1917, Maulana Azad and Mohandas Gandhi in 1922) helped mould

[11] For a speculative but illuminating discussion of the reasons that may have motivated the change in Ambedkar's thinking—which also reveals other tensions in the Constitution-making process—see Nirja Jayal's excellent analysis of this issue. Nirja Gopal Jayal, *Citizenship and Its Discontents: An Indian History* (Cambridge, MA, Harvard University Press, 2013) 144–58.

[12] Abhinav Chandrachud, *An Independent, Colonial Judiciary: A History of the Bombay High Court During the British Raj, 1862–1947* (New Delhi, Oxford University Press, 2015) 22.

public opinion in favour of the growing nationalist movement by creating a perception that colonial rule, law and courts were deeply unfair in their application to Indians. However, this impression did not extend to all legal and judicial institutions uniformly. As scholars have argued, while some of the lower courts did become instruments of colonial policy in very clear ways, this tendency did not extend to superior courts in general. Further, the High Courts in particular had begun a process of indigenisation well before independence, so that by the time of independence, the prominent High Courts in particular were considered more Indian than British.[13]

All this goes to explain why the framers of the Indian Constitution did not seem eager to completely supplant the colonial structure of courts and decided instead to continue many parts of that legal order, albeit with important adaptations and modifications, which we will focus upon in the remaining part of this section.

By the 1920s, the High Courts had become established in several parts of India. Appeals from the High Courts lay to the Judicial Committee of the Privy Council in London, which was a time- and money-consuming effort and was an avenue open to very few Indians. By the 1930s the colonial government had also established the Federal Court of India by the Government of India Act 1935. This became necessary because that law also introduced a federal element into the colonial Indian legal order for the first time, and the Federal Court was thought to be necessary to resolve disputes between the federal units. Notably, however, the Federal Court had a limited original jurisdiction and its decisions were still subject to appeal before the Privy Council, factors that inhibited its evolution into a robust judicial forum.

Within the Constituent Assembly, deliberations on the judiciary began with some common agreement. The colonial system of courts would be retained but important changes would be made. Appeals to the Privy Council would be abolished—a decision that was unusual as many other former British colonies retained such appeals for long after formal independence—and a new Supreme Court would be established. Although this new institution would retain the role of

[13] ibid 299–307. Note that Chandrachud's work focuses on the Bombay High Court but his analysis is plausibly extendable to the other High Courts in Calcutta, Madras, Allahabad, Patna and Lahore.

the Federal Court in being an arbiter of federalism disputes, its main purpose would be to safeguard the new Bill of Rights that would be introduced in Part III of the Constitution. The new Supreme Court was also to have a much wider jurisdiction than the Federal Court in other matters, including, as we saw in Section II, in the range of appeals and original cases it would take on. The framers gave this new institution a wider range of powers because of their belief that the unity that the country needed in perilous times could not be achieved exclusively by the strong Union government that they would establish. For KM Munshi, 'the unconscious process of consolidation which a uniformity of laws and interpretation involves makes the unifying unconscious and more stable'.[14] BR Ambedkar similarly felt that an integrated judicial system coupled with the uniformity of law were 'essential to maintain the unity of the country'.[15]

As noted earlier, the framers invoked multiple strategies to ensure that the judges of the superior courts would be independent. However, in light of the expansive role undertaken by the judiciary in later years, to which we will turn in the succeeding section of this chapter, it is important to emphasise what kind of role the framers had in mind for the judiciary. One of the great champions of judicial autonomy and independence in the Assembly was Alladi Krishnaswamy Aiyar. On this question, he had a precise explanation:

> While there can be no two opinions on the need for the maintenance of judicial independence, both for the safeguarding of individual liberty and the proper working of the Constitution, it is also necessary to keep in view one important principle. *The doctrine of independence is not to be raised to the level of a dogma so as to enable the judiciary to function as a kind of super-Legislature or super-Executive.* The Judiciary is there to interpret the Constitution or adjudicate upon the rights between the parties concerned. … the Judiciary as much as the [Legislature] and the Executive, is depending for its proper functioning upon the cooperation of the other two.[16] [emphasis added]

It is important to place this statement in context. While the framers of the Constitution were keen to have an independent judicial institution

[14] KM Munshi, *Note to the Ad Hoc Committee on the Union Judiciary*, cited in Granville Austin, *The Indian Constitution: Cornerstone of a Nation* (New Delhi, Oxford University Press, 1966) 184.

[15] CAD VII 1, 37.

[16] CAD XI 9, 837.

that would safeguard rights and be an important check on the abuse of power, they were equally clear that the main engine of activity in the constitutional scheme was the executive government acting with the support of an active and vigilant Parliament. It appears that their vision sought to combine in hybrid form the parliamentary sovereignty of the British type with judicial review of the US type. In such a vision the judiciary was to have strong powers and a defined role but was nevertheless still to play a subordinate role to Parliament and the government of the day, which enjoyed a majority in Parliament. This is certainly how the role of the judiciary was envisaged by Prime Minister Nehru, who was an ardent champion of judicial review and independence but also believed that it was Parliament and the government of the day which would have the final say on policy decisions. Interestingly enough, this was also the position of the early judges of the Supreme Court, all of whom had been members of its predecessor, the Federal Court, and had been steeped in the values of the British judiciary, which did not have any powers to strike down Parliamentary law and viewed the law in 'technocratic' rather than 'political' terms.[17]

As we will see in the next section, the situation in post-independence India evolved very differently from the framers' vision for judiciary–executive relations.

IV. THE SUPREME COURT AND ITS ROLE AS GUARDIAN OF THE RIGHTS PROVISIONS (1950–2016)

It is important to emphasise that the High Courts in India have, both in theory and in practice, played an important role in advancing rights jurisprudence in India. However, space constraints preclude a close examination of their record here. The descriptive survey of the work of the Supreme Court provided here is both summary and reductive since the volume of case law that has been generated across this period is enormous and complex. The survey is also thin on doctrinal detail

[17] 'Technocratic' is the term used by Professor Sathe to describe the worldview and self-perception of the early Supreme Court. See, SP Sathe, *Judicial Activism in India: Transgressing Boundaries and Enforcing Limits* (New Delhi, Oxford University Press, 2003) 40.

because there is now a well-developed body of academic work which can provide a reader with access to such analysis.[18]

This section seeks to provide an overview of the process by which the Supreme Court of India evolved from being a cautious new institution in 1950 to the point by the early part of the 21st century when it was perceived by many political commentators as the most powerful political actor in the Indian constitutional landscape. Although this is a narrative that has been detailed by many scholars,[19] only the broad sketches of that transformation can be outlined here. In identifying the major phases of the working of the Supreme Court, I broadly follow the trajectory and phases employed in Chapter 2 to describe the evolution of the political landscape in India.

A. Phase I: The Supreme Court as Loyal Opposition During the Nehru Era: Establishing Judicial Review and the 'Technocratic' Phase of the Supreme Court (1950–66)

On 28 January 1950, two days after the Constitution was formally adopted, the Supreme Court of India was officially inaugurated. Its first judges were the six Indian judges who had been part of the Federal Court of India with Chief Justice Harilal J Kania becoming the

[18] The publication, in 2016, of the *Oxford Handbook of the Indian Constitution* is an important landmark in public law scholarship in India. Its 56 chapters provide an overview of how the various important institutions and rights conceived by the Constitution have evolved and developed across 66 years of the working of the Constitution. The volume as a whole focuses on doctrinal development of the law and is an excellent resource for tracking individual cases, analytical insights into the Court's doctrine and overall trends on specific subjects. See Sujit Choudhry, Madhav Khosla and Pratap B Mehta (eds), *The Oxford Handbook of the Indian Constitution* (Oxford, Oxford University Press, 2016) 1048 pp. A leading practitioner text on the Constitution of India which assiduously tracks the large volume of cases on each article of the Constitution is Mahendra P Singh (ed), *V.N. Shukla's Constitution of India*, 12th edn (Lucknow, Eastern Book Co, 2013) 1236 pp.

[19] See generally, Rajeev Dhavan, *The Supreme Court of India: A Socio-legal Critique of Its Juristic Technique* (Bombay, NM Tripathi, 1977); Upendra Baxi, *The Indian Supreme Court and Politics* (Lucknow, Eastern Book Company, 1981); Upendra Baxi, *Courage, Craft and Contention: the Indian Supreme Court in the Eighties* (Lucknow, NM Tripathi, 1985); and S.P. Sathe, *Judicial Activism in India: Transgressing Borders and Enforcing Limits*, 2nd edn (New Delhi, Oxford University Press, 2002).

first Chief Justice of the Supreme Court. It is important to recall the political context of the time. Prime Minister Nehru headed a Cabinet composed of many stalwarts of the nationalist movement, which also consisted of leaders from beyond the ranks of the Indian National Congress: Dr Ambedkar was at the time the Minister for Law and Shyama Prasad Mookherjee was the Minister for Industries. The first Cabinet represented a 'national' government that extended beyond the Congress and was an indication of the early fervour displayed by Indians, in the first flush of independence, to put nation ahead of partisan political affiliation. Within two years, Prime Minister Nehru had led the Congress party to a major victory in the first General Elections, garnering well over a two-thirds majority in the Lok Sabha. The opposition parties were splintered and were quite ineffectual both in and outside Parliament.

In keeping with the image of the Federal Court, which had had a relatively quiet and modest existence,[20] it was perhaps expected that the Supreme Court would be an important institution but would align with the nationalist mission outlined in the Constitution. In some ways, this is what the Court did. However, what is significant is that on a range of issues, from its very inception, the Supreme Court was also willing to stand up to the Nehru Government where the text of the Constitution seemed to favour a litigant challenging government action. Since there was virtually no other actor which was in a position to do so, it is helpful to think of the Supreme Court as performing the role of a loyal but weak opposition during this first crucial phase of the new Republic. The claim is not that the judges of the Supreme Court *intended to* act as a loyal opposition, but that their actions can be viewed from that standpoint with the benefit of hindsight and a full awareness of their context.

This assessment is informed by the judgments delivered by the Supreme Court in a range of early decisions. In its very first decision, *AK Gopalan v State of Madras*,[21] the Supreme Court had to confront a challenge to a parliamentary law that authorised preventive detention.

[20] Rohit De, 'The Federal Court and Civil Liberties in Late Colonial India' in T Halliday, L Karpik and M Feeley (eds), *Fates of Political Liberalism in the British Post-Colony: The Politics of the Legal Complex* (Cambridge: Cambridge University Press, 2012) 59–90.

[21] *AK Gopalan v State of Madras*, AIR 1950 SC 27.

The petitioner, a communist politician, who had been detained under an existing law, argued that the law violated his rights under Articles 19 and 21 of the Constitution. Although the Court by a majority of five to one upheld the constitutionality of the law as a whole, it emphasised that it had the power of judicial review over legislative action and held one provision of the law to be ultra vires the Constitution, striking it down for violating Article 22(5) of the Constitution. While one can see this decision as validating the action of the government of the day and upholding the parliamentary law in question, the decision of the majority also gave hope to vigilant citizens because, in its very first decision, the Supreme Court had shown that it would not hesitate to strike down a portion of a parliamentary statute. This approach of the Court was more evident in its free speech decisions—*Brij Bhushan* (1950),[22] *Romesh Thapar* (1950)[23] and *Shailabala Devi* (1952)[24]—where the Supreme Court struck down efforts at curbing free speech in the context of pre-censorship. Similarly, in the *VG Row* case (1952),[25] the Supreme Court did not hesitate to strike down an amendment to a criminal law passed by the Madras legislature for unreasonably transgressing the right to association conferred on citizens by Article 19(1)(c) of the Constitution. Although the striking down of a legislative instrument now seems routine, it has to be remembered that this was extremely unusual for a judicial system which had existed for over a century in India and had perceived itself as a loyal ally of the regime. In the initial years, the Indian Supreme Court exercised this power quite liberally. Going beyond the freedoms guaranteed by Article 19, the Supreme Court questioned affirmative action policies when it struck down a provision for community-specific seats in the early case of *State of Madras v Champakam Dorairajan* (1951).[26] These might not, by themselves, have aggravated matters, but the Nehru government became concerned when the Patna High Court struck down a Bihar land reform enactment in the *Kameshwar Singh* case (1951).[27]

[22] *Brij Bhushan v State of Delhi*, AIR 1950 SC 129.
[23] *Romesh Thapar v State of Madras*, AIR 1950 SC 124.
[24] *State of Bihar v Shailabala Devi*, AIR 1952 SC 329.
[25] *State of Madras v VG Row*, AIR 1952 196.
[26] *State of Madras v Champakam Dorairajan*, AIR 1951 SC 226.
[27] *Kameshwar Singh v The State of Bihar*, AIR 1951 Patna 91.

Land reforms had been one of the primary policies of the Nehru government and it moved quickly and effectively to amend the Constitution through the First Amendment to the Constitution. The First Amendment sought to address all the issues listed above—it increased the restrictions which could be imposed on free speech to circumvent the reasoning employed by the courts; and it expressly permitted admission of backward classes of citizens into educational institutions to overcome the *Champakam Dorairajan* ruling's effect. Most significantly, the First Amendment introduced Articles 31A, 31B and the Ninth Schedule to immunise land reform measures from constitutional scrutiny by the judiciary. This had the effect of temporarily freezing a festering dispute over the right to property between the Parliament and the judiciary. This is a debate which raged for a considerable period and is of crucial significance in understanding both the nature of Indian constitutionalism and the relations between its Parliament and judiciary over the first quarter-century of its existence. However, this issue is better addressed in Chapter 7, while focusing more squarely on the subject of constitutional amendment where the right to property features in a major way.

Reverting to our narrative, the successful passing of the First Amendment had the desired effect on the judiciary. Prime Minister Nehru's standing in the country and within government ensured that the judiciary would not take on his government by stretching the language of the Constitution. This was helped also by his own statesmanlike conduct in relation to differences with the judiciary. Moreover, the judges of the Supreme Court accepted, as noted earlier, the superior representative capacity of Parliament and yielded to the logic that Parliament had the final say on a question that had been decided through a constitutional amendment, even if this was done expressly to overrule a judicial verdict. From then on until Nehru's death in 1964, the judiciary maintained a respect for the powers and authority of Parliament in matters relating to the Constitution, often by adhering to the text of the Constitution.

B. Phase II: The Post-Nehru Years Until the Emergency: The 'Teleological' Phase of the Supreme Court (1966–77)

In this phase Indian democracy experienced the after-effects of the passing of a giant in Indian politics. The Prime Ministers who succeeded

Nehru—Shastri and Indira Gandhi—struggled to establish their presence over their party colleagues and were unable to obtain the same level of authority to push policies through. Equally, other constitutional actors felt less inhibited in challenging their decisions and asking fundamental questions about their policies. This was true of the judiciary as well, which was already accustomed to this role. However, in this phase, the judiciary showed itself willing to go beyond the text of the Constitution, to raise more profound questions relating to the very purpose of government and the Constitution. The trend of raising questions did not last all the way through to the end of this phase as the Court seemed to buckle under the consequences of having raised such questions consistently for nearly a decade.

As will be examined more closely in Chapter 7, the power of Parliament to amend the Constitution to advance its socio-economic policies had been a source of tension between the judiciary and the other two wings of government since the early days of the Republic. During Prime Minister Nehru's tenure, these tensions were resolved through the route of successive constitutional amendments to various provisions of the Constitution, including the Fundamental Rights chapter, which came to be accepted by the Supreme Court. However, soon after Nehru's death and following Prime Minister Lal Bahadur Shastri's untimely passing in 1965, Indira Gandhi's ascent to the office of Prime Minister created political uncertainty given her own precarious position within the Congress party. The old certitudes became shaky and this was reflected also in the approach of the Supreme Court in a series of cases decided in fairly quick succession.

In the case of *Golakh Nath v State of Punjab* (1967),[28] which involved a challenge to the First, Fourth and Seventeenth Amendments for foreclosing judicial review of the right to property, an 11-judge bench of the Supreme Court held that Parliament did not have the power to pass any amendment which had the effect of taking away any of the Fundamental Rights guaranteed by Part III of the Constitution. Chief Justice Subba Rao's majority judgment went beyond the text of the Constitution and asked what the broader purposes of a written Constitution might be in reaching its conclusion that some aspects of the Constitution may be beyond the amendment power of Parliament. Chief Justice Subba Rao appeared to be motivated by 'the argument

[28] *Golakh Nath v State of Punjab* (1970) 1 SCC 248.

from fear' which stemmed from a perception that Prime Minister Gandhi would be far less principled in her approach to policy making while being sensitive to constitutional values and Fundamental Rights, especially when compared to Nehru. Things were not helped by the fact that shortly after this judgment, Chief Justice Subba Rao resigned from the Court and was a candidate for the Presidential elections where he garnered support from parties who were seen as aligned with landowners and supporters of the right to property.

As Prime Minister Indira Gandhi struggled to increase her base of support in a bid to defeat the old guard of the Congress party, which was trying to undermine her authority, the Supreme Court continued to flex its muscles and struck down two other important policies of her government. In the case of *R.C. Cooper v Union of India* (1970)[29] the Supreme Court held that Prime Minister Gandhi's much-heralded policy of bank nationalisation was unconstitutional as the amount of compensation paid to those whose banks were taken over by the government was illusory. Then, soon afterwards, in the case of *Madhavrao Scindia v Union of India* (1971),[30] the Supreme Court heard a challenge to a Presidential order which discontinued the practice of disbursing privy purses to members of the families of the rulers of the Princely States who had agreed to join the Indian Union at the time of independence on this basis. In upholding the legal and constitutional rights of the members of the erstwhile royal families, the Supreme Court again undermined the authority of Prime Minister Gandhi's government. In the process, however, the Supreme Court ended up being projected as a champion of the rights of landowners, rich owners of private banks and members of the families of the once fabulously wealthy princely rulers.

Prime Minister Gandhi campaigned aggressively against the judiciary in the General Elections held in 1971. Her campaign asserted that she was seeking to advance socialist goals but was thwarted by her opponents, which included the judiciary, that had struck down important planks of her platform. Upon winning a comprehensive majority in Parliament, Prime Minister Gandhi unleashed a range of constitutional amendments designed to expressly reverse specific judgments of the Supreme Court.

[29] *R.C. Cooper v Union of India* (1971) 1 SCC 85.

[30] *Madhavrao Scindia v Union of India*, AIR 1971 SC 530.

Some of these amendments were the subject of challenge in the landmark case of *Kesavananda Bharathi v State of Kerala* (1973),[31] which was decided by a 13-judge bench by a narrow majority of 7:6. The judges in the majority sought to achieve a fine balancing act. They reversed the decision in *Golak Nath* and held that Parliament did have wide powers of constitutional amendment which would extend to every part of the Constitution, including Part III and the Fundamental Rights. They also upheld the constitutional amendments passed by the Indira Gandhi Government but imposed a check on the amending power by holding that Parliament's power of amendment would not extend to the 'basic features' or the 'basic structure' of the Constitution. Although the majority judges gave some illustrative examples of what would amount to the 'basic structure', it was evident even from a bare reading of the judgment that the concept was ambiguous and this ambiguity would, over time, be something to the advantage of the judiciary, which could potentially use it to augment its own power. Once again, this judgment witnessed the Court moving away from the text of the Constitution to arguments from philosophical foundations and first principles as to the purpose of vesting amending powers in Constitutions that were designed to endure through the ages. The long-term impact of the judgment was monumental. Once the Supreme Court reserved to itself the power to decide which constitutional amendments enacted by Parliament would pass muster, its power in relation to lesser matters would be far greater.

In the short term, however, the judgment of the majority, despite its attempt to be more sensitive than the *Golakh Nath* judgment to the balance of power between Parliament and the judiciary in respect of the power of constitutional amendment, was perceived as a slight by the Indira Gandhi Government. Within a day of the pronouncement of the judgment in *Kesavananda*, the President issued an order appointing AN Ray (who had joined the minority judges in supporting the stance of the Indira Gandhi Government) as the next Chief Justice of India, superseding the three judges who had been in the majority in *Kesavananda* and had been in line to be Chief Justice ahead of AN Ray. The decision created shockwaves in the country and within the legal profession in particular, which viewed the decision as a blow, not only

[31] *Kesavananda Bharathi v State of Kerala* (1973) 4 SCC 225.

to the independence of the judiciary, but also to democratic constitutionalism in India.

Although this action seemed to restrain the judges of the Supreme Court, Prime Minister Gandhi's troubles with the superior judiciary as a whole continued. On 12 June 1975 Justice Jagmohan Lal Sinha of the Allahabad High Court delivered judgment in *State of Uttar Pradesh v Raj Narain* (1975),[32] which had commenced in 1971 when Raj Narain had alleged that Prime Minister Gandhi's election from the Rae Bareilly constituency in Uttar Pradesh should be set aside for the commission of a 'corrupt practice' as she had used State resources for her personal campaign, an electoral offence under the applicable law. Justice Sinha's judgment found the Prime Minister guilty of the offence, which had the consequence of putting into doubt her position as Prime Minister. Within a fortnight of the judgment, after the Supreme Court in an intriguing order issued by Justice Krishna Iyer granted her an interim stay on the judgment, Prime Minister Gandhi advised President Fakhruddin Ali Ahmed to issue a Proclamation of Emergency.

The Emergency officially lasted from 25 June 1975 to 21 March 1977 and was, as noted earlier, a cataclysmic event in India's political and constitutional history. Its imposition weakened several institutions in India, some of which have yet to recover fully. The immediate effect on the Supreme Court was palpable and caused a shift in the trends towards constitutional adjudication it had exhibited over the last decade. The most drastic evidence of this shift was to be found in the Supreme Court's judgment in the case of *ADM Jabalpur v Shivkant Shukla* (1976).[33] The case involved a challenge to a repressive preventive detention law (the Maintenance of Internal Security Act 1971) under whose aegis several hundred thousand political opponents of the regime had been detained during the Emergency. The petitioners had also challenged the Proclamation of Emergency as well as a Presidential Order of 27 June 1975 which suspended the right to move the courts for the protection of rights guaranteed under Articles 14, 21 and 22. The judgment of the Supreme Court, by a majority of 4:1, upheld the government's claims in their entirety. The Court held that

[32] *State of Uttar Pradesh v Raj Narain*, judgment and order dated 12 June 1975 of the Allahabad High Court in Election Petition No 5/1971.

[33] *ADM Jabalpur v Shivkant Shukla*, AIR 1976 SC 1207.

during the period of Emergency all governmental actions were immune from judicial scrutiny. To hold so, they had to also find that the rights to life and personal liberty were gifts by the State to citizens, which could therefore be simply revoked in times of Emergency. In his stirring dissent, Justice Khanna held that the imperatives of the rule of law demanded that the rights to life and personal liberty could not be suspended even during an Emergency, and that the legality of a detention was open to question. For his courage, Justice Khanna was rewarded by being passed over for becoming Chief Justice, a position that the Gandhi Government awarded to Justice Beg, who had delivered the most cloying judgment in favour of the government's position in the *ADM Jabalpur* case. With this, the capitulation of the judiciary to the will of an authoritarian regime seemed complete.

The Supreme Court's judgment in *ADM Jabalpur* is universally regarded as its lowest point and was a return to a formalistic worship of the text, while being oblivious to the foundational, philosophical premises that underlay the text.

C. Phase III: The Court's Turn to Populism: The Flowering of Public Interest Litigation and the Turn to the Directive Principles (1977–89)

After the Janata Government came to power in 1977, its major policy decisions, including the passing of the 44th amendment to undo the damage inflicted by the 42nd amendment, did much to restore the power of the Supreme Court. For its part, the Supreme Court seemed eager to retrieve its credibility by delivering important judgments such as the one in *Maneka Gandhi v Union of India* (1978),[34] where it strove to bolster its civil libertarian credentials by overruling the *Gopalan* case (which was by then perceived as a rigidly conservative decision) and giving to Article 21 an expansive interpretation which would also lay the foundation for further capacious interpretation in later cases. At the same time, the Court started developing its jurisdiction in Public Interest Litigation (PIL) cases, where it sought to address issues relating to the poor and marginalised sections of Indian society. The seeds for

[34] *Maneka Gandhi v Union of India*, AIR 1978 SC 597.

this jurisdiction had been laid in some cases in the early 1970s[35] but the most significant cases that led to the frenetic use of PIL in the 1990s were decided in the aftermath of the Emergency.[36] The constitutional scholar Upendra Baxi has argued that the Court's activism on behalf of the poor and the marginalised in the aftermath of the Emergency was an attempt to 'bury its emergency past'.[37]

Following the return of Prime Minister Indira Gandhi's government in 1980, some judges of the Supreme Court continued to pursue PIL cases knowing that, given her public commitment to eradicating poverty, she would find it hard to adopt the kind of aggressive policies against the judiciary that she had undertaken in the past. This phase saw some of the most progressive decisions of the Court, especially on socio-economic rights issues, many of which were housed in the Directive Principles. The Indian Supreme Court initially adopted the approach that the words in Article 37 that rendered the Directive Principles unenforceable were to be interpreted to mean that they were inferior in constitutional status to Fundamental Rights. The constitutional scholar PK Tripathi wrote a withering critique of this position

[35] Arun K Thiruvengadam, 'In Pursuit of "the Common Illumination of our House": Trans-judicial Influence and the Origins of PIL Jurisprudence in South Asia (2008) 2 *Indian Journal of Constitutional Law* 67–103.

[36] There is a large body of literature on PIL extending across three decades. For a selection, see generally Upendra Baxi, 'Taking Suffering Seriously: Social Action Litigation in the Supreme Court of India' (1985) 4 *Third World Legal Studies* 107–32; SK Agarwala, *Public Interest Litigation in India: A Critique* (Bombay, NM Tripathi, 1985); Clark D Cunningham, 'Public Interest Litigation in the Indian Supreme Court: A Study in the Light of American Experience' (1987) 29 *Journal of the Indian Law Institute* 494–523; TR Andhyarujina, *Judicial Activism and Constitutional Democracy in India* (Bombay, NM Tripathi, 1992); Charles Epp, *The Rights Revolution: Lawyers, Activists and Supreme Courts in Comparative Perspective* (Chicago, IL, University of Chicago Press, 1998); Ashok H Desai and S Muralidhar, 'Public Interest Litigation: Potential and Problems' in BN Kirpal et al (eds), *Supreme But Not Infallible* (New Delhi, Oxford University Press, 2000); Mayur Suresh and Siddharth Narrain (eds), *The Shifting Scales of Justice: The Supreme Court in a Neoliberal Era* (New Delhi, Orient Blackswan, 2014); Shyam Divan, 'Public Interest Litigation' in Sujit Choudhry, Madhav Khosla and Pratap Mehta (eds), *The Oxford Handbook of the Indian Constitution* (Oxford, Oxford University Press, 2016) 662–79; and Anuj Bhuvania, *Courting the People: Public Interest Litigation in Post Emergency India* (New Delhi, Cambridge University Press, 2016).

[37] Upendra Baxi, *The Indian Supreme Court and Politics* (Lucknow, Eastern Book Company, 1980).

in 1954 but it was not until the decision in *Minerva Mills v Union of India* (1980)[38] that the Supreme Court acknowledged that both Directive Principles and Fundamental Rights were of equal status in the Indian constitutional scheme, and are to be harmoniously construed. Until this issue was resolved, Indian courts could not actively seek to implement the Directive Principles.

After the pronouncement in the *Minerva Mills* case, the Indian judiciary felt more confident in addressing social rights issues and tackled a raft of such cases across the 1980s. It then proceeded to decide a range of important cases relating to the rights to livelihood and housing (*Olga Tellis v Bombay Municipal Corporation* (1985)[39] and *Ahmedabad Municipal Corporation v Nawab Khan* (1997)),[40] education (*Mohini Jain v State of Karnataka* ((1992)[41] and *Unni Krishnan v State of Bihar* ((1993)[42]) and health (*Consumer Education and Research Centre v Union of India* (1995)[43] and *Paschim Banga Khet Samity v State of West Bengal* (1996)[44]). In all these cases, the Court expressly cited and relied upon the relevant Directive Principle to bolster its expansive reading of Article 21 to include the particular social right.

D. Phase IV: The Rise of the 'Good Governance' Court in the Era of Coalition Politics, and the Age of Judicial Supremacy (1989–2014)

As the Indian political space entered the era of coalitional politics, the next quarter-century witnessed a period of political instability, with several short-lived governments at the Centre. Even when governments lasted their full term, they were either dependent on 'outside support' of other parties, or were composed of multi-party coalitions which impeded quick and firm policy making. All this resulted in a set of circumstances where, in the face of weak governments that were slow

38 *Minerva Mills v Union of India*, AIR 1978 SC 1789.

39 *Olga Tellis v Bombay Municipal Corporation*, AIR 1985 SC 180.

40 *Ahmedabad Municipal Corporation v Nawab Khan* (1997) 11 SCC 123.

41 *Mohini Jain v State of Karnataka*, AIR 1992 SC 1858.

42 *Unni Krishnan v State of Bihar* (1993) 1 SCC 645.

43 *Consumer Education and Research Centre v Union of India*, AIR 1995 SC 922.

44 *Paschim Banga Khet Samity v State of West Bengal*, AIR 1996 SC 2426.

to act since they lacked political will, the authority of the judiciary grew by leaps and bounds, to the point where the Court became a much more prominent institution of policy making and agenda setting than the framers of the Constitution could have anticipated. This period also coincided with the introduction of policies of economic liberalisation to which the Court, over time, lent its support and actively aided.[45] This eventually led to contradictions between the image of the populist, pro-poor court it had pursued in the 1980s and was also the subject of bitter critique by social activists and progressive scholars, who dubbed it a 'middle class' court.[46] Some scholars ascribed the label of a 'good governance' court to describe the various interventions undertaken by the Supreme Court on matters relating to public policy and governance.[47]

To illustrate briefly what these changes entailed, we may refer to a comprehensive survey of PIL cases that were decided during the period 1997–98. In the conclusion of the survey, S Muralidhar presciently observed: 'The cases that were taken up for detailed consideration by the courts reflected a perceptible shift to issues concerning governance'.[48] This was the period during which the Supreme Court became proactive in its efforts towards: (1) cleaning up the political process by focusing on corruption at the highest levels of the political set-up in the Hawala and the Fodder Scam cases; (2) solving the chaotic traffic and pollution in Delhi; (3) cleaning up the Taj and its surrounding area; (4) regulating the disposal of hazardous waste; (5) regulating the manufacture and sale of pesticides; (6) addressing the issues of sexual harassment and female foeticide; and (7) regulating the collection and distribution of blood by blood banks.[49]

[45] See generally, Narrain and Suresh (eds) (n 36).

[46] See generally, Usha Ramanathan, 'In the Name of the People: The Expansion of Judicial Power' in Siddharth Narrain and Mayur Suresh (eds), *The Shifting Scales of Justice: the Supreme Court in a Neoliberal Era* (New Delhi, Orient Blackswan, 2014); Balakrishnan Rajagopal, 'Judicial Governance and the Ideology of Human Rights: Reflections from a Social Movement Perspective' in C Rajkumar and K Chockalingam (eds), *Human Rights, Justice and Constitutional Empowerment* (New Delhi, Oxford University Press, 2007) 200–36.

[47] Nick Robinson, 'Expanding Judiciaries: India and the Good Governance Court' (2009) 8 *Washington University Legal Studies Journal* 1–69.

[48] S Muralidhar, 'Public Interest Litigation' (1997–98) *Annual Survey of Indian Law* 33–34.

[49] The cases referred to are: *Vineet Narain v Union of India* (1998) 1 SCC 226; *Union of India v Sushil Kumar Modi* (1997) 4 SCC 770; *Suo Moto proceedings in re: Delhi*

Even as the Supreme Court's focus shifted from rights of the marginalised to the rights of the middle class in the 2000s, the other two wings of government began to focus more squarely on the social and economic rights of the marginalised sections, in part because of pressure from civil society activists. This resulted in a spate of welfare laws—the Right to Information Act 2005, the National Rural Employment Guarantee Act 2005, the Right to Free and Compulsory Education Act 2009 and the Right to Food Security Act 2013. Some scholars have argued that these laws can be traced back to the activism of the Supreme Court in earlier eras and some significant decisions,[50] while others have noted that these laws, though much needed, fall significantly short of fulfilling the requirements of universal welfare services, or even the actual needs of the poor and marginalised sections of India's population.[51] While subject to some debate, the general view of commentators has been that the Supreme Court became less focused on the rights of the weakest sections of Indian society during this period.

To showcase the interpretive audaciousness that was a typical feature of the Court's *modus operandi* during this time, one could pick a range of issues and cases. I focus on a crucial issue that was also integral to the Court's institutional strength: safeguarding its own independence.[52] Apart from expanding its authority and jurisdiction many times over, the Supreme Court displayed an anxiety about controlling appointments to its ranks in a series of cases which began in the late 1970s, but whose outcome was radically transformed by the greater power enjoyed by the judiciary in the 1990s.

Transport Department (1998) 9 SCC 250; *M.C. Mehta v Union of India* (1998) 9 SCC 711; *Research Foundation for Science and Technology v Union of India* (1997) 5 SCALE 495; *Dr. Ashok v Union of India* (1997) 5 SCC 10; *Vishaka v Union of India* (1997) 6 SCC 241.

50 Sanjay Ruparelia, 'A Progressive Juristocracy? The Unexpected Social Activism of India's Supreme Court', Kellogg Institute Working Paper #391, University of Notre Dame, 2013), available online at <https://ndigd.nd.edu/assets/172934/a_progressive_juristocracy.pdf>.

51 Jayal (n 11) 163–98.

52 See generally, BN Srikrishna, 'Judicial Independence' in Sujit Choudhry, Madhav Khosla and Pratap Mehta (eds), *The Oxford Handbook of the Indian Constitution* (Oxford, Oxford University Press, 2016) 349–66.

As noted earlier, the framers were deeply concerned with ensuring the independence of the judiciary and sought to achieve this objective by ensuring that a number of different constitutional actors would have a say in the appointments process. This is reflected in the language of Articles 124 and 217, which deal with appointments to the Supreme Court and High Courts respectively. Article 124 stipulates that appointments to the Supreme Court are to be made by the President (who is to act on this issue on the basis of the aid and advice offered by the Cabinet) 'after consultation with such of the Judges of the Supreme Court and of the High Courts in the states as the President may deem fit for this purpose'. In the case of the High Courts, Article 217 requires the President to also consult the Governor of the State and the Chief Justice of the High Court. The language of these provisions has been the subject of conflicting interpretations in a series of cases decided across four decades.

It is important to bear the background context in mind when appreciating these cases. The two rounds of judicial supersessions deployed by the Indira Gandhi Government in the 1970s were seen as extremely damaging to the spirit of independence of the judiciary. The Gandhi Government also sought to transfer High Court judges who did not take positions amenable to it. During the short life of the Janata Government, efforts were taken to restore both the credibility and independence of the judiciary. However, the disturbing practice of injecting political appointees into the superior courts was exacerbated during the 1980s after the return to power of Prime Minister Gandhi.

The first case that considered the meaning of these provisions was that of *Union of India v Sankalchand Seth* (1977).[53] In its judgment, the Supreme Court, while interpreting the word 'consult', held that it imposed a requirement on the executive to consult the Chief Justice of India and the view of the chief judge should normally be accepted. A few years later in the case of *S.P. Gupta v Union of India* (1981),[54] the judgments of the Court appeared to dilute this requirement when they held that 'the Chief Justice of India, the Chief Justice of the High Court and such other judges … are only constitutional functionaries having a consultative role and the power of appointment results solely

[53] *Union of India v Sankalchand Seth* (1977) 4 SCC 193.
[54] *S.P. Gupta v Union of India* (1981) Supp SCC 67.

in the Union government'.[55] *S.P. Gupta* also held that 'the opinion of none of the constitutional functionaries is entitled to primacy'.[56] It must be remembered that this judgment was delivered in the early 1980s after Prime Minister Gandhi's triumphant return to power.

The political landscape had altered considerably by the time the next major case came up for decision. The position in *S.P. Gupta* was soundly reversed in the early 1990s, in the Supreme Court's judgment in *Supreme Court Advocates-on-Record v Union of India* (1993) ('*SCAORA*').[57] A seven-judge bench of the Court held by a majority that primacy in the matter of appointments of judges to the Supreme Court vested in the judiciary. The Supreme Court read into the word 'consult' a binding requirement that the view of the Chief Justice of India be accounted for. It further held that the Chief Justice of India would form this view by taking into account the views of the two senior-most judges of the Supreme Court. Thus was constituted, out of whole cloth, the all-important 'collegium' which would become the pivotal body for deciding judicial appointments over the next quarter-century. The majority judgment of Justice Verma further outlined other measures by which the collegium was to represent collectively the views of the relevant courts and judges.

Six years later, as a result of several problems emerging in the working of the collegium system, the President referred the matter of judicial appointments to a nine-judge bench which gave its judgment in the case known as *Special Reference No. 1 of 1998*.[58] The Court reiterated the judgment in the *SCAORA* case but tweaked the collegium system, expanding the number of judges from three to five in the Supreme Court and from one to three at the High Court level. As a result of these two rulings, Indian judges came to enjoy the unique position of being exclusively in charge of appointments to their own institution. The working of this system was seen as problematic for several reasons, not least because it was a closed mechanism and did not allow for any substantial inputs by actors beyond the judiciary, thereby affecting the democratic legitimacy of superior court judges. Even those who had initially complained about the naked political interference in the 1980s

55 ibid 29 (judgment of Bhagwati J).

56 ibid 30.

57 *Supreme Court Advocates-on-Record v Union of India* (1993) 4 SCC 441.

58 *Special Reference No. 1 of 1998* (1998) 7 SCC 739.

began to voice their doubts about a system which had shifted across to the other extreme by being completely without any input from the democratically more legitimate actors. However, given the weak state of the executive and legislature under successive coalition governments from 1999 to 2014, there was little done to change this situation.

E. Phase V: The Court as Counterweight to a Powerful Executive: Back to Basics? (2014–present)

As will be examined more closely in the concluding chapter, the elections held to constitute the 16th Lok Sabha in May 2014 represent a landmark in Indian political history. After a quarter-century of relatively weak governments at the centre, these elections resulted in a Central government that had a clear majority in the lower house of Parliament. For the purposes of our focus on the judiciary, this phase has seen the judiciary revert to its more conventional role of being a check on a powerful executive authority. The BJP government has taken an aggressive stance towards dissent and towards those who have opposed its agenda of 'development with a Hindu focus'. With a decimated opposition in Parliament and a systematic manpower change in national institutions, the judiciary is one of the few institutions that seems capable of standing up to the authority of the Central government. Not surprisingly, one of the first major policy initiatives of Prime Minister Modi's government was to push through a constitutional amendment to replace the infamous collegium system with one where the executive would have a definitive say on judicial appointments. With this objective in mind, the Modi Government moved the 99th amendment to the Constitution along with the National Judicial Appointments Commission (NJAC) Act 2014. This framework put in place a system which gives the executive considerable say in the appointments process. Article 124A established a six-member NJAC of which three members were to be sitting judges, and the remaining three were to be the Union Minister for Law and two 'eminent persons'. These last two were to be nominated by the Prime Minister, the Chief Justice of India and the Leader of the Opposition in the Lok Sabha. The result of this was that judges, while still having a dominant say in the process, would not be in the majority in the appointments commission and their 'primacy' was therefore altered.

Both the Amendment and the Act were challenged before the Supreme Court. In its judgment in the *Supreme Court Advocates-on-Record Association v Union of India* (2015) ('*SCAORA II*'),[59] a five-judge bench, by a majority of 4:1, held that the 99th Amendment and the NJAC Act were in violation of the Constitution for being in breach of the doctrine of basic structure. The effect of the Court's judgment was that the NJAC became redundant and the collegium system was revived. The Modi Government expressed its displeasure openly and at the time of writing, matters have come to a near deadlock in terms of appointments as the Court and the government grapple over the contents of a Memorandum of Procedure to smoothen the process of appointing judges to the superior courts.

While some judges and courts across the nation have sought to fulfil the traditional role of 'check and balance', somewhat expectedly, the Supreme Court as a whole has been less willing to push back against the government and the legislature on issues where its own interests have not been at stake. This has led one commentator to accuse the Supreme Court of adopting a policy of 'judicial evasion' in significant cases decided from 2015 onwards—challenging the flagship policies of 'Demonetisation' and 'Aadhaar' initiatives of the Modi Government.[60] As our survey shows, this trend is consistent with earlier phases where the Supreme Court adopted quiescent positions to avoid ruffling feathers in strong executive governments. Yet that is precisely what the Court was designed to do, should be doing, and will hopefully resume doing in the near future.

V. THE CRISIS OF BACKLOG AND DELAY IN THE INDIAN JUDICIARY

The gridlock between the Modi Government and the judiciary has drawn attention to a looming crisis in the Indian judicial system

[59] *Supreme Court Advocates-on-Record Association v Union of India*, 2015 SCC Online SC 964.

[60] Gautam Bhatia, 'O, Brave New World: The Supreme Court's Evolving Doctrine of Constitutional Evasion', *Indian Constitutional Law and Philosophy* blog, available online at <https://indconlawphil.wordpress.com/2017/01/06/o-brave-new-world-the-supreme-courts-evolving-doctrine-of-constitutional-evasion/>.

which has been simmering for decades and now threatens to spill out of control. The Indian judiciary handles the largest number of cases in the world and also experiences some of the longest delays and backlogs. Some statistics will bear out these claims.

The Indian judiciary as a whole consists of about 12,000 courts. Below the Supreme Court are arraigned 24 High Courts, 3,150 District courts, 4,816 munsif/magistrate courts and 1,964 class II magistrate and equivalent courts. The total number of cases before the judicial system has been growing steadily since the colonial era. To begin at the top, the Supreme Court of India has a superior managerial capacity to handle backlog and delay. In 1950 the number of cases pending before the Supreme Court was only 771. By 1978 that number had grown to 23,092, crossing 100,000 in 1983. Following a series of measures, this number came down to as low as 19,806 in 1998 but has continued to increase thereafter, standing at 60,938 as of September 2016.[61] This is an extraordinary increase within a single court. The Supreme Court has generally been better than the rest of the judicial hierarchy in handling its backlog.

The crisis has been much more severe in the High Courts and lower judiciary. At the first conference of Chief Ministers held in 1957, Prime Minister Nehru reported that the total number of arrears in the entire judicial system was 164,000 cases.[62] By 1982 that number had swelled to 600,000 within only the High Courts and Supreme Court. As of March 2013 the total number of cases had reached a colossal 31.39 million: 64,330 in the Supreme Court, 4.5 million in the 24 High Courts, and 26.83 million in the district and subordinate courts.[63] The backlog has also resulted in long delays. News reports of cases being decided nearly 20 years after they were instituted are becoming distressingly common.

It is important to recognise that delay and backlog were a problem even during the colonial period, as is evident from a perusal of the 1924 report of the Justice Rankin Commission. However, it is clear

[61] Information gathered from the website of the Supreme Court of India. Supreme Court of India, Court News (July–September 2016), available at <http://supremecourtofindia.nic.in/courtnews/2016_issue_3.pdf>.

[62] Granville Austin, *Working a Democratic Constitution: A History of the Indian Experience* (New Delhi, Oxford University Press, 1999) 139.

[63] Supreme Court of India, Court News (Jan–March 2014), available at <http://supremecourtofindia.nic.in/courtnews/2014_issue_1.pdf>.

that the constitutional scheme contributes to the much bigger scale of the problem now. The vast jurisdiction of the Supreme Court is certainly a contributing factor to its massive backlog. Added to this is the unanticipated consequence of adopting a provision such as Article 136: special leave petitions under this single provision count, astonishingly, for a very large proportion of cases before the Supreme Court. Other factors that contribute to this problem are the lack of training of judges and other personnel to people the vast judicial system, the low judge-to-population ratio in India when compared with other countries, and the lack of incentives which restrain the best lawyers from taking up positions as judges.

As efforts to reform the Indian legal and judicial system are undertaken in response to calls from all quarters, the challenge will be to carry out reforms which do not compromise the hard-earned reputation for independence that the courts in India have come to enjoy.

VI. CONCLUSION

This chapter has sought to describe the provisions relating to the Fundamental Rights and the Directive Principles in the Constitution of India, while also covering the manner in which the Indian judiciary has sought to both safeguard and implement the Rights and Principles. The chapter has also sought to provide an overview of the different phases of the evolution of the Indian Supreme Court across its 67-year history, while trying to identify the central characteristic features of each of the phases. The chapter concluded by drawing attention to the massive problems of backlog and delay which threaten to undermine the high reputation that the Indian judiciary enjoys for upholding constitutional claims and values in difficult times.

FURTHER READING

Granville Austin, *Working a Democratic Constitution: A History of the Indian Experience* (New Delhi, Oxford, 1999).

Upendra Baxi, *The Indian Supreme Court and Politics* (Lucknow, Eastern Book Company, 1981).

Upendra Baxi, *Courage, Craft and Contention: The Indian Supreme Court in the Eighties* (Lucknow, NM Tripathi, 1985).

Anuj Bhuvania, *Courting the People: Public Interest Litigation in Post Emergency India* (New Delhi, Cambridge University Press, 2016).

Sujit Choudhry, Madhav Khosla and Pratap Mehta (eds),*The Oxford Handbook of the Indian Constitution* (Oxford, Oxford University Press, 2016).

Rajeev Dhavan, *The Supreme Court of India: A Socio-legal Critique of Its Juristic Technique* (Bombay, NM Tripathi, 1977).

George Gadbois, *Judges of the Indian Supreme Court 1950–1989* (New Delhi, Oxford University Press, 2011).

Madhav Khosla, 'Making Social Rights Conditional: Lessons from India' (2010) 8 *International Journal of Constitutional Law* 739.

BN Kirpal et al (eds), *Supreme But Not Infallible: Essays in Honour of the Supreme Court of India* (New Delhi, Oxford, 2000).

Pratap Bhanu Mehta, 'India's Judiciary: The Promise of Uncertainty' in Devesh Kapur and Pratap Mehta (eds), *Public Institutions in India: Performance and Design* (New Delhi, Oxford University Press, 2005) 158–93.

Pratap Bhanu Mehta, 'The Indian Supreme Court and the Art of Democratic Positioning' in Mark Tushnet and Madhav Khosla (eds), *Unstable Constitutionalism: Law and Politics in South Asia* (Cambridge, Cambridge University Press, 2015) 233–60.

Burt Neuborne, 'The Supreme Court of India' (2012) 1 *International Journal of Constitutional Law* 476–510.

Lavanya Rajamani and Arghya Sengupta, 'The Supreme Court' in Niraja Gopal Jayal and Pratap Bhanu Mehta (eds), *The Oxford Companion to Politics in India* (New Delhi, Oxford, 2010) 80–97.

SP Sathe, *Judicial Activism in India: Transgressing Boundaries and Enforcing Limits*, 2nd edn (New Delhi, Oxford University Press, 2002).

5

Technocratic Constitutional Institutions

The Comptroller and Auditor General – the Election Commission – New regulatory institutions

I. INTRODUCTION

IN THE PREVIOUS few chapters our focus was on conventional institutions of constitutional democracy. In this chapter we turn to some unconventional institutions that have gained high reputations for safeguarding constitutional and democratic values in contemporary India. Two of these institutions—the offices of the Comptroller and Auditor General of India and the Election Commission—owe their origin to the sagacious vision of the framers of the Indian Constitution who entrenched provisions relating to these institutions within the original Constitution. We will explore their reasons for doing so and the manner in which the evolution of these institutions over time has conformed to the expectations of the framers. The third set of institutions—broadly referred to as new regulatory institutions—cannot be traced back to the framers' explicit understandings but have come to play crucial roles in upholding constitutional and democratic values in India since the significant constitutional moment that accompanied the liberalisation of the Indian economic and constitutional order in the early 1990s. The chapter thus seeks to provide a descriptive narrative of the evolution of these three sets of institutions. In the next section the focus is upon the motivating logic of such a move on the part of the framers of India's Constitution. Thereafter, the subsequent sections focus on each of the three institutions in turn.

II. REFLECTING ON THE MOTIVATIONS OF THE FRAMERS FOR ENTRENCHING TECHNOCRATIC CONSTITUTIONAL INSTITUTIONS

The framers of the Indian Constitution sought to incorporate within the Indian polity a particular version of constitutional democracy. However, in doing so, they were not insensitive to the defects of parliamentary democracy and sought to insert institutional safeguards which would guard against the natural tendencies of democracies to become self-destructive. As we noted earlier, one such move was by strengthening greatly the role of the Indian judiciary, especially when contrasted with the powers enjoyed by the colonial judiciary. This is typically justified as incorporating a counter-majoritarian check on the institutions of the executive and the legislature, which are designed to represent majoritarian values and choices.

What is interesting about the choice of the framers in respect of the institutions under focus is their prescience. In the contemporary discourse around constitutional democracy there is a certain fatigue and resignation about the limits of 'electoral democracy'. In sum, this is an expression of frustration with an inability to control elected leaders in the period between elections when there are few checks on their actions. While electoral processes are an essential mechanism for regulating and renewing the life blood of constitutional democracies, they are, by their very nature, time bound and episodic. Indian democracy, in common with many others, is seen as crippled by the absence of equally effective mechanisms to keep elected leaders focused on being accountable and responsible to the people. The institutions under study here have the advantage that they are able to monitor the functioning of governments and political leaders at different times and can exert pressure on them to be accountable and responsible. In some cases they serve checking and oversight functions; in other cases they help in the implementation of policies and thereby enforce accountability and responsibility. Each of the three institutions involves the exercise of technocratic functions and skills and calls for competence, and knowledge of specific technical abilities. For this reason, appointments to these positions take on even greater importance. One question to focus upon is the extent to which these institutions are able to live up to their founding expectations in practice and over time.

III. THE OFFICE OF THE COMPTROLLER AND AUDITOR GENERAL

The first institution that this chapter focuses upon is the office of the Comptroller and Auditor General (CAG) since it clearly falls into the category of institutions that were meant to perform a checking and oversight function. This section begins with a brief overview of the institution during the colonial era, followed by a section that examines the original intentions of the framers of the Indian Constitution for the institution, which was modified from its colonial era avatar. The third section charts the progress of the institution across six decades of India's independence, concluding with its recent phase.

A. History and Original Design

The office of the Auditor General was an important institution in the colonial administration of India. As noted in Chapter 1, the East India Company developed a reputation for corruption and exploitation fairly early on, and this office was created for the purpose of conducting audits and maintaining and monitoring accounts in a bid to stave off similar criticism of the Crown's rule in India after it formally took over the reins of power in 1858. The first Auditor General in British India was Edmund Drummond, who served from 1860 to 1862. Prior to the enactment of the Government of India Act 1935, the Auditor General reported to the Secretary of State for India. The Act of 1935 changed this by stipulating that the Auditor General would report to the governments and legislatures in India, while also adding to the status of the office by providing the same permanency of tenure as a federal court judge. This increased stature, motivated by securing the independence of the office, was a significant move and, as we shall see later, contributed to the rise of the institution in more contemporary times. Although the Act of 1935 is now recognised as having introduced important federal elements into the colonial constitutional order that were retained in the independence Constitution, it is noteworthy that the office of the Auditor General was retained as a centralised institution. The Act of 1935 did conceive of provincial Auditors General but these were created to play supplemental roles rather than to supplant the office of the Auditor General, which continued to be in charge of both the audits and accounts of all the provinces. The Act of 1935 stipulated that the reports prepared by the Auditor General on the accounts of the federation and the provinces should be laid before the respective legislatures. In order to make the office more independent, the Act of 1935 further provided that the person occupying the office of the Auditor General would be ineligible for taking up further employment in government.

When the draft Constitution was prepared by BN Rau, the constitutional adviser, in October 1947, it contained separate provisions for the appointment of Auditors General at the federal and State levels, reflecting the greater commitment to federalism in the overall document. In important respects, however, this draft Constitution continued with the vision and scheme of the Act of 1935 for the institution of the office of the Auditor General. As the draft provisions progressed through the various stages of Constitution making in the Assembly, they went through several changes. The Expert Committee on the Financial Provisions of the Union Constitution, in its report of 5 December 1947, favoured retaining a single, centralised office for the Auditor General and expressed the hope that individual provincial governments would not appoint their own Auditors General.

The draft provisions then came up for consideration before the Constituent Assembly on 30 May 1949, where several members suggested amendments. TT Krishnamachari moved amendments seeking to change the designation of the office; he argued that adding 'Comptroller' would signify that the duties of the offices went beyond auditing and included control over government spending. Krishnamachari also argued that the Comptroller and Auditor General should take an oath similar to that of the judges of the Supreme Court; that the entire administrative expenses of the office should be charged upon the revenues of India, putting it beyond the purview of voting in Parliament; and that the conditions of service of the staff of the office should be secured as well. BD Das moved an amendment to the effect that the appointment of the Comptroller and Auditor General should be made by warrant of the President under his hand and seal, to ensure that the status of the office was secure. HN Kunzru argued that Parliament should be able to confer additional powers on the Comptroller and Auditor General.

Responding to these and other amendments, Dr BR Ambedkar accepted the suggestions listed above while rejecting some others. In so doing he expressed his own belief that 'This dignitary or officer is probably the most important officer in the Constitution of India'.[1] He went on to state that the duties of this office 'are far more important than the duties even of the Judiciary'.[2]

B. Constitutional Provisions Relating to the Office of the Comptroller and Auditor General

Part V of the Constitution sets out provisions relating to 'The Union'. Chapter V of this part is entitled 'Comptroller and Auditor General of India' and contains four provisions, Articles 148–151. Article 148, following the amendment by HN Kunzru, stipulates that the Comptroller and Auditor General of India shall by appointed by the President 'by warrant under his hand and seal'. It also provides that the procedure for removing the Comptroller and Auditor General is the same as that for impeaching a Supreme Court judge, thereby setting a very high bar. Article 148(2) provides that the Comptroller and Auditor General shall take an oath to uphold the Constitution; Article 148(3) declares that his salary shall be determined by Parliament and neither his salary nor the terms of his employment can be varied to his disadvantage after the appointment. The provision continues with its goal of insulating the office from political influence by stipulating that the Comptroller and Auditor General will not be eligible for further office under the government of India or that of the States. Clause 5 of the same provision seeks to provide some security to the members of the Indian Audit and Accounts Department, which aid the Comptroller and Auditor General in discharging his functions, by prescribing that the conditions of service of such persons be prescribed by rules made by the President. Finally, the last clause of the provision stipulates that all administrative expenses of the office shall be charged to the Consolidated Fund of India.

[1] CAD VIII 407–08.

[2] ibid.

Article 149 declares that the Comptroller and Auditor General will perform the functions that were being discharged by his predecessors in colonial India, while also enabling Parliament to add to these duties. Parliament enacted the Comptroller and Auditor-General (Duties, Powers and Conditions of Service) Act 1971, setting out the conditions of service of the Comptroller and Auditor General as well as outlining the duties and powers of the office, including the entities that can be subjected to audits.

Article 151 requires the Comptroller and Auditor General to submit reports relating to accounts for the Union to the President, who is in turn required to lay them before each house of Parliament. Similarly, the reports prepared for the accounts of each State are to be submitted to the Governors of States who are required to lay them before the State legislatures.

C. Functioning of the Office of the Comptroller and Auditor General in the Post-independence Era

For the first four decades after independence the office of the Comptroller and Auditor General appears to have functioned in an efficient yet low-key manner. Its impact was also limited. This is in part due to structural features of the institution. It relies on other institutions being vigilant and proactive in acting upon the audit reports being submitted by the office of the Comptroller and Auditor General. As is widely known, the two parliamentary financial committees designed to examine audit reports—the Public Accounts Committee and the Committee on Public Undertakings—have rarely examined the audit reports closely.[3] Some of the fears of the framers have also proven to be correct. In the Assembly, Dr Ambedkar had noted that giving the power to appoint the Comptroller and Auditor General to the executive was 'incongruous' as the executive would have little incentive to appoint persons with a strong inclination to check the government. Since independence in 1947, India has had 13 men serve in the office of Comptroller and Auditor General. The first four holders of the office were

[3] Ronojoy Sen, 'Going Beyond Mere Accounting: The Changing Role of India's Auditor General' (2013) 72(4) *Journal of Asian Studies* 801–11, 808.

from the Indian Audit and Account Service. However, the last nine incumbents have all been from the powerful Indian Administrative Service. What is more troubling is the fact that several of the occupants of the office were on the verge of retirement.[4] Obtaining positions which are in effect post-retirement jobs makes the incumbents inclined to be grateful to the government which appoints them. The highly centralised nature of the organisation has also hampered its ability to function in a country as vast and complex as the Indian Union. Although the office of the Comptroller and Auditor General has a vast number of staff, especially when contrasted to its counterparts in countries like the UK and the US, it revolves around the office of the Comptroller and Auditor General located in Delhi and suffers from an overly centralised managerial style.

However, despite these shortcomings in its structure, the office of the Comptroller and Auditor General has played a significant checking and controlling function, especially in the last few decades.[5] In 1989 an audit report on the Bofors scam shook the foundations of the Congress government led by Prime Minister Rajiv Gandhi, leading to the walk-out of the entire opposition in Parliament. In 1996 an audit of the Bihar government exposed the 'fodder scam', which eventually led to the resignation of Chief Minister Lalu Yadav. Around the turn of the century, audit reports submitted by the office of the Comptroller and Auditor General on the 'migration package' granted to telecom operators exposed massive concessions granted to private players in a sector which has generated some of the biggest financial scandals in post-liberalisation India. In 2001 an audit report raised questions about the way the army procured goods for use during the Kargil war of 1999, creating doubts about the overall procurement process employed by the Ministry of Defence. These reports garnered a lot of public attention but resulted in little by way of actual prosecutions and convictions of those who were responsible for the fraudulent acts. Nevertheless, these episodes pointed to the important role performed by the office of the Comptroller and Auditor General and generated both publicity and a degree of credibility for the office in the minds

4 SK Das, 'Institutions of Internal Accountability' in Devesh Kapur and Pratap Bhanu Mehta (eds), *Public Institutions in India* (New Delhi, Oxford University Press, 2005) 128–57, 134.

5 See generally, Sen (n 3) 808–09.

of the press and the public. These would become crucial aids that later occupants of the office could draw upon to shine a light on acts of corruption in public life.

In 2008 Vinod Rai, a senior member of the Indian Administrative Service, was appointed the 11th Comptroller and Auditor General and served in that capacity until 2013. Rai's tenure saw a flurry of audit reports that travelled beyond auditing and raised questions about the direction of public policy more generally. In so doing he was unapologetic and defiant. The title of his book, published a year after his retirement, is *Not Just an Accountant.* In it he argues that the office of Comptroller and Auditor General was constitutionally envisioned to perform a checking function on the executive, which is what he sought to do over the five years of his tenure. To this end, Vinod Rai adopted a much higher profile than his predecessors and took to convening press conferences to announce more controversial audit reports.

Of the many audit reports released during the tenure of Comptroller and Auditor General Rai, we focus upon three here. In 2010 the office of the Comptroller and Auditor General released a report on the allotment of telecom (2G spectrum) licences. This related to the 122 2G spectrum licences that had been issued by the Central government's Ministry of Telecommunications in 2008 in what the report termed as a decision riddled with problems and arbitrariness. The report of the Comptroller and Auditor General charged that the 'presumptive loss' to the exchequer as a result of the misallocation of the telecom licences was to the tune of US$40 billion. In its report on the allocation of coal blocks released in 2012, the office of the Comptroller and Auditor General objected to the way in which 142 coal blocks were allocated by the Central Ministry of Coal from 2004 onwards, resulting in 'financial gain' for the private players to the tune of US$33 billion. The two audit reports on the 2010 Commonwealth Games held in New Delhi, issued in 2009 and 2011, narrated a record of irregularities and other problems in the conduct of the largest sporting event held in India, which led to cost inflation and long delays on a massive scale.

These and other reports were issued during the scam-ridden second term of Prime Minister Manmohan Singh's leadership of the United Progressive Alliance coalition government (2009–14). The government attacked the reports for exaggerating the costs involved and, more significantly, going far beyond the ambit of an auditor's report, and questioned the neutrality of the office of the Comptroller and Auditor General and his staff. Nevertheless, the reports led to criminal prosecutions and the resignation of some key players in each episode. This in turn burnished the image of the Comptroller and Auditor General in the eyes of the press and the larger public. Political commentators speculated that the defeat of the United Progressive Alliance in the 2014 General Elections could be attributed, at least in part, to the severe damage inflicted by the audit reports issued by the office of the Comptroller and Auditor General upon the image of the United Progressive Alliance coalition in governing effectively.

Somewhat predictably, when Vinod Rai retired in 2013, his chosen successor, though picked from the ranks of the higher echelons of the Indian Administrative Service, opted for a much lower profile. At the time of writing, the office of the Comptroller and Auditor General has largely stayed away from news headlines. This, once again, points to the dangers of having appointments to such crucial constitutional posts being made exclusively by the government of the day, with no corresponding obligation upon it to seek inputs from non-partisan individuals and representatives of civil society. That said, the experience of the Election Commission (to which the chapter turns in the next section) shows that once a dormant constitutional office has been awakened by a single activist office holder, its subsequent incumbents do tend to use the powers that become available to them to exercise their checking function over time.

Early in its history, the office of the Comptroller and Auditor General had to face questions about the proper scope of its supervisory functions. As is clear from more recent history during the tenure of Vinod Rai, these debates continue. But the trend is more towards expansive interpretation of the office's powers, especially in the changed circumstances since economic liberalisation in the early 1990s, which has resulted in a number of traditional State functions being transferred to private entities. Thus, there have been calls for the scope of the office of the Comptroller and Auditor General to extend to Public Private Participation projects and other ventures which involve private entities. Some of these questions led to court cases where the judiciary had to intervene. Thus, for instance, a decision of the Supreme Court in 2013 held that the office of the Comptroller and Auditor General was justified in conducting performance audits as this was within the powers conferred upon it by section 15 of the

Comptroller and Auditor General Act 1971.[6] In the final section of this chapter we will examine how the post-1991 situation in India will continue to throw up such questions, making it reasonably certain that the office of the Comptroller and Auditor General will continue to be relevant in the future.

IV. THE ELECTION COMMISSION OF INDIA

At first glance, the Election Commission does not present itself as a checking or oversight institution since its mandate is to oversee the conduct of elections. However, given the central importance of elections for conferring legitimacy to governments in constitutional democracies, it seems clear that institutions to oversee this crucial function are also worthy of close attention. The Election Commission is a particularly important institution since it oversees the very process which provides legitimacy to the constitutional and democratic order.

A. History and Original Design

The institution of the Election Commission is one of the genuine innovations of the Indian Constituent Assembly. It did not exist in colonial India, where signalling the low priority accorded to them by the imperial authorities, elections were left to the executive, which handled them at the provincial and the Central levels. It is interesting that the framers of the Constitution decided on the importance of an independent institution for monitoring elections through a tangential route. Their principal concern arose out of the fact that in colonial India only a very small proportion of the population was eligible to exercise the right to vote. So, for instance, it was estimated that in the provincial elections of 1919 only 3 per cent of the total population was eligible to vote.[7] Not surprisingly, therefore, from a very early stage, the

[6] *Arvind Gupta v Union of India* (2013) SCC 293.

[7] 'Franchise and Elections' in B Shiva Rao, *The Framing of India's Constitution: A Study*, vol 5 (Delhi, Universal Law Publishing Company, 1968, reprinted 2010) 459–72, at 470.

draft articles which were approved by the Fundamental Rights Sub-Committee on 29 March 1947 contained a provision which guaranteed the right to vote, which would be both free and secret. It was to safeguard this right that the Sub-Committee first conceived of the role of an Election Commission.

As the issue developed, some influential members, including C Rajagopalachari, felt that it would not be proper to include the issue of universal adult franchise and the institutions needed to safeguard it within the Fundamental Rights chapter. It was ultimately decided to include the right to vote along with the provisions relating to the Election Commission in a part separate from the Fundamental Rights chapter. Some commentators saw deeper implications of the decision not to include the right to universal adult franchise as a fundamental right, given how much this issue had been an integral part of the nationalist movement.[8] It is certainly a noteworthy, and puzzling, omission for which the original documents do not provide adequate explanation.

Conceived similarly to the office of the Comptroller and Auditor General as a centralised institution, some of the initial debates among Assembly members were over the structure of the Election Commission and whether it should be a body with component units in the States. Equally, there was a suggestion that in order to protect the rights of minorities—another broad theme across issues that were discussed in the Constituent Assembly—there should be separate representation for minorities on the Election Commission.[9] Both these suggestions were eventually discarded. When these matters were discussed on the floor of the Constituent Assembly on 15 June 1947, BR Ambedkar strongly argued in favour of a centralised institution because of his sense that in some provinces, executive governments were preventing people from specific racial, cultural and ethnic backgrounds from being

[8] Mithi Mukherjee cites this as an example of the form of 'imperial justice' that the Congress believed was to be continued in independent India, abandoning the more radical form of justice that Gandhi had sought to insert into the nationalist movement. Mithi Mukherjee, *India in the Shadows of Empire: A Legal and Political History, 1774–1950* (New Delhi, Oxford University Press, 2010) 211–15.

[9] This suggestion was advanced, interestingly enough, by Syama Prasad Mukherjee, who was both a member of Nehru's first Cabinet and the founder of the Bharatiya Jana Sangh, a predecessor to the Bharatiya Janata Party.

brought onto the electoral rolls. He was supported by KM Munshi, but they were opposed by Kuladhar Chaliha from Assam, who complained that the centralisation of the Constitution as a whole was reducing the States to municipal bodies. He did so with a rhetorical flourish that goes to the heart of the link between legitimacy and (dis)trust: 'If you cannot trust the honesty of your own individuals, you can never make a success of democracy'.[10] HN Kunzru also felt that the provisions gave too much power to the President, and thereby to the Central government in appointing the Chief Election Commissioner and the other Election Commissioners. As a compromise, KM Munshi, who supported the broad plank adopted by Ambedkar in favour of a centralised institution, suggested that an amendment be made to clarify that the President's power to intervene in the powers of the Election Commission could be made subject to parliamentary law.

This strategy, of leaving the structure of the Election Commission as relatively flexible and providing Parliament the option of stepping in to change the composition of the Election Commission if it became necessary, was followed on other contentious issues as well. Thus, when some members wondered whether the Commission should be a permanent body or created from time to time when elections were due, it was decided that the body would consist of a permanent Chief Election Commissioner with other commissioners being appointed as and when their presence became necessary. When the provisions relating to the Election Commission were debated on the floor of the Assembly on 15 June 1949, Shibben Lal Saxena correctly predicted that over time the task of conducting elections would keep the Commission occupied consistently, for which it lacked a more robust structure and more personnel. Saxena also sought to entrench the position of the Chief Election Commissioner to avoid a situation where a Prime Minister appointed a 'party man' as an Election commissioner in the future.[11] In his response to these and other amendments, Dr Ambedkar conceded that the provision 'does not contain anything to provide against nomination of an unfit person to the post of the Chief Election Commissioner or the other Election Commissioners'.[12] To remedy the problem, Dr Ambedkar moved an amendment indicating that the

[10] CAD VIII 919.

[11] CAD VIII 905–07.

[12] ibid 920–21.

President's power to appoint the officers of the Election Commission would be subject to any law enacted by Parliament for this purpose.

It thus appears that some members of the Assembly had correctly anticipated some problems the future Election Commission would face. These include being swamped with work and not having enough personnel to discharge the onerous task of conducting elections, as well as the tendency of particular governments to want to pack the Election Commission with pliant appointees. The framers on the whole felt, however, that these could not be dealt with at the time of the framing and would have to be dealt with as the institution evolved. While some may see their inability to address these issues at the founding as an inability or weakness (even though they were aware of these potential problems), some others may see this as a recognition that some problems would have to be tackled by the emerging constitutional culture as it evolved.

B. Constitutional Provisions and Parliamentary Laws Relating to the Election Commission

The provisions discussed above are to be found in Part XV of the Constitution, which bears the title 'Elections' and consists of Articles 324–329. Article 324, the first provision, declares that the 'superintendence, direction and control of the electoral rolls for, and the conduct, of all elections' including to Parliament, the State legislatures, and the offices of the President and Vice-President will vest in the Election Commission. It further stipulates that the Election Commission will consist of a permanent Chief Election Commissioner and such other Election Commissioners as may be appointed by the President from time to time. The Chief Election Commissioner can be removed from office in a manner and on grounds similar to those for a judge of the Supreme Court; the security of tenure of other Election Commissioners is relatively less fortified and only requires a recommendation for their removal from the Chief Election Commissioner. The conditions of service and tenure of office of the Election Commissioners are to be determined by the President through rules but are subject to laws made by Parliament. These provisions thus reflect the compromises reached by the Assembly members on the structure of the Commission.

Article 325 declares that there shall be one electoral roll for every territorial constituency in elections for the Parliament and State legislatures and no person can be made ineligible for any such election on grounds of religion, race, caste, sex or any of them. This has to be viewed against the historical pattern of separate electorates (based primarily on religion) that were introduced by the colonial authorities and were viewed by the nationalist movement as having spread communal feeling and tensions. This provision reflects the great antipathy felt by the framers towards the idea of separate electorates in a free and democratic India.

Article 326, which as we have seen was the reason for having a separate chapter dealing with elections, states that elections to Parliament and the State legislatures shall be on the basis of universal adult suffrage and that every person above the age of 18 (originally set at 21, amended by the Rajiv Gandhi Government in 1989) will be qualified to be registered as a voter. The constitutionally specified grounds of disqualification for voters are non-residence, unsoundness of mind, crime, or corrupt or illegal practice. Although this is an important provision which goes to the foundation of constitutional democracy in India, it has sometimes been ignored or under-appreciated, including by the Supreme Court,[13] somewhat vindicating the fears of those who had cautioned against its being housed outside of the Fundamental Rights chapter.

Article 327 enables Parliament to make laws relating to elections to Parliament and the State legislatures, including on the preparation of electoral rolls. Article 328 bestows a similar power upon State legislatures, though subject to the power of Parliament in this regard. Finally, Article 329 places limits on the power of courts to intervene in matters of elections. Clause (a) bars the courts from intervening in issues relating to the delimitation of constituencies or allotment of seats to such constituencies if laws to this effect are enacted under Articles 327 or 328. Clause (b) stipulates that elections to Parliament and the State legislatures can be called into question only through election petitions as provided by relevant laws. Other constitutional provisions also relate to the working of the Election Commission in so far as they set out the

[13] See the decision by Chalemeshwar J of the Supreme Court in *Rajbala v State of Haryana* (2016) 1 SCC 463.

mode of presidential and vice-presidential elections (Articles 51–74); outline the parliamentary structure (Articles 79–104); and set out the composition and electoral basis of State legislatures (Article 168–193).

A number of parliamentary laws affect the working of the Election Commission. The Representation of the People Acts 1950 and 1951 deal with issues such as the delimitation of constituencies as well as processual details and the basis of the electoral system. In 1991 Parliament enacted the Chief Election Commissioner and other Election Commissioners (Conditions of Service) Act 1991, which established a permanent three-member Election Commission. This law was passed to resolve long-standing controversies over the power of the incumbent government to appoint and remove the Election Commissioners.

C. The Functioning of the Election Commission in Post-independence India

The primary duties of the Election Commission, as set out in the constitutional provisions mentioned above, consist of the following: 'the delimitation of constituencies, the drawing up of electoral rolls, the supervision of the nomination of candidates, the administration of the electoral process, and the surveillance of the probity of electoral conduct'.[14] Many of these elements involve technical issues of electoral law and are not the focus of analysis here. The attempt, instead, is to provide a broad sweep analysis of the working of the institution over time. A scholar who has insightfully analysed electoral politics in India divides the history of the Election Commission across post-independence India into three phases: (i) Establishment (1950s–late 1960s); Quiescence (late 1960s–1990); Activism (1990–present).[15]

(i) Phase I (1950–Late 1960s)

The first test for the newly established institution arose soon after its creation, when it had to conduct the first General Elections for the

[14] Alistair McMillan, 'The Election Commission' in Nirja Jayal and Pratap Mehta (eds), *The Oxford Companion to Politics in India* (New Delhi, Oxford University Press, 2010) 100.

[15] ibid 111–13.

Lok Sabha. The scale and size of India meant that this would be the largest exercise in democratic elections in history. Given the challenges involved, the first Chief Election Commissioner of India, Sukumar Sen (1950–58), decided to hold them after taking time to visit each State to personally oversee preparations. The elections were eventually conducted over a period of four months, between October 1951 and February 1952, and were generally regarded, despite some teething troubles, as a success and a considerable democratic achievement. Under the tenure of Sen and his successor, KVK Sundaram (1958–67), the Election Commission sought to establish itself and its credibility as an effective conductor and monitoring agent of democratic elections across the country. In this it was largely successful, even as it adopted a low profile and sought to correct its initial mistakes and learn from them. In the public imagination, however, the distinctiveness and separate identity of the institution was not always clear.

(ii) Phase II (Late 1960s–1990)

By the late 1960s the Congress no longer enjoyed the dominant presence of the Nehru years. Under Indira Gandhi's successive governments, the political culture of respect for institutional independence waned and any institution which was perceived as a threat to the Prime Minister's office was forced to stand down. This was more true of the Election Commission as an institution than certain other institutions because although there were high-profile controversies regarding the conduct of elections, the Election Commission appeared to play no role in their resolution. During this period seven men served as Chief Election Commissioners for shorter tenures than the first two incumbents. Towards the end of this phase, in 1989, the Rajiv Gandhi Government sought to appoint two more commissioners just before the Lok Sabha elections. This was perceived as seeking to undermine the independence of the institution and the VP Singh Government, which came to power in 1990, removed the two commissioners (SS Dhanoa and VS Seigal) and appointed the mercurial TN Seshan as India's 10th Chief Election Commissioner.

(iii) Phase III (1990–Present)

TN Seshan's tenure as Chief Election Commissioner, lasting from 1990 to 1996, had a dramatic effect on the role, impact and public perception of the Election Commission as an institution. Perhaps because he took office at the start of the coalition era in Indian politics, Seshan felt he had far more room to flex the institutional muscle power of the Election Commission. He undertook a series of initiatives that while not always successful on the ground, propelled Seshan and the institution of the Election Commission (in that order, which is also why Seshan was often legitimately criticised for seeking personal prominence) into the national limelight on a regular basis. These initiatives included efforts at overcoming the problem of voter registration, candidate fraud and electoral corruption through the introduction of voter identity cards. This scheme was caught up in administrative difficulties and over time undermined rather than strengthened the perception of the Election Commission as an efficient organisation. Seshan also threatened to use the power of the Election Commission to delay elections if his initiatives were not accepted. In at least some cases, these were often the result of his own preferences for cleaning up the political system and were not derived from the legally authorised powers of the Commission. Seshan's somewhat cavalier approach to questions of the basis of authority caused legal difficulties. For some of these actions Seshan faced strictures from judicial bodies, which only seemed to increase his populist appeal. Seshan's successors in office, MS Gill (1996–2001) and JM Lyngdoh (2001–04) were able to consolidate the new gains in terms of profile by bringing in innovative measures to improve the conduct of elections, such as the process of computerisation for updating electoral rolls and the introduction of electronic voting machines, which are, as of 2003, now used across elections. A long-standing effort of the Election Commission has been the Model Code of Conduct for parties and candidates, which was first used in Kerala in 1960. Seshan and his successors sought to elevate the status of the Code to impose sanctions on errant political parties and figures, though they were not always successful in such efforts. Since 1997 the Election Commission has sought to address the vice of the increasing criminalisation of Indian politics by seeking to influence which candidates are nominated by political parties for elections. Some critics have asserted that in so doing, the Election Commission's technocratic focus loses sight of the important democratic questions—such as the right of voters to choose candidates freely—that underlie such issues. Similarly, it has sought to place restrictions on the reporting of electoral campaigns by the media, which has been criticised as unfairly restricting the freedom of speech. However, the Commission's efforts at bringing about internal democracy within India's many political parties—almost all of which function like feudal systems, characterised by dynasties and the hold of charismatic forms of authority—have had little success so far.

While the activist decisions of the Election Commission have at times been criticised by academics and experts, it has gained great popularity and prestige as an institution that seeks to safeguard the integrity of the electoral process. Surveys indicate that the Election Commission enjoys the highest rates of public trust/confidence among India's public institutions; it ranks higher, for instance, than the judiciary, government, political parties and police.[16] However, its institutional independence remains a virtue that needs to be constantly monitored. As recently as in January 2009 there was a controversy over the appointment of Navin Chawla as the Chief Election Commissioner, in view of his perceived closeness to the Congress Party. As in the case of the Comptroller and Auditor General of India, the fact that the appointment process of the Chief Election Commissioner remains exclusively within the discretion of the elected government of the day means that there is always the possibility that a person favourable to the ruling dispensation will gain office. Nevertheless, the high public profile enjoyed by the institution in contemporary times, and the provisions to ensure security of tenure, provide hope that the incumbent will be able to take on the government which appointed him or her if the occasion so demands.

The Election Commission of India has been recognised as an institution that has contributed in a robust manner to the consolidation of constitutional democracy across the post-independence phase.[17] Its role during the 1990s, when India underwent a period of significant socio-political and extra-constitutional change, has been particularly appreciated. It is to this tumultuous phase of constitutional development in India that the chapter now turns its focus.

[16] Subrata K Mitra and VB Singh, *Democracy and Social Change in India: A cross Sectional Analysis of the National Electorate* (New Delhi, Sage, 1999) 260.

[17] For a recent analysis of the Election Commission, see E Sridharan and Milan Vaishnav, 'Election Commission of India' in Devesh Kapur, Pratap Mehta and Milan Vaishnav (eds), *Rethinking Public Institutions in India* (New Delhi, Oxford University Press, 2017) 417–73.

V. THE INTRODUCTION OF NEW REGULATORY INSTITUTIONS IN THE AFTERMATH OF THE CONSTITUTIONAL MOMENT OF 1991

As we have noted, the early 1990s witnessed a series of significant shifts in the economic, political and sociological landscape of India. These shifts have collectively led to a 'constitutional moment' in India. The term, coined by the US constitutional scholar Bruce Ackerman, refers to constitutional transformations that occur outside the formal amendment framework established by the text of the Constitution.[18] In other chapters we have focused on changes in the political and sociological dimensions; in this section, the focus is on the economic sector.[19]

There are many theories and explanations for the reasons behind the advent of economic liberalisation in India. We focus here, instead, on the consequences of this dramatic change. The changes have been described as transforming a 'centralized, tutelary, interventionist state whose political and administrative elites were committed to the notion that they knew best and could do best' into 'an increasingly decentralized regulatory state and market economy whose politicians and entrepreneurs turned to voters, consumers and investors for ideas and action'.[20] While this description may be articulating the difference too starkly (as it is clear that the pre-1991 State was not cut off abruptly and many of its aspects continue in the contemporary State), it does delineate some elements that merit closer scrutiny.

On the economic front, what is striking is the emergence in India of what has been described as the 'regulatory state'. This is characterised

[18] There is considerable debate over the correctness and applicability of Ackerman's theory, which has generated a large literature. For present purposes, it is sufficient to rely on one early articulation of the theory of constitutional moment in Ackerman's work: Bruce Ackerman, *We, the People* (Cambridge, MA, Belknap Press, 1991) 3–5.

[19] This section draws upon my previous work: Arun K Thiruvengadam, 'Flag-Bearers of a New Era?: The Evolution of New Regulatory Institutions in India (1991–2016)' in Susan Rose Ackerman and Peter Lindseth (eds), *Comparative Administrative Law*, 2nd edn (Cheltenham, Edward Elgar Publishing, 2017) 218–33.

[20] Lloyd Rudolph and Susanne Rudolph, *In Pursuit of Lakshmi: The Political Economy of the Indian State* (Chicago, University of Chicago Press, 1987) 129.

by a few specific features: an expanded role for markets, greater private sector participation in all facets of society, and withdrawal of the State from the direct provision of services and as the dominant employer. The new regulatory State is thus marked by 'greater reliance on institutions operating at arm's length from government, insulated from daily political pressures, and embedding their decisions in technical expertise'.[21] These institutions, usually termed as independent regulatory authorities, have emerged in several sectors in India, although their form and structure varies. In this section, we focus on a select few among the many new regulatory institutions that have emerged in India since the early 1990s.

It is important to recognise that the new regulatory institutions have no constitutional basis or grounding. The framers of the Indian Constitution appear not to have anticipated the need for such institutions. While they went beyond more traditional Constitutions that only set out the traditional three wings of government and provided constitutional status to unconventional institutions such as the Comptroller and Auditor General, the Election Commission and the Finance Commission, they did not intervene in details of institutions housed in the traditional executive. This may also have been because the framers, being themselves framed by the thinking of their times, were almost uniformly committed to the idea of a strong State that would lead and dominate functioning in the economic realm. It is important to recall that while the framers were at work, their peers in government were the Democrats in the US (who, under President Truman, were still engaging with the New Deal State erected by President FD Roosevelt), the Labour Party in the UK (which, under Prime Minister Clement Atlee, was engaged in creating the modern British welfare state) and the Communist Party in the Soviet Union (where General Secretary Stalin had already erected the Command model of State control over the economy). Not surprisingly, therefore, the framers of the Indian Constitution assumed that control over economic decisions should primarily rest in the traditional wings of government.

Nevertheless, it could be argued that the rise of the new regulatory institutions in India in the 1990s has something in common with the

[21] Navroz K Dubash and Bronwen Morgan, 'The Rise of the Regulatory State of the South' in Navroz K Dubash and Bronwen Morgan (eds), *The Rise of the Regulatory State of the South* (Oxford, Oxford University Press, 2013) 2.

vision of the framers, who had already created technocratic, counter-majoritarian constitutional institutions including the two we have already examined in this chapter.

At the time of independence, India's economy was significantly located in private ownership. Although there was not much by way of industrial and commercial infrastructure, the steel mills, jute industries and banks that existed were in private hands. The framers adopted a socialist philosophy (and enshrined aspects of it within the Directive Principles of State Policy) and the imperative of a planned economy. By the late 1960s this had resulted in a process whereby all institutional economic activity was under public control.[22]

During the subsequent decades and lasting until 1990, public sector firms were the dominant actors in the economy. These public sector units and the departments of government to which they were subordinate functioned simultaneously in the capacities of operator, manager and regulator.

In the post-1991 situation, such a situation became unsustainable. The rationale for introducing independent regulators varied across sectors. In the utilities sector it was to build confidence among private actors, who had to compete with government public sector companies while remaining confident that the rules of the game would not be changed to their disadvantage. In the securities and financial sector, regulation sought to (i) protect investors from misleading and fraudulent practices; (ii) establish fair, transparent and efficient markets; and (iii) reduce systematic risks (including through capital and internal control requirements).[23]

In contemporary India there now exist nearly 25 Central regulatory authorities.[24] Some of these owe their origin to the pre-1991 era, such as the Reserve Bank of India, which was established in 1935 as a functionally autonomous regulator of fiscal and monetary policy. Nevertheless, the majority of these Central regulatory institutions bear

[22] Saugata Bhattacharya and Urijit Patel, 'New Regulatory Institutions in India' in Devesh Kapur and Pratap Mehta (eds), *Public Institutions in India* (New Delhi, Oxford University Press, 2005) 420–21.

[23] ibid 417–18.

[24] TV Somanathan, 'The Administrative and Regulatory State' in S Choudhry, M Khosla and PB Mehta (eds), *The Oxford Handbook of the Indian Constitution* (Oxford, Oxford University Press, 2016).

the hallmark of 'regulatory state' institutions as they seek to ensure a level playing field between the government on the one hand, and private actors on the other, in several sectors.

The first statutory independent regulatory commission was the Securities and Exchange Board of India (SEBI), which was established in 1992. Prior to its creation, the financial regulators were the Ministry of Finance, the Department of Company Affairs and the Reserve Bank of India, besides the individual stock exchanges. SEBI now interacts with all these agencies in regulating the financial sector. Similarly, prior to the creation of the Telecom Regulatory Authority of India (TRAI) in 1997, the telecommunications sector was regulated by the Department of Telecommunications located within the Ministry of Communications of the Central government.

Being relatively young institutions, both SEBI and TRAI have had to evolve quite quickly to meet the demands of the rapidly changing sectors that are under their respective charge. The narrative trajectory of the evolution of TRAI has been particularly rocky as the original TRAI set up in 1997 was disbanded and reconstituted in 2000, in part because the initial avatar, headed by a retired Chief Justice of a High Court who adopted a robust view of the powers available to the institution, was perceived by those within government as being overly activist and keen to undermine the role of the government. This led to the clipping of TRAI's wings in 2000 and a careful vetting of subsequent heads of TRAI, who were invariably drawn from the ranks of retiring members of the bureaucracy and rarely showed a willingness to take on their former employers.[25] As in the case of the Comptroller and Auditor General and the Election Commissioner, the government's power to appoint personnel to these institutions assumes a crucial dimension. The problem with the new regulatory authorities is that, unlike the other two institutions examined in this chapter, they have no security of tenure akin to constitutional authorities and thus remain even more vulnerable to pressure from government and other sources. There are

[25] This is the truncated story of TRAI's origin and evolution. For fuller details see Arun K Thiruvengadam and Piyush Joshi, 'Judiciaries as Crucial Actors in Regulatory Systems of the Global South: The Indian Judiciary and Telecom Regulation (1991–2012)' in Navroz Dubash and Bronwen Morgan (eds), *The Rise of the Regulatory State of the South* (Oxford, Oxford University Press, 2013) 136–62.

other challenges, including the fact that most regulatory institutions have few powers of enforcing their rulings and their parent statutes do not unambiguously delineate their coercive powers.[26]

That said, however, one must recognise that even with constitutional safeguards to protect their independence, it took several decades for the Comptroller and Auditor General and the Election Commission to flex their institutional muscles. Given that these new regulatory institutions are yet to complete a quarter-century, they may need more time to develop a culture of independence and efficient functioning. It is nevertheless clear that they are playing an increasingly important role on the national scene and this will only continue to grow in the times to come.

VI. CONCLUSION

The three sets of institutions that have been briefly reviewed in this chapter play pivotal roles in safeguarding constitutional values in contemporary India. Yet they are unusual institutions and would not typically find mention in constitutional discourse in many nations. Two of these owe their origin and status as constitutional authorities to the vision and sagacity of the framers of the Indian Constitution. The third set of institutions is the creation of geopolitical and transnational factors that occurred nearly four decades after the adoption of the Indian Constitution. They were brought in to respond to challenges that the framers of the Indian Constitution could not be expected to have anticipated. Yet, we can find commonalities between the vision of the framers of the Indian Constitution and the rationale for establishing these new regulatory institutions. Given current political realities, each of these institutions can be expected to continue to play important roles in safeguarding the values of Indian constitutionalism.

[26] Thiruvengadam (n 19) 229–31, 'Flag-Bearers of a New Era?: The Evolution of New Regulatory Institutions in India (1991–2016)' in Susan Rose Ackerman and Peter Lindseth (eds), *Comparative Administrative Law*, 2nd edn (Cheltenham, Edward Elgar, 2017).

FURTHER READING

SK Das, 'Institutions of Internal Accountability' in Devesh Kapur and Pratap Bhanu Mehta, *Public Institutions in India: Performance and Design* (New Delhi, Oxford University Press, 2005) 128–57.

Peter Ronald D'Souza, 'The Election Commission and Election Reforms in India' in DD Khanna et al (eds), *Democracy, Diversity and Stability: 50 Years of Indian Independence* (New Delhi, Macmillan India, 2008) 51–98.

Navroz Dubash and Bronwen Morgan (eds), *The Rise of the Regulatory State of the South* (Oxford, Oxford University Press, 2013).

Devesh Kapur, Pratap Bhanu Mehta and Milan Vaishnav (eds), *Rethinking Public Institutions in India* (New Delhi, Oxford University Press, 2017).

A McMillan, 'The Election Commission of India and the Regulation and Administration of Electoral Politics' (2012) 11(2) *Election Law Journal: Rules, Politics, Policy* 187–201.

Vinod Rai, *Not Just an Accountant: The Diary of the Nation's Conscience Keeper* (New Delhi, Rupa, 2014).

E Sridharan and Milan Vaishnav, 'Election Commission of India' in Devesh Kapur, Pratap Mehta and Milan Vaishnav (eds), *Rethinking Public Institutions in India* (New Delhi, Oxford University Press, 2017) 417–73.

R Sridharan, 'Institutions of Internal Accountability' in Devesh Kapur, Pratap Mehta and Milan Vaishnav (eds), *Rethinking Public Institutions in India* (New Delhi, Oxford University Press, 2017) 271–296.

6

Constitutional Regulation of India's Multiple Identities

Introduction – Constitutional provisions – Relevant constitutional history – Evolution and development of post-independence constitutional jurisprudence – Role of the Parliament, the executive and judiciary and other constitutional actors – Conclusion

I. INTRODUCTION

WHILE IT IS well known that India has a diverse and heterogeneous population, its scale and detail need to be appreciated to obtain an understanding of the complexities involved in regulating issues that are generated as a result of this diversity. The scholar Ramachandra Guha has argued that India's societal contestations can be understood across five often-intersecting axes: religion, caste, language, class and gender.[1]

India's population, according to the most recently conducted census in 2011, stands at 1.2 billion. The census, incidentally, has historically been a catalyst for creating, transforming and sharpening identities in India. Introduced during the period of the British Raj, the first census results in 1872 enabled the colonial authorities to 'see' and learn about their subjects along enumerated categories. In the process, the colonial subjects had to learn to adopt some identities which were new for them as well. The process of 'classification' and 'counting' contributed to the sharpening of identities which were more fluid and less clear than

[1] Ramachandra Guha, *India After Gandhi* (Picador India, 2007) xix–xx.

was evident in the precise and clean-cut figures of the census results. Scholars have noted how the categories of 'religion', 'caste' and even a category as 'objective' as age came to be viewed as ideologically charged and capable of both confusion and manipulation in census surveys and calculations.[2]

With these caveats in mind, let us examine the categories of Indian identity identified earlier, starting with religion. Of the 1.2 billion Indians, Hindus, who account for nearly 80 per cent of the population of India, are at 966 million. Hindus are divided by the category of caste into five broad segments (the four *varnas* and the fifth unnamed category for the former Untouchables); these *varnas* are further divided into more than 3,000 sub-categories (*jatis*). India's 172 million Muslim citizens constitute its largest minority religion, accounting for 14.23 per cent of its population. This makes India the country with the third-largest Muslim population in the world. Indian Muslims are further divided into Sunnis, Shias, Bohras, Ismailis and Ahmadiyyas. The Hindu population is divided into even more sects. Other numerically significant religious minorities in India are Christians (27.8 million), Sikhs (20.8 million), Buddhists (9.25 million), Jains (4.4 million) and Parsis (57,264).

India's linguistic diversity is particularly striking—part of the difficulty in identifying the number of languages spoken within it arises from the problem of distinguishing between languages and dialects. The 2001 census reported that there are 122 major languages and 1,599 languages/dialects that are currently in use across the territory of India. Of these, 30 languages are spoken by more than a million native speakers, while 122 are spoken by more than 10,000 people. Many of

[2] From among the vast literature, see generally, Kevin Walby and Michael Haan, 'Caste Confusion and Census Enumeration in Colonial India, 1871–1921' (2012) XLV(90) *Histoire sociale/Social History* 301–18 (showing that for the census reports between 1871 and 1921 epistemological problems with envisioning and enumerating caste were the rule rather than the exception); Timothy L Alborn, 'Age and Empire in the Indian Census, 1871–1931' (1999) 31 *Journal of Interdisciplinary History* 61–89 (demonstrating that even the relatively prosaic category of age was treated in problematic ways by census gatherers between 1871 and 1931). See generally, Barbara D Metcalf and Thomas R Metcalf, *A Concise History of India* (Cambridge, Cambridge University Press, 2002) (challenging the notion that a continuous meaning can be applied to social categories such as 'caste', 'Hindu', 'Muslim' or even 'India').

these languages are written in different scripts and are not easily accessible to people who do not speak or read them. Hindi, which is spoken by the largest number of people in the country, is used by only about 40 per cent of the overall population, which, as we will see, became a source of contention in the Constituent Assembly when deciding upon the language for the conduct of the work of government and public works. Given this diversity, it may seem either puzzling or only logical that the language in which much of the business of governance is conducted in India is English, which was spoken by less than 1 per cent of Indians at the time of independence.

A distinctive social category in India is that of caste. Although an attribute of the Hindu majority, what makes its effects so invidious is that nearly all religions in the Indian subcontinent were also influenced by the caste system. Thus, caste has sociological, political and legal implications for all religious groups in India. Nevertheless, the greatest impact of the caste system has been on Hindu society. The Constitution of India seeks, as we shall see, to tackle the long-term effects of one of the most insidious forms of discrimination devised in any human society. These policies include 'reservations' (or quotas) in legislatures, educational institutions and government employment. The primary focus of these ameliorative measures are the worst off in caste Hindu society: the Scheduled Castes, or the category formerly known as the Untouchables. Scheduled Castes—who have at various times been referred to as 'Depressed Classes', 'Harijans' and 'Backward Classes' and self-identify in the contemporary period as 'Dalits'—constitute 16.6 per cent of the overall population and include 1,206 main castes that were considered 'untouchable' within the Hindu traditional system. Scheduled Tribes, who can rightfully claim to be the indigenous population of India, presently number about 105 million across 701 distinct tribes. They constitute 8.6 per cent of India's population and are spread across parts of central, southern and north-eastern India. The Constitution also provides for benefits including 'reservations' (or quotas) for other categories of Hindus, which are termed 'Other Backward Classes' (OBCs). Unlike Scheduled Castes and Scheduled Tribes, the OBCs are sociologically less distinct. At the broadest level, they can be described as the middle category between the upper castes and the Scheduled Castes, but since one official estimate of their numbers is about 52 per cent of the overall population of India, this amounts to a very large middle. Many of the OBC castes are socially and economically heterogeneous, which makes problems of identifying the populations in need of ameliorative policies more difficult. Some OBC groups are economically well off and have political support even though their representation in higher education, government employment and services more generally remains low. At the same time, those among the OBCs who were located just above the former Untouchables were also subject to levels of discrimination which were very similar. It is the range and quality of discrimination experienced by OBCs and the sheer numbers and diverse experiences involved that makes the extension of reservations to the category as a whole problematic. Reservations for OBCs have unsurprisingly, therefore, remained very controversial and have affected the overall perception of legitimacy of reservation and affirmative action policies.

In terms of class, India was historically a segmented and unequal society (in part due to the caste system), especially in relation to access to basic needs. Nearly two centuries of colonial rule exacerbated these problems, leading to widespread destitution and staggering levels of poverty at the time of independence. This backdrop shaped, as noted in earlier chapters, the nature of the constitutional compact, the setting of national priorities in the fundamental text, and the policies of State-led development that were followed in the crucial initial years. India's Human Development Indices (HDIs) in the twenty-first century continue to be indicative of a society that, nearly seven decades after formal independence, has yet to pull a significant proportion of its population out of dire poverty. According to a report issued by the UN Millennium Development Goals, in 2015 more than a fifth of India's population (21.5 per cent) was living below the poverty line, which it defined as earning less than US$1.25 per day. This is a staggering number, especially when understood against the rising affluence of the middle and upper classes in India, many of whose members now enjoy an unparalleled level of prosperity, especially in urban centres. The rising affluence of the small section of those who comprise these classes in India only heightens the growing inequality of Indian society as a whole. The starkness of these statistics becomes even more acute when one takes into account the absence of universal welfare measures in Indian society. Despite the socialist rhetoric employed liberally in the Constitution, actual welfare measures were not statutorily enforced until the first decade of the twenty-first century. Even these are not universal, are regarded as woefully inadequate, and have yet to gain a firm footing.

The issue of gender continues to be extremely salient in contemporary Indian society. Some of the issues relating to gender discrimination are a function of the widespread poverty and underdevelopment adverted to earlier, but many of the social ills that afflict women in India can be traced to cultural practices which disadvantage women in very specific ways. The preference for male children has led to horrific acts of female foeticide and exclusion of women from schools, workplaces and the public domain in extreme ways. Over time this has led to a skewed ratio of men to women, which will have disastrous consequences in the long term. It is also important to recognise that issues of gender in India are also affected by intersectionality of identities. Women who are either from lower castes or from minority communities face special challenges and issues. The intersecting of issues relating to caste, religion and gender creates new and vexing problems for multiculturalism and the legal regulation thereof.

As we will see later in this chapter, each of these five categories that cause social disruption and conflict in contemporary India were very much in the minds of the framers of India's Constitution. What makes the Indian constitutional experiment a truly ambitious exercise is its attempt to devise constitutional strategies to address these seemingly intractable issues simultaneously. As we shall see, while Indian constitutionalism is generally regarded as an exemplar in liberal constitutionalism, its provisions relating to issues of multiculturalism exhibit departures from mainstream liberal theory especially in its commitment to group rights in the context of reservations and rights of minority religious groups.

This chapter will focus on the constitutional provisions relating to the five issues identified above and will then track the evolution of constitutional doctrine, law and politics around these issues. The principal focus will be on the following issues: freedom of religion and secularism; the provisions relating to affirmative action (consisting of quotas for seats in the legislature, public employment and education) for those affected by caste discrimination; and the provisions that seek to achieve equal rights for women. The complex politics of language in India, which were a source of deep contention within the Constituent Assembly, were to some extent addressed and resolved by the linguistic reorganisation of States that was covered in Chapter 3.

They are therefore less the focus of analysis here. Similarly, issues of class were sought to be partially addressed in the Directive Principles and have been a major driver of policy changes, but are not fully addressed here.

In the evolution of the law and politics on all these issues the major institutions of government—the legislature, the executive and courts—have played crucial roles, and the chapter will seek to provide an overview of how these institutions have interacted to develop policies that have changed over time.

Independent India has had a disturbing record of consistent communal violence, with at least one major outbreak of communal/religious violence in each of the last four decades. In the last quarter-century, the rise of Hindu right wing parties, which have gone on to form governments at the Centre and in several States, have posed a serious challenge to India's model of secularism. This chapter will also provide a brief overview of India's unique form of legal pluralism, where different religious communities are allowed to be governed by their separate personal laws.

As is evident, issues of multiculturalism pose complex problems in India's multi-stratified society and this chapter will be able to provide only a broad overview of the most salient of such issues. The chapter will, in keeping with the rest of the book, make selective use of examples to describe the overall terrain.

II. RELEVANT CONSTITUTIONAL PROVISIONS

This section provides a brief overview of the provisions that deal with the five markers of identity in India addressed earlier. The attempt here is only to provide a textual overview. There are a large number of such provisions—numbering nearly 50—and this survey seeks to emphasise only the most important aspects. As expected, most such provisions are from Parts III and IV of the Constitution, which house the Fundamental Rights and Directive Principles.

The Preamble to the Constitution declares that it seeks to constitute India into a *sovereign, socialist, secular, democratic republic.* In so doing, the aspiration is to secure the following, among other, societal goals: *Justice* (understood as a multifaceted concept, focusing on social and economic dimensions beyond the political), *Liberty* (including of belief, faith and worship) *Equality* (of both status and of opportunity) and *Fraternity* (understood as assuring the dignity of the individual). All these concepts and their identified dimensions have implications for the Indian Constitution's vision of multiculturalism and its approach towards issues of religion, caste, class, language and gender.

Since issues of protective discrimination are linked to questions of equality, they are tackled within the provisions relating to the Right to Equality, namely, Articles 14–18. Beyond the general guarantee of equal protection of the laws specified in Article 14, Article 15(1) proscribes any discrimination by the State against any citizen on the following named grounds: religion, race, caste, sex, place of birth, or any of them. The three markers of religion, gender and caste are specifically named grounds upon which discrimination is prohibited. Clause 2 of Article 15 makes clear that the prohibition against discrimination also extends horizontally, to citizens and non-State institutions, as it guarantees access to 'shops, public restaurants, hotels, and places of public entertainment' as well as 'the use of wells, tanks, bathing ghats, roads and places of public resort'. This specific naming of sites from which lower caste individuals were historically excluded is significant. Article 15(3) makes clear that the general prohibition against discrimination does not prevent the State from 'making any special provision for women and children'. This is a form of protective discrimination, which, some feminists have found problematic. Article 15(4), which, as will be explained shortly, was inserted through the First Amendment to the Constitution within a year of its adoption, similarly enables the State to take special steps 'for the advancement of any socially and educationally backward class of citizens or for the Scheduled Castes and Scheduled Tribes'. The Scheduled Castes and Scheduled Tribes are, interestingly, mentioned separately from backward classes.

Article 16 focuses on equality in the context of public employment. Clause (1) promises equality of opportunity (to be distinguished from equality of result) for all citizens in matters of employment relating to 'any office under the State'. This entails, per clause (2), a guarantee of non-discrimination on the grounds named in Article 15: religion, race, caste, sex, descent, place of birth, and residence. Clause (4) enables the State to override the prohibition on discrimination to provide for 'reservations of appointments or posts in favour of any backward class of citizens' to ensure adequate representation in State services. Article 17 formally abolishes the practice of Untouchability, and declares that anyone practising caste discrimination against the former Untouchables would be committing an offence.

Together, Articles 15 and 16 enable the State to make special provisions to combat the historical discrimination faced by groups such as women, children, lower caste groups, Scheduled Castes and Scheduled Tribes, and any other marginalised section which qualifies as 'backward'. While these special provisions could encompass many situations, the State is specifically empowered to take concrete steps in the spheres of education and public employment. What is striking is that the Indian State is entrusted with the duty and responsibility of ensuring that marginalised sections of Indian society, who had historically been excluded from the mainstream, are protected from further discrimination and are actively encouraged to join the new national project, which is founded on egalitarian and humanistic principles, reflected also in the Preamble.

The next set of relevant provisions are Articles 25–28, which are housed within a section entitled 'Right to Freedom of Religion'. Article 25(1) guarantees to all *persons* (and not only to citizens) the freedom of conscience and the right to freely 'profess, practise and propagate' religion. It further provides that these freedoms are subject to restrictions based only on grounds of 'public order, morality and health'. Clause (2) connects these freedoms to the non-discrimination provisions examined earlier, by empowering the State to provide for social welfare and reform measures in relation to Hindu religious institutions, by ensuring that they are open to all sections of Hindus. This is deeply tied to the practices of caste Hinduism, which excluded lower castes, the former Untouchables and women from temples. As we shall in greater detail later, this is one of the paradoxes of the Indian model of secularism, which promises freedom of religion but also places an obligation on the State to reform religion and social practices based on religion, especially in respect of Hinduism. Explanation II to Article 25(2) highlights another distinctive feature when it provides that for the purposes of the Constitution, reference to Hindus includes references to Sikh, Jain or Buddhist religions. All three groups, which consider themselves distinct from Hinduism, are nevertheless legally treated as included within Hinduism.

Article 26 vests in every religious denomination in India certain rights, including that of establishing and maintaining institutions for religious and charitable purposes; managing its own affairs in matters of religion; and owning, acquiring and administering movable and immovable property. These rights are subject to general considerations of 'public order, morality and health' but have been guaranteed to enable religions to have the conditions to flourish in concrete and practical terms, giving content to the more abstract right to freedom of religion guaranteed by Article 25. The next two provisions add important negative dimensions to the freedom of religion. Providing further specificity, Article 27 allows immunity to all persons from taxes that are designed to benefit a specific religion. Article 28 prohibits the imparting of religious instruction in institutions run entirely out of State funds. Clause 3 of the provision further provides than any student attending an educational institution cannot be compelled to participate in religious instruction or ceremonies held in the premises. Taken together, Articles 25–28 seek to provide both positive and negative protections to the freedom of religion, while also enabling the State to carry out reforms specifically focusing on the Hindu religion.

Another group of provisions that are directly relevant for this chapter are entitled 'Cultural and Educational Rights' and stand guaranteed under Articles 29–30. Article 29, which seeks to protect the 'interests of minorities', stipulates that 'any section of the citizens who reside in India and have a distinct language, script or culture of their own' have the right to conserve it. This has the effect of defining the concept of a minority in an expensive sense, travelling beyond religion to also cover linguistic and cultural aspects of the human personality. Clause (2) limits itself to the context of educational institutions that are either fully or partially administered by the State, and prohibits them from discriminating against anyone on the following grounds: religion, race, caste or language. Article 30 declares that all religious and linguistic minorities in India have the right to administer educational institutions of their choice.

Several provisions from Part IV of the Constitution, dealing with Directive Principles of State Policy, are also relevant for the issues analysed here. Three of these have implications for the way the legal regulation of religion has developed. Article 44 is an example of the way the framers often deferred resolving a contentious issue, and urges the State 'to endeavour to secure' a Uniform Civil Code throughout the territory of India. This has implications for the personal law system that the colonial authorities had inserted into the Indian legal order and is a continuing site for contestation. The personal law system in India enables Indians of four major religious communities—Hindu (a category which is deemed to include Sikhs, Buddhists and Jains), Muslim, Christian and Parsi—to be governed by their respective religious laws in matters of family law relating to marriage, divorce, succession, adoption, guardianship and maintenance. These laws sit uneasily with the constitutional commitment to equality and respect for gender rights, given that all these religious laws privilege men over women in both blatant and subtle ways. However, these tensions, as we shall see, have not been resolved seven decades on given the sensitivities involved.

Article 48 deals with the issue that has always been important for the Hindu nationalist forces, that of 'cow slaughter'. It couches the need for preventing the slaughter of cows within the need for organising agriculture and animal husbandry and urges the State to 'endeavour' to achieve this goal. The third provision, Article 46, provides additional justification for special provisions for Scheduled Castes, Scheduled Tribes 'and other weaker sections' by exhorting the State to 'promote with special care' the 'educational and economic interests' of all three categories of persons.

There are several other provisions in the Directive Principles which address the category of class identified earlier and seek to protect the interests of working class people and those of workers in general. By way of illustration, Article 39 exhorts the State to provide equal pay for equal work; to take efforts to avoid concentration of wealth and means of production; and to initiate policies that seek to secure the health and strength of workers. Article 42 separately urges the State to attain just and humane conditions of work and maternity relief. Article 43 recommends a living wage and conditions of work that allow time for leisure and social and cultural opportunities for workers. These more specific facets of workers' interests are sought to be protected more generally by the language of Article 39(b) and (c). The former encourages the State to distribute 'the ownership and control of the material resources of the community' to 'subserve the common good'. Article 39(c) calls upon the State to ensure that 'the operation of the economic system does not result in the concentration of wealth and means of production to the common detriment'.

The provisions relating to language are located outside Parts III and IV. The most important ones are located in Part XVII, a standalone section which bears the title 'Official Language'. Consisting of four chapters and nine provisions, this Part deals with the language of business in the Union and State governments, as well as in the courts of law. There are still other provisions—such as Articles 120 and 210—which deal with the language of legislative proceedings, and the Eighth Schedule, which lists out the number of languages recognised by the Constitution (22 at the time of writing). Article 343 states that the official language of the Union of India shall be Hindi in the Devanagari script. Clause (3) of the same provision states that for the first 15 years from the commencement of the Constitution (in 1950), English will continue to be used for all the official purposes of the Union. In effect, English has continued to be the official language of business of the Union and several State governments. This is also because of Article 348, which stipulates that the language to be used in Parliament, the Supreme Court and the High Courts is English, until Parliament decides to make a change. Article 345 provides that State legislatures may provide for a regional language or Hindi to be used as the official language for the conduct of business in that State.

The final set of provisions that are relevant for this chapter are those from Part XVI of the Constitution, entitled 'Special provisions relating to certain classes'. The 13 provisions (Articles 330–342) primarily provide for legislative reservations/quotas for Scheduled Castes, Scheduled Tribes and Anglo-Indians within the Lok Sabha and the State legislative assemblies, based on the proportion of their populations within each State and the nation as a whole. Besides this, they also mandate that the Union and State governments make efforts to ensure adequate representation of members of these communities within their services. This is secured through Article 335, which places a positive obligation on the State to account for the claims of Scheduled Castes and Tribes in relation to government positions both at the Centre and at the State level, while bearing in mind 'the maintenance of efficiency of administration'. Other provisions in this Part mandate the creation of the National Commission for the Scheduled Castes and the National Commission for Scheduled Tribes, which are now permanent bodies charged with tracking issues relating to the socio-economic development of both communities and with protecting the rights and privileges guaranteed to them. Another provision provides for the creation of a Backward Classes Commission on a non-permanent basis for conducting studies relating to the socio-economic conditions of the backward classes.

Taken together, these various provisions provide a wide range of measures by which the rights and privileges of religious, linguistic and cultural minorities, women and peoples historically discriminated against on grounds of caste or tribe are sought to be protected and guaranteed. As we have noted above, some of these provisions also empower sections of the Hindu majority, while also enabling the State to focus on reforms within that religion specifically, and thus represent a complex model of multiculturalism. Scholars have noted the extraordinary commitment of the framing generation to openly and candidly confront the historical injustices perpetrated against marginalised sections of the Indian populace and to enable the Indian State to address these injustices through a positive programme of reform and change. Whether the institutions that were created by the Constitution have been able to deliver on these promises is a task that will be addressed in Section III of this chapter. But, first, we turn to the debates among the framers that informed their thinking in making these textual choices and commitments.

One of the striking aspects of these provisions is that they recognise both individual and group rights, and the Indian Constitution is regarded as one of the earliest constitutional orders to entrench group rights for specific communities. While the framers of the Indian Constitution did make some innovative choices here, it is important to recognise that they were responding to the colonial legal order's recognition of various group identities, which structured the content and form of the colonial legal system in significant ways. This is the focus of the next section of this chapter.

III. RELEVANT CONSTITUTION-MAKING HISTORY

In choosing to entrench the constitutional provisions examined in the previous section, the framers of the Indian Constitution were seeking to make radical departures from the colonial policies in relation to religion, caste and ethnic groups in India, some of which had been in place since the late nineteenth century. As with several other parts of the Constitution, what was eventually adopted was a fascinating mix of continuities and departures from the colonial legal order. The historical context is particularly important to understand the motivations and reasons for the bewildering array of options that are present in the actual constitutional provisions.[3]

A. The Emergence and Ascendance of Group-based Representation and Privileges in Colonial India (1860s–1947)

As we saw in Chapter 1, the colonial authorities began taking hesitant steps to involve Indians in their own governance in the aftermath of the revolt of 1857, and especially after the formal transfer of power from the East India Company to the British government in 1858. The 1872 census was an attempt by the colonial government to better understand the native population, and since at the time they primarily viewed Indians through the lens of religion, the census sought to classify Indians by religion. Religion remained an important marker of the Indian colonial subject's identity throughout the period of colonial rule. Later, the categories of caste, race and language were added to the potent mix of colonial identity. The overriding tendency of the colonial authorities was to view Indians primarily in terms of group affiliation rather than as individuals. What the colonial authorities learned in India (one of the early British colonies in Asia and Africa) about group identities marked by religion and race was repeated across the British Commonwealth with respect to other native populations, and these understandings were reflected in the legal categories that were created as a result and persist in many post-colonial orders across Asia and Africa.

The concessions to self-governance by the native populations took the form of group representation in the colonial legislatures. Attributable both to the colonial imperative of maintaining peace between different sections of the native population, and to the general British tendency to view natives through compartmental units, early British attempts at providing representation were in the form of groups

[3] There is a considerable body of scholarship which has focused on the complex dynamics of group rights in colonial and pre-independent India, leading up to the debates and final resolution in the Constituent Assembly. I rely on the recent scholarship of Rochana Bajpai whose monograph is an excellent resource on the subject. Rochana Bajpai, *Debating Difference: Group Rights and Liberal Democracy in India* (New Delhi, Oxford University Press, 2011).

that prioritised minority interests. An early form of this was in the nature of 'separate electorates', which were instituted at the national level by the Government of India Act 1909. These devices had been in place at the local government level in provinces such as the Punjab since the 1880s. Moving beyond the markers of religion and race, the colonial authorities gradually began to provide for legislative representation for groups along social and economic criteria. Through this process, landholders, universities and trade associations came to have representation in legislative bodies over time.

As this process evolved across the early twentieth century, colonial authorities bestowed group representational rights upon a greater variety of groups, along a broader range of institutional options. Beyond separate electorates, these included reserved seats in legislatures, weightage (guaranteed representation of minorities that was greater than their enumerated share in the population) nomination and combinations of these mechanisms. So, the Government of India Act 1919 not only catered for separate electorates for Muslims but included special measures for other minorities such as Sikhs, Indian Christians, Anglo-Indians and Europeans. The colonial government also recognised groups within the Hindu population, granting 'non-Brahmins' reserved seats in legislatures, and enabling members of the 'Depressed Classes' to become nominated members. This was reflected in the scheme of the Government of India Act 1935, which provided reserved seats in provincial legislatures for as many as 13 communal and socio-economic categories.[4] This trend of having reserved seats for religious and caste minorities was also in place in some of the Princely States such as Mysore.

A second measure to improve the representation and involvement of members of minority groups was effected at the executive level. A convention was developed by which minority representation at the Cabinet level was secured across the provinces, especially by the time the Government of India Act 1935 was in force.

A third strategy towards this overall objective of inclusivity was through group quotas in government employment. The originators for such policies were the Princely States. In 1874 Mysore instituted

[4] Granville Austin, *The Indian Constitution: Cornerstone of a Nation* (Oxford, Clarendon Press, 1966) 144.

reservations for backward classes in order to counter Brahmin dominance in the public services. Other Princely States such as Kolhapur, Travancore and Cochin followed suit and were later emulated by Madras and Kerala. In British India, the government of Punjab introduced a policy of balancing Hindu and Muslim members in government administration as early as in the 1880s. Over the next seven decades and by 1947, various policies were instituted, the consequence of which was that religious minorities (including in some cases caste and linguistic minorities) were 'proportionately represented, often over-represented, in national and provincial government employment'.[5]

Rochana Bajpai identifies three different phases of the evolution of group rights and privileges across the colonial period.[6] In the first stage, lasting until the 1920s, the colonial government's effort was to grant recognition of an entitlement to representation to communities such as Muslims that were viewed as an important and distinct element of Indian society. The Congress party at this early stage was not the mass party it became later and was not unduly concerned about the recognition extended to Muslims and the Depressed Classes. By the 1920s, things had changed. The Congress-led national movement, under the charismatic leadership of Gandhi, had expanded greatly in scope and its self-understanding. The colonial government now began to dispense group representation and recognition as a way to 'safeguard' minorities against Congress and Hindu numerical dominance. By doing so, the colonial authorities also sought to legitimise colonial rule by offering protection to various minority groupings. The Congress in turn became wary of minority safeguards, viewing them as a colonial device to perpetuate British rule by dividing Indians. The groups which benefited the most from group rights and understandably championed them were the Muslims and the Depressed Classes/Scheduled Castes. In the months preceding independence and the negotiations over a new Constitution, the Congress party was forced to be open to a range of options in relation to minority groups.

As Bajpai explains, there were two broad types of provisions that were to be negotiated. The first consisted of 'political' safeguards

[5] Steven Wilkinson, *Votes and Violence: Electoral Competition and Ethnic Riots in India* (Cambridge, Cambridge University Press, 2004) 106.

[6] Bajpai (n 3) 37–43.

which sought to ensure representation for minority groups in legislatures, executives and government employment positions. These were essentially a continuation of the colonial policies which ensured separate electorates, reserved and nominated seats in legislatures, quotas for minorities in cabinets and quotas in government posts and services. The second category consisted of 'cultural rights and privileges' that sought to secure religious, cultural and educational rights for minority groups. This second category was an innovation in that they had not been introduced by colonial policies given the British antipathy to rights discourse in general. These rights and privileges did, however, have precursors in the draft Constitutions prepared by the nationalist movement since 1895.

B. The Abolition of Political Safeguards for Religious Minorities and the Transformation of Minority Discourse in the Constituent Assembly (1947–50)

The convening of the Constituent Assembly in December 1946 marked the third and decisive phase. The Congress party was, at least initially, quite open to both categories of minority provisions, eager as it was to ensure that its actions did not give the Muslim League a reason to boycott the Constituent Assembly. However, things changed drastically within a few months. Jinnah's decision to boycott the Assembly and the fast-paced events that led to the violence of Partition completely altered the relative balance of power between the contestants for constitutional power. Following Partition, the main political parties which had advocated strong group rights for religious minorities—the Muslim League and the Sikh Panthic Party—disintegrated. In general, the supporters of political safeguards for religious minorities were considerably weakened overall. This did not apply to the other minority groups such as the backward classes, whose leader, Dr BR Ambedkar, continued to wield power within the Constituent Assembly and was able to secure political safeguards for the Scheduled Castes and Scheduled Tribes. What this meant was that the political safeguards that had applied during the colonial period to both religious minorities and backward classes were scaled back completely for the former. As adopted in the final Constitution, the category of political safeguards was to apply only to Scheduled Castes and Scheduled Tribes. Religious minorities no longer had any political safeguards in the form of separate electorates or reserved or nominated seats in the legislature. Nor were quotas in the executive or in government posts made available to them. Such political safeguards were extended, as noted in the previous section, only to Scheduled Castes, Scheduled Tribes and to Anglo-Indians. Religious minorities were instead extended the second category of group rights, which were designed to advance general rights to freedom of religion and cultural and educational rights in tandem. Even here, the finally adopted provisions were attenuated when compared to what was originally demanded.

The standard explanation for these limitations is the aftermath of Partition, and how conditions became unfavourable for demands such as political safeguards for religious minorities to be prosecuted. Bajpai's novel insight is that the liberal nationalist vision of the nationalist movement in general and the Congress party in particular is an independent explanatory factor that accounts for this change. Through a detailed and careful examination of the preparatory documents and the debates in the Assembly, Bajpai argues that nationalist discourse 'comprised a set of inter-related concepts' including 'secularism, democracy, social justice, national unity and development', all of which were invoked by the nationalists within the Assembly to resist special provisions for groups. In this liberal, nationalist vision, group preference as a general matter was deeply problematic to the vision of nationalism that was being advanced. However, this nationalist vision was more accommodating of the interests of Scheduled Castes and Tribes since they could be justified as rectifying social disadvantage. The Congress and the nationalists generally considered group-differentiated rights legitimate as a temporary measure only for lower castes and tribals, but not for religious minorities. This liberal, nationalist vision was more open to broad liberal guarantees of the right to freedom of religion, and to cultural and educational rights that would enable minority religions to flourish. This explains the commitment to the rights to freedom of religion guaranteed under Articles 25–28 and the rights to cultural and educational rights guaranteed under Articles 29–30. This is also why the political safeguards extended in Articles 330–342 apply only to Scheduled Castes, Tribes and Anglo-Indians.

C. Debates Within the Constituent Assembly on Gender and Language

This section provides a brief overview of the major debates relating to gender and language in the Constituent Assembly. To continue with the discussion of political safeguards, it is notable that the women in the Assembly were strongly averse to any form of legislative reservations or quotas on the basis of gender. Both Hansa Mehta and Renuka Ray—among the most prominent of the women members of the House—spoke clearly against the idea of reserved seats, quotas or separate electorates for women, and argued instead for a robust form of equality that would encompass social, economic and political justice.[7] The idealism of the framing generation of women appears to have been tempered by the reality of Indian political life: by the early 1990s, women's groups had come around to advocating for legislative quotas for women in Parliament and other representative institutions. In the mid-1990s, a constitutional amendment proposing that at least 33 per cent of seats should be reserved in Parliament and the legislative assemblies was moved, but failed to pass on four separate occasions. However, as noted in Chapter 3, through the passage of the 73rd and 74th constitutional amendments, quotas for women at the village and municipality levels were translated into reality. The question of legislative quotas for women continues to be a live issue in contemporary Indian politics.

An issue that has come to dominate debates relating to women in post-colonial India is that of personal laws. This phenomenon stemmed from the fact that the British had, from the early days of colonial rule in India, established a dual-track system of legal administration. Subjects that were considered secular were dealt with by British legal norms in one track, while those relating to family were adjudicated according to British understandings of Hindu or Muslim law. The British thought that the latter category involved issues of a 'religious' nature and sought to govern Indians according to their own religious laws, particularly in matters involving family law. The colonial authorities believed that Indians were divided into two main categories: Hindu and Muslim.

[7] For Mehta's views, see Constituent Assembly Debates, Vol. 1, 138. For Ray's views, see Constituent Assembly Debates, Vol 4, 668.

These laws were termed 'personal laws' to indicate that they would apply regardless of domicile and were laws inherent to their personal status. Personal laws were delimited to matters involving religion, caste and family. What is significant is that while the system was conceptualised as applying to Indians their own religious laws in matters involving inheritance, marriage and similar issues, the colonial State took on the role of defining and adjudicating that religious law.[8] This enabled the colonial State to maintain a stance of neutrality in general while intervening in specific cases where it felt the need to do so. As we will see, the post-colonial State in India continued this simultaneous adoption of non-intervention and intervention in the sphere of 'religious' law.

The colonial State viewed India as an agglomeration of communities, with religion and caste forming the primary building blocks of Indian society. This rendered religious community rather than the individual as the unit of legal and political recognition, and also constituted Hindus and Muslims as separate legal subjects governed by different sets of laws. The consequence of this was that a variety of legal disabilities were visited upon women specifically, according to the religious community to which they belonged.[9] As we have seen in the previous section, the framers of India's Constitution were keen to dislodge the centring of identities of Indians in groups and communities, and sought to replace it in great measure by making the individual the focus of a rights regime. However, the fundamental liberties created by the Constitution also bestow rights upon groups and communities in specific contexts. The effects of the personal law system on women's rights was also deliberated upon, though this did not garner as much attention as would seem necessary in retrospect.

When the Fundamental Rights Sub-Committee first discussed the freedom of religion provision in March 1947, its two women members—Hansa Mehta and Rajkumari Amrit Kaur—were concerned that the right to freedom of religion should be articulated in such a way as not to render impossible the enactment of future legislation for eradicating several customs practised in the name of religion that were detrimental to the interests of women such as child marriage, polygamy

[8] Rachel Sturman, *The Government of Social Life in Colonial India* (Cambridge, Cambridge University Press, 2012) 8.

[9] ibid.

and unequal laws of inheritance.[10] This concern was accepted eventually, resulting in Article 25(2), which clearly stipulates that the freedom of religion guaranteed in Article 25(1) does not prevent the State from intervening in religious matters to uphold social welfare and engage in social reform. As we will see, this enabled the Indian State to bring about crucial reforms relating to Hindu women and to a lesser extent, for women in minority religious communities. The muted effect in respect of the latter was a consequence of another debate in relation to what became Article 44 in the Part on Directive Principles, which, as noted earlier, declares that 'the State shall endeavour to secure for the citizens a Uniform Civil Code throughout the territory of India'.

Article 44 was numbered as draft Article 35 in the Draft Constitution and was discussed in the Constituent Assembly on 23 November 1948. Several Muslim members of the Assembly sought an amendment that expressly excluded personal laws from the ambit of a Uniform Civil Code.[11] They expressed the concern that Muslims in particular would have their identity effaced if their personal laws were tampered with in the name of legal homogeneity. The seriousness of the charge is reflected in the fact that three important members—KM Munshi, AK Ayyar and Ambedkar—spoke to allay concerns of the Muslim members. Scholars have noted that Nehru and others in the Congress party became convinced that Muslims and other minorities needed special guarantees in the aftermath of Partition, and they therefore allowed religious minorities the right to preserve and practise their personal laws in the post-independence period.[12] This had an unfortunate and direct effect on women in all communities but more so in religions other than Hinduism since Nehru's government felt that a way to show their good secular credentials was by beginning reforms with the Hindu community by codifying their personal laws first. Thus, as we shall see in a subsequent section, Hindu women had a somewhat better situation as a consequence.

[10] B Shiva Rao, *The Framing of India's Constitution: Select Documents* (New Delhi, Universal Law Publishing Co, 1968, reprinted 2010) vol 5, 'Fundamental Rights', 170–318, at 260.

[11] CAD VII 540–52. As many as seven Muslim members supported such an amendment.

[12] Susanne Rudolph and Lloyd Rudolph, 'Living with Difference: Legal Pluralism and Legal Universalism in Historical Context' in Gerald J Larson (ed), *Religion and Personal Law in Secular India* (Delhi, Social Science Press, 2001) 48–49.

Austin notes that the provisions relating to language in the Constitution were among the most bitterly contested ones in the entire text, taking as long as three years to be resolved.[13] In the years before the making of the Constitution, there was a steady demand for reshaping the territorial boundaries of provinces based on language, with the Congress party itself being a votary of the concept since at least 1917.[14] However, closer to the time of formal independence, again due to the communal violence experienced during Partition, the Congress leadership became wary of igniting further disharmony on the basis of language. Leaders such as Nehru, Patel, Rajagopalachari and even Gandhi issued statements expressing concerns about the issue. Within the Assembly, the demand for linguistic division of provinces was emphatically rejected on the logic that it would cause the new nation to revert to the 'centuries-old India of narrow loyalties, petty jealousies, and ignorant prejudices engaged in mortal conflict'.[15]

However, the issue of what should be the national language of India posed greater difficulty. As Austin notes, at the start of the process the overwhelming majority within the Congress and the Constituent Assembly—including important leaders such as Nehru and Gandhi—felt that Hindi should be adopted as the national language of the Indian nation. This view, broadly speaking, arose from a sense that the world's largest and most diverse democracy would need to build a common national citizenship to sustain its unity, especially in the aftermath of the horrors of Partition. It was felt that to build a mass, democratic, national politics that was free from the divisions bred by linguistic and cultural multiplicity, it was important to have a common, indigenous language that would foster communication between Indians, which would also lead to better economic development.[16] However, across three years of Constitution making, the resistant views of non-Hindi

[13] Austin (n 4) 313.

[14] Guha (n 1) chapter 9, 180–200.

[15] The quotation is from the Report of the Linguistic Provinces Commission (the Dar Commission) appointed by the Constituent Assembly to study the issue of linguistic provinces. See Report of the Linguistic Provinces Commission (Government of India Press 1948) 13.

[16] Sujit Choudhry, 'Language' in Sujit Choudhry, Madhav Khosla and Pratap Mehta (eds), *The Oxford Handbook of the Indian Constitution* (Oxford, Oxford University Press, 2016) 181.

provinces became more and more entrenched. Non-Hindi speakers did not necessarily disagree with the goal of unity and integration, but feared that the privileging of Hindi would distribute economic and political power towards Hindi speakers and away from them. Ultimately, a consensus decision was reached to defer the decision on the national language.[17] Hindi was declared the 'official language' of the Union while English was to continue as the language for official purposes for 15 years. This consensus is reflected in the provisions relating to language that were summarised in the previous section.

IV. POST-INDEPENDENCE EVOLUTION OF THE LAW ON THE MARKERS OF INDIAN IDENTITY

This section will attempt the difficult task of summarising the actions of Indian institutional actors—principally, the Parliament, the executive and the judiciary but including other actors such as people's movements and political mobilisations—in shaping the post-independence developments relating to the identity markers we are focusing upon across nearly seven decades. This will necessarily have to be a brief, truncated overview but the references cited provide greater detail and nuance for those who seek a thicker description. The focus will be on the major trends and shifts in such an evolution. Due to limitations of space, only three of the markers—language, caste and religion—will be focused upon here. Regrettably, gender and class are only tangentially addressed—in the sections on religion and caste respectively.

A. Language

As noted earlier, the issue of language was one of the most contentious within the Constituent Assembly. It was therefore natural to expect that this would be one of the most divisive issues in post-independence India. In many other post-colonial societies—Pakistan and Sri Lanka, to name two in the region—the politics of language caused the break-up

[17] Hannah Lerner, 'The Indian Founding: A Comparative Perspective' in Sujit Choudhry, Madhav Khosla and Pratap Mehta (eds), *The Oxford Handbook of the Indian Constitution* (Oxford, Oxford University Press, 2016) 63–64.

of nations or led to civil wars that ruptured the national fibre irreparably. In India, this was averted through a combination of statesmanship, good fortune and the common anxiety among decision makers that the sheer size and diversity of India's vast population would require greater accommodation in decision making. The tensions involved were nevertheless very serious throughout and the issue of language continues to be a source of tensions in moulding the national identity and project. The nature of tensions and the content of the debates has, however, changed over time.

As we saw in the section on constitutional history, the issue of language in Indian politics has centred on the issues of linguistic provinces and the indigenous language that should be adopted as the national language to replace English, which had served as the language of official business of government in India since the colonial era. Although the Constituent Assembly had resolved not to divide provinces on the basis of language, the mass movement which advocated for this issue did not subside, and continued to press its case in the immediate years after independence. Although Prime Minister Nehru and his most influential Congress Cabinet Ministers continued to be against the policy, things came to a head when the movement for a new State for the Andhra people in the South (whose language, Telegu, was the second most widely spoken language after Hindi) picked up momentum. This occurred in October 1952, when Potti Sriramulu—who had been a follower of Gandhi among other things—began a fast unto death in the city of Madras. This was not taken seriously by the Nehru Government but when Sriramulu died in December 1952 it caused great public unrest as well as violence. To quell the further potential of violence, two days after the death of Sriramulu, Prime Minister Nehru announced that a new State of Andhra Pradesh would come into being, which eventually occurred on 1 October 1953, within a year of the announcement. As Nehru had feared, this gave fresh impetus to long-standing demands by other groups, such as the powerful movement for a new State of Maharashtra to replace the bilingual State of Bombay. Nehru's government then appointed an independent commission to decide the issue across the country. The States Reorganisation Committee was established in 1953; it took two years to travel across the country and submitted its report in 1955. Based largely on its recommendation that language be accepted as the principal basis for reorganisation of States, Parliament enacted the States Reorganisation Act 1956, replacing the existing three-fold categorisation of States into Part A, B and C States with a two-category classification into States and Union Territories. A number of new States were created in the process; within the next decade, the new States of Gujarat and Maharashtra (in 1960) and Punjab and Haryana (in 1966) were also created. This process has been described by one scholar as the 'largest and most peaceful reconfiguration of political space under the rule of law, without recourse to mass violence in the history of liberal democracy'.[18] There were, as we saw in Chapter 3, further changes in the nature and form of States in India, with the most recent occurring when the 29th Indian State of Telangana was created in 2014. The general view of scholars is that despite the fears of the Nehru Government, linguistic reorganisation may well have contributed to the goal of national unity and constructively channelled linguistic sentiment, which had threatened to spiral out of control.[19]

Tensions around the issue of Hindi's status as national language re-emerged in the early 1960s, as the 15-year time limit set by the framers of India's Constitution for resolving the question of India's national language neared. In 1955 the government set up a commission to develop a plan for the transition from English to Hindi. Delivering its report in 1956, a majority of the Kher Commission reiterated the democratic case for conferring official language status solely on Hindi. They also recommended that the examinations for the prestigious and influential Indian Administrative Service be held solely in Hindi. The Commission also had dissenting voices, which strongly argued against this move, focusing on the neo-colonial effect on non-Hindi-speaking States, because of the important role performed by officers of the Indian Administrative Service in State bureaucracies. Parliament sought to head off the looming crisis by debating the Official Languages Act Bill two years ahead of the deadline in 1965. Enacted in 1963, this law sought to extend the compromise between Hindi and non-Hindi speakers by providing that while Hindi would become the sole official language in 1965, English would continue to be an 'associate additional official language'. Prime Minister Nehru gave assurances on the floor of Parliament that there would be no attempt to impose Hindi on

[18] Choudhry (n 16) 180.
[19] Guha (n 1) 200.

non-Hindi-speaking States. However, some ambiguity about whether English could be retained pursuant to a parliamentary review committee's findings remained. In 1964 the Ministry of Home Affairs issued a directive that sought to find out how States planned to implement Hindi as the sole official language after the deadline of 26 January 1965. This, among other things, caused an outbreak of violence in Tamil Nadu; riots broke out, leading to 66 deaths. This in turn resulted in a meeting of various political leaders, which was reflected in an amendment made in 1967 to the Official Languages Act 1963. This amendment clearly stipulated that the resolution of the language issue was to opt for a bilingual approach: both Hindi and English would be used in Parliament; Hindu would be used for communication between the centre and Hindi-speaking States, while English would be used between the centre and non-Hindi-speaking States. More importantly, the examinations for entry into the Indian Administrative Services and other important Union Services would be conducted in multiple languages. As a result, in practice, English has remained the dominant language of communication in the elite wings of government and the private sector as a whole.[20] This may seem ironic given the anti-colonial sentiment that was prevalent at the time of independence, but it is the nature of linguistic diversity in India and the absence of a single alternative language which are explanatory factors.

One consequence of the linguistic reorganisation of States has been that issues affecting linguistic minorities within States have become more prominent. While the judiciary had had little to do with linguistic reorganisation or the choice of official language for the nation as a whole, it is in this narrower issue involving language that the role of the courts has been more prominent. This has become necessary to resolve the new tensions that have emerged in the wake of linguistic reorganisation, as a consequence of a clash between efforts by State governments to build respect for the official language of the State by requiring the regional language to be the language of instruction in schools, and the demands of linguistic minorities to be allowed to choose the language of instruction for their children. These conflicts have resulted in several court cases where the main battleground has been the text

[20] Paul Brass, *The Politics of India Since Independence* (Cambridge, Cambridge University Press, 1994) 158–69.

of Article 30 of the Constitution, which grants linguistic minorities the right to establish and administer educational institutions of their choice.[21] As Choudhry's analysis shows, courts have adopted somewhat contrasting approaches, but in general have sought to uphold the Article 30 right of linguistic minorities to make autonomous choices about the education of their communities and their children. In other issues relating to identity, however, the courts have—as we shall see—played a much more prominent role.

B. Caste (and Class)

This section provides a brief overview of the development of the system of reservations in India across seven decades. It does so by identifying issues on which the judiciary clashed with the executive and the legislature and by noting significant policy initiatives adopted by the latter two wings on reservations.

The original text of the Constitution provided for multiple forms of benefits for Scheduled Castes, Scheduled Tribes and for 'backward classes' and/or 'weaker sections' of citizens. As noted earlier, the last two phrases are ambiguous and in some places were understood as including Scheduled Castes and Scheduled Tribes, but in other places were used to denote groups such as the OBCs. As we shall see, the practice of affirmative action has witnessed a great deal of continuing support for policies aimed at ameliorating the socio-economic conditions of Scheduled Castes and Tribes. The OBCs have increasingly become claimants of policies of affirmative action in India; this development has been far more contentious. A leading scholar of the working of caste in Indian law and society has used the phrase 'compensatory discrimination' to categorise these various measures, whose purpose is defined as seeking 'to redistribute resources and opportunities to those who enjoy the fewest advantages'.[22] Using the term 'discrimination' highlights the fact that such policies do not involve 'benign policies of inclusion' and some people are indeed left out; however, the purpose

[21] A number of these cases are examined in Choudhry (n 16) 189–94.

[22] Marc Galanter, *Competing Equalities: Law and the Backward Classes in India* (New Delhi, Oxford University Press, 1984).

is 'not exclusion and relegation but inclusion and recompense both for historic deprivations and to offset present handicaps'.[23]

Scheduled Castes and Tribes and Anglo-Indians were, as noted earlier, guaranteed legislative representation through quotas for the first 10 years after the coming into force of the Constitution. As we shall see in the next chapter, this period has been extended for 10 years every decade; six constitutional amendments have ensured that the time limit for legislative quotas was extended in every decade, with the last amendment passed in 2009. As we shall see, reservations for OBCs were resisted by some political parties, including the Congress party in its hegemonic phase up to 1989; however, the extension of legislative reservations for Scheduled Castes and Tribes has had unanimous support across the political spectrum. Whether these have enabled legislators to advance the interests of Scheduled Castes and Tribes through legislative policies is a more debatable question.[24]

The original Constitution also provided, as noted earlier, for reservation in public employment for Scheduled Castes and Tribes. While these too have support across the political spectrum, in practice their effectiveness has been limited by the fact that 'the quotas were never filled, due to a lack of qualified candidates or a lack of willingness on the part of those in charge of filling them'.[25] However, other scholars have noted that more recent statistics reveal some improvement: the proportion of Scheduled Castes in the highest levels of government employment (Classes I and II) had increased from 4.5 per cent in 1965 to 22.7 per cent in 1995.[26] This shows some impact even if more could have been expected given the time span involved. At the same time, this also goes to show how entrenched societal patterns of discrimination against the Scheduled Castes have been. The statistics are worse for the Scheduled Tribes, who have even lower rates of education and employment. Of the 105 million people who fall within Scheduled Tribes, as many as 49.5 per cent live below the official poverty line. Seven decades of reservations have had little positive effect on this group

[23] ibid 2.

[24] Christophe Jaffrelot, 'The Impact of Affirmative Action in India: More Political than Socioeconomic' (2006) 5(2) *India Review* 173–89, 176–77.

[25] ibid.

[26] Guha (n 1) 613–14. See also Josy Joseph, *A Feast of Vultures: The Hidden Business of Democracy in India* (New Delhi, Harper Collins India, 2016).

of Indian citizens. Their traditional lives have instead been devastated by the effects of conscious State policies of displacement in the name of economic development that have led to large-scale mining and the destruction of the natural habitat of the tribal people, and their eviction from national parks and sanctuaries in the name of environmental protection.[27] It is clear that far more urgently than policies of reservations, what the Scheduled Tribes need is a reversal of deleterious State policies that are destroying their habitat and environment. They remain, in the words of one scholar, the 'most vulnerable and victimized of Indians'.[28]

The social group that has benefited most, relatively speaking, from the constitutional system of reservations are the OBCs. However, even here the impact has been more political than socio-economic. Many sections of the OBC population continue to be among the worst off in terms of human development indicators. Any progress that they have achieved overall is only relative to that of the Scheduled Castes and Tribes.

The trajectory of how reservations have developed and came to be extended in India is complex and convoluted because different wings of government have, at different times, been either for or against the very idea of reservations or have opposed their extension to new groups such as the OBCs. In what follows, I seek to provide a broad overview, relying on authoritative accounts that can be referenced for further details.

The narrative of the clashes between different institutions of the State over the evolution of policies of reservations began early. The original Constitution, as noted, did not provide for reservations in education (the subject of Article 15). The Supreme Court and the judiciary as a whole were initially quite hostile to the idea of reservations, especially in the education sector. In 1951, issuing judgment in the case of *Champakam Dorairajan v State of Madras*,[29] the Supreme Court struck down a set of regulations in Madras which enabled a selection committee to make allocations in medical and engineering colleges according to a formula which explicitly factored in caste.

[27] Ramachandra Guha, 'Tribal Tragedies in Independent India' in Ramachandra Guha, *Democrats and Dissenters* (Gurgaon, Allen Lane/Penguin, 2016) 104–28.

[28] ibid 128.

[29] *Champakam Dorairajan v State of Madras*, AIR 1951 SC 226.

Ms Dorairajan, a Brahmin woman who had not actually applied to a medical school—a fact that was curiously downplayed by the courts—challenged the regulations as being in violation of her right under Article 29 not to be discriminated against 'only' on grounds of 'religion, race, caste, language'. Both the Madras High Court and the Supreme Court upheld the argument of violation of Article 29(2), rejecting the argument of the government that the policies were pursuant to Article 46. Justice Das pointedly noted that while Article 16(4) specifically provided for reservations in the context of public employment, Article 15 did not contain any such provision.

The response of the Nehru Government was swift. As part of the wide-ranging First Amendment to the Constitution (which, as we saw earlier, inserted the Ninth Schedule and made significant changes to the right to property and free speech regulation) a new clause (4) was added to Article 15 which empowered the government to 'make special provision' for the Scheduled Castes and Tribes *and* 'any socially and educationally backward classes of citizens'. This was clearly a direct response to Justice Das' reasoning in the *Champakam Dorairajan* case. It was also an attempt to draw a link to Article 340, which used the phrase 'socially and educationally backward classes' and envisaged the appointment of a commission to identify its constituents.[30] During the debate over the new provision, Prime Minister Nehru set out his government's approach to the issue by stating thus: 'So we arrive at a peculiar tangle. We cannot have equality because in trying to attain equality we come up against some principles of equality'. Nehru recognised that trying to bring about social reform in India's complex social structure required a 'balance between the existing fact as we find it, and the objective and ideal that we aim at'.[31] By doing so, Nehru acknowledged that the interests of those who enjoyed a dominant position in the status quo would also have to be considered. This statement reveals the relatively moderate stance of the Nehru Government on issues of reservations, which became evident in its reluctance to accommodate the OBCs as a group, to which we shall turn shortly.

The judiciary deferred to Parliament's decision to overrule the basis of its decision in *Champakam Dorairajan* but continued to try and limit

[30] Galanter (n 22) 164.

[31] Quoted in Samaraditya Pal, *India's Constitution: Origins and Evolution* (Haryana, Lexis Nexis, 2014) vol 1, 692.

the concept and extent of reservations in both educational and employment contexts. In *Balaji v State of Mysore* (1963)[32] the Supreme Court declared that caste could not be the sole basis for determining the backward status of a community and also held that the maximum permissible proportion of quotas was 50 per cent. Its doctrinal holding that Article 15(4) 'has to be read as a proviso or as an exception to Articles 15(1) and 29(2)' was reiterated in a series of cases over the next decade and resulted in a number of obstacles for State governments which sought to expand reservations.[33] This trend was halted by the decision of a seven-judge bench of the Supreme Court in *NM Thomas v State of Kerala* (1976) (the bench split 5-2).[34] The judges in the majority emphatically held that Article 16(4) was not an exception but an integral part of the scheme of Article 16, which sought to pursue 'real, not formal, equality'. The *Thomas* decision signalled to the rest of the judiciary the willingness of judges at the apex level to support reservations and give up the abstemious approach it had adopted earlier. This was the trend for nearly two decades before the judiciary had to pronounce on the constitutionality of the Mandal Commission report. Before we turn to that, some background on OBC reservations is necessary.

As mentioned earlier, Article 340 envisages the creation of a commission to report on the state of 'socially and educationally backward classes'. Given the difficulties involved in getting a sense of who constituted these classes and what their conditions were, it was expected that this commission would be established early on in the life of the republic. The Nehru Government did as much in 1953. The Commission, known as the Kalelkar Commission after its chairperson, submitted its report in 1955, recommending that 2,399 castes be classified as socially and educationally backward. It suggested reservations for backward classes in government services, ranging from 25 to 40 per cent. The Nehru Government found fault with the tests applied to determine backwardness and delayed its discussion in Parliament. When the report was finally discussed in Parliament after Nehru's death, in

[32] *Balaji v State of Mysore*, AIR 1963 SC 649.

[33] For a listing of these decisions, see Marc Galanter, 'Symbolic Activism: A Judicial Encounter with the Contours of India's Compensatory Discrimination Policy' in Marc Galanter, *Law and Society in Modern India* (Delhi, Oxford University Press, 1989) 258–65.

[34] *NM Thomas v State of Kerala*, AIR 1976 SC 490.

1965, the government decided not to accept its recommendations. From the 1960s onwards, however, various State governments initiated reservations for OBCs, following varying criteria and considerations. As a result, there is great variety among the States in measures taken to advance the socio-economic interests of people identified as falling within the OBC category.

At the national level, the issue was revived during the Janata Government's tenure, in 1978, when the Second Backward Classes Commission was appointed. The Mandal Commission report was submitted in 1980 and it stipulated the use of caste as the primary criterion for its finding that 3,248 castes, amounting to 52 per cent of the population, were in need of reservations. By that time, Indira Gandhi's Congress Government was in power and, in keeping with its long-standing policy, the Congress Government did not implement the report's recommendations. In 1990 Prime Minister VP Singh's coalition National Front Government, led by the Janata party, decided to implement the Mandal Commission's report and announced that up to 27 per cent of government posts would be reserved for the OBCs. Taken together with the 22 per cent reservations for Scheduled Castes and Tribes, this pushed the total number of reserved seats close to the 50 per cent limit set by the Supreme Court.

The decision to implement the Mandal Commission recommendations sparked protests and violence across North India, where OBC reservations were, unlike in the southern States, a relatively new phenomenon.[35] The government's decision was challenged before the courts and in *Indra Sawhney v Union of India* (1992)[36] a nine-judge bench of the Supreme Court largely upheld the government's decision to provide reservations for OBCs pursuant to the Mandal report. In doing so, the Supreme Court also signalled a further dilution of its long-standing resistance to extension of policies of reservations.

A little over a decade later, the Supreme Court tried, once again, to limit the extent of reservations by holding in *PA Inamdar v State of Maharashtra* (2005)[37] that reservations could not be extended to private educational institutions, especially those that did not receive

[35] Brass (n 20) 250–53.

[36] *Indra Sawhney v Union of India* (1992) Supp (3) SCC 217.

[37] *PA Inamdar v State of Maharashtra* (2005) 6 SCC 537.

aid from the State, as this would violate their Article 19(1)(g) right to occupation. The response of Parliament was to enact the 93rd Constitutional Amendment, which inserted clause (5) into the text of Article 15. This provision makes clear that private educational institutions, whether receiving aid or not, are subject to reservations. The only exception that is recognised in this context is for minority educational institutions (in view of Article 30). Three years later, in *Ashok Kumar Thakur v Union of India* (2008),[38] the Court followed this trend by upholding the extension of education quotas by the Central government to Central universities. In recent years, the judiciary has continued to try and set limits to what it perceives as politically opportunistic attempts at extending reservations. However, given the overwhelming support for reservations across the political spectrum, the judiciary has limited its intervention to narrow issues such as that of reservation in super-speciality posts; the 'carry-forward' rule; and reservations in promotions.[39]

The most profound effect of the Mandal Commission report has been not so much in the arena of public employment (the focus of its recommendations) but on the mobilisation of the vast OBC population in the political sphere that it engendered. The anti-Mandal protests by upper caste students led in turn to counter-protests by OBC groups. Political parties such as the Samajwadi party and the Bahujan Samaj party were instituted to represent the political aspirations of the OBCs and the Scheduled Castes. Starting from the 1991 elections, these parties and the pre-existing Janata Dal began to obtain the OBC vote to significant effect, at first in State elections but later in national elections as well.

This brief overview also shows that while the judiciary has sought to rein in the executive and the legislature's policy choices in the area of reservations to offset caste discrimination, the main actors in this arena have—as asserted by a recent scholarly account—been the executive, Parliament and political parties.[40] Unlike in the area of language, courts

[38] *Ashok Kumar Thakur v Union of India* (2008) 6 SCC 1.

[39] For details of these cases and the logic employed by the courts, see Vinay Sitapati, 'Reservations' in Sujit Choudhry, Madhav Khosla and Pratap Mehta (eds), *The Oxford Handbook of the Indian Constitution* (Oxford, Oxford University Press, 2016) 728, 734 and 735–37.

[40] ibid 740–41.

have had a say in determining post-independence-era policies on the issue of caste, but this too has been limited, especially in recent years, where the action has been dominated by the dynamics of electoral politics.

C. Religion (and Gender)

In providing an overview of developments in the sphere of religion and the law, this section also tracks the way the executive and the legislature have evolved policy decisions, on some occasions in response to the actions of the judiciary. In comparison to its role in moulding developments relating to language and caste, the judiciary has had a more dominant role in influencing the orientation of the law around religion. All such attempts were, as is perhaps to be expected in a polity that is as deeply religious as India, deeply contested. This section focuses, selectively, on issues relating to reform of religious practices and personal laws, the rights to religious freedom and practice, and minority educational and cultural rights. It ends with a brief discussion on Indian secularism.

In the initial stages, in keeping with the Nehru Government's zeal to pursue specific constitutional goals, it was the executive and the Parliament which took the lead in pursuing change on important issues relating to religion. This is exemplified by the various attempts to enact what came to be known as the Hindu Code.[41] Prime Minister Nehru insisted that the Hindu community, being the majority, would have to subject its religious law to reform first, also to demonstrate that it was serious about progressive reforms and would not use reform as a pretext to persecute minority religions.

Preliminary efforts to draft a new Hindu Code began in 1941 and gathered steam within the Constituent Assembly in 1948. Initially entrusted to the Rau Committee, the draft was revised by Ambedkar and sought to pursue change in aspects of Hindu succession, marriage and adoption law, most of which would result in better rights for women. The Hindu Code was to apply also to Sikhs, Buddhists and

[41] For an authoritative account, see Archana Parashar, *Women and Family Law Reform in India* (New Delhi, Sage, 1992) 79–134.

Jains and sought to codify rules of Hindu law drawing from customary laws as well as judicial precedents of the High Courts and the Privy Council.

The draft of the Hindu Code Bill was met with stiff opposition from the many representatives of Hindu orthodox groups within the Assembly, including powerful members of the Congress party itself such as the President of the Constituent Assembly (and later the first President of the new republic) Rajendra Prasad. Opposition to the Bill grew outside the Assembly through several people's movements across the country, which objected to the granting of divorce and property rights to Hindu women.[42] After the formation of the first government, Nehru sought to move the Bill in Parliament during 1950–51, where it was championed by Ambedkar in his capacity as India's first Law Minister. However, the Bill could not be passed in Parliament. In October 1951 Ambedkar resigned as India's first Law Minister citing this as one of the grounds for his decision. Nehru changed strategy and after securing greater power to himself within the Congress party by strengthening his core base, moved the Hindu Code Bill again in 1955–56. While the original law was a single comprehensive one, the new Bills were split into the following to forestall opposition to them: the Hindu Marriage Act 1955, the Hindu Succession Act 1956, the Hindu Minority and Guardianship Act 1956 and the Hindu Adoption and Maintenance Act 1956. This 'piecemeal' approach did 'expand the inheritance rights of daughters in the family property and established the right of divorce' but, crucially, 'retained the Hindu male coparcener and its inequities and exclusions intact'.[43] Scholars have argued that much was lost from the more radical Hindu Code Bill of 1951. The new law, more problematically, codified Hindu rituals as valid law and made the situation of women worse in some cases.[44] Some of the original changes were enacted into legislation as late as 2005, nearly five decades later. Nevertheless, the reforms sought to bring nearly

[42] For a vivid description of these events and an overview of the entire process of enactment of the Hindu Code laws, see Guha (n 1) 226–41.

[43] Sturman (n 8) 233–34.

[44] For a sharp critique of the achievements of the Hindu Code law, see Flavia Agnes, 'Personal Laws' in Sujit Choudhry, Madhav Khosla and Pratap Mehta (eds), *The Oxford Handbook of the Indian Constitution* (Oxford, Oxford University Press, 2016) 907–08. See also Werner Menski, *Hindu Law Beyond Tradition and Modernity* (Oxford, Oxford University Press, 2003) 24–25.

60 million Hindu women within their purview and represented a hard-fought victory for the government across nearly 15 years. They remain some of the most wide-ranging legislative interventions in the sphere of religion to date. When asked why similar reforms were not being considered for minority religions, Prime Minister Nehru cited time (and presumably the proximity to Partition, which had made Indian Muslims insecure about their status) as a reason and felt that enacting the Hindu Code was a move in that direction.[45] Legislative reforms for women of other communities were much slower to be effected. Christian law reforms were spearheaded by Christian women; their efforts across two decades bore fruit when the Indian Divorce Act 1869 was amended in 2001 and egalitarian grounds of divorce were introduced for Christian women. A similar campaign by Parsi community leaders and legal scholars brought reforms to the Parsi Marriage and Divorce Act 1936 in 1988. Muslim law has never been reformed since independence. However, in the aftermath of the infamous *Shah Bano case* (1985),[46] the Rajiv Gandhi Government passed the Muslim Women (Protection of Rights on Divorce) Act 1986 to override the judgment. This law was perceived by women's groups as retrograde in respect of advancing the rights of Muslim women. Several years later, the Supreme Court tried to minimise the damage through a creative judgment in *Daniel Latifi v Union of India* (2001).[47]

The constitutionality of personal laws has always been a point of contestation given the obvious tensions between the constitutional guarantees of equality and non-discrimination and the existence of gender-discriminatory personal laws. Individuals affected by these tensions have continuously approached the courts, giving rise to a steady stream of judicial decisions which have not always been consistent in the approach taken. Flavia Agnes has argued that these decisions reveal a further tension between the supremacy of the text of the Constitution in a legal culture of pluralism where the sources of law and legal authority are multiple. Covering the development of case law across seven decades, she describes the existence of two broad

[45] Guha (n 1) 241.

[46] *Mohd. Ahmed Khan v Shah Bano Begum*, AIR 1985 SC 945. For the background and analysis of this significant case and event, see generally, Parashar (n 41) chapter 4; Bajpai (n 3) 177–224.

[47] *Daniel Latifi v Union of India* (2001) 7 SCC 740.

trends. In the initial years, when courts were, as we have seen, eager not to encroach upon territory that they felt belonged to the other two wings of government, a 'non-interventionist' approach was adopted. This is exemplified by the decision of the Bombay High Court in *State of Bombay v Narasu Appa Mali* (1952)[48] where a citizen who challenged a progressive law that sought to prohibit bigamy among Hindus argued that this was discriminatory as Muslims were allowed to have multiple marriages by virtue of their personal law. While upholding the law relating to Hindus, the High Court held that personal laws were not 'laws in force' under Article 13 and were immune from constitutional scrutiny. Although the legal reasoning behind this decision is open to multiple objections, it was viewed as both properly deferential and pragmatic and has been endorsed in several Supreme Court decisions rendering it valid law. Agnes notes that as the judiciary gained in confidence, and it became clear that there would be no political consensus or initiative to reform personal law, courts began to move away from the earlier stance and began intervening in specific ways. This has included two broad strategies: seeking to reconcile tensions between fundamental rights and personal laws by 'reading down' a statutory provision;[49] or striking down offending provisions as being in violation of fundamental rights.[50]

In several decisions rendered more recently, the Supreme Court has exhorted the executive and the legislature to initiate the project of a Uniform Civil Code. For a variety of political factors, this remained dormant, but has been activated more recently. After the advent of Prime Minister Modi's BJP-led government in 2014, there has been a change of guard at the Law Commission of India—the official body charged with recommending law reform—and the current incumbent

[48] *State of Bombay v Narasu Appa Mali*, AIR 1952 Bom 84.

[49] This was the strategy used in *Githa Hariharan v Reserve Bank of India* (1999) 2 SCC 228, where the Hindu Minority and Guardianship Act 1955, which provided that only the father could be the natural guardian of a child, was creatively interpreted to include the mother as well.

[50] This trend, begun in the 1980s, has gathered steam in more recent years as courts have shown a greater urgency in upholding the fundamental rights at stake. See, eg, the decision of the Kerala High Court in *Ammini EJ v Union of India*, AIR 1995 Ker 252, which struck down section 10 of the Indian Divorce Act 1869, that placed a higher burden on women than men while seeking divorce. This decision, among others, led to the eventual amendment of the law in 2001.

chairperson has declared an intention to examine the issue, making it a live issue again. In mid-2017, a Constitution Bench of the Supreme Court heard an important case relating to the constitutionality of the practice of 'triple talaq' which will have significant implications for the continuance of personal laws.

I now turn the focus of this section to the rights guaranteed under Articles 25–28 and how they have been interpreted by the judiciary. Scholars have noted that the Indian constitutional design has dictated the practice that has followed in the post-independence era. Gurpreet Mahajan has noted that through these provisions, the framers of the Indian Constitution dealt with the issue of religion 'by endorsing the principle of non-establishment of religion but without advocating the separation of religion from politics'.[51] The implication of this choice is that 'the State was to have no religion of its own, but [at the same time] religion was not … viewed as a personal or private matter: it was placed squarely in the public domain and the State was expected to be involved in a variety of ways with religion'.[52] This choice was a recognition on the part of the framers that for many, if not most, Indians 'religion was a constitutive element of personal identity'. Having constituted religion as an integral part of the public domain, the Constitution also empowered the State to intervene in matters of religion. This is most clearly exhibited in Article 25(2), which places an obligation on the State to pursue social welfare and reform and specifically to open Hindu religious institutions to all classes of Hindus. The specific terms of Article 25(2) have been generally understood as placing an obligation on the State to tackle discriminatory and pernicious practices within Hinduism as a whole. The Indian State also takes on regulation of institutions of other religions. A case in point is the regulation by the Indian federal government of the Central Wakf Council, a statutory body that supervises Wakf Boards and administers movable and immovable properties designated for Muslim religious purposes. However, such regulation of Muslim and Christian religious institutions falls far short of the extent of intervention in Hindu religious institutions that is described below.

[51] Gurpreet Mahajan, 'Religion and the Indian Constitution' in Rajeev Bhargava (ed), *Politics and Ethics of the Indian Constitution* (Oxford, Oxford University Press, 2008) 301.

[52] ibid 301–02.

As noted already, the Nehru Government undertook the enactment of the Hindu Code as a way of discharging this obligation in more general terms. The specific mandate of Article 25(2) in respect of Hindu religious institutions has been undertaken by the individual States, especially those in South India, from very early on in the life of the new republic.

One of the first State laws was the Madras Hindu Religious and Charitable Endowment Act 1951, which was challenged in the case of *Commissioner, Hindu Religious Endowments, Madras v Sri Lakshmindra T.S. of Sri Shirur Mutt* (1954).[53] The main challenge here was to the comprehensive system of regulation of religious endowments which the petitioner argued were in violation of its right to administer religious institutions guaranteed by Article 26. While upholding the law—and thus signalling to other States that such laws should be enacted, which they were in quick succession—the Supreme Court sought to strike a balance between the interests of the State and the religious denomination. It did so by devising what it called 'the essential practices' test. Created as a defensive measure, the test consisted of assessing what is the essential part of a religion, which the Court held could not be regulated by the State. However, in later years, the test was used in a series of cases to the opposite effect: of depriving what the judiciary sought fit to term as a 'non-essential' practice of any constitutional protection whatsoever. Rajeev Dhavan has carefully tracked how this process occurred over time and has led to a situation where the judiciary has gradually increased its own powers.[54]

The regulation of Hindu religious institutions has, over time, extended to very great lengths, especially in the States of Tamil Nadu, Kerala, Andhra Pradesh and Karnataka. In all these States, temple boards and committees operate to regulate temple lands and finances, appoint middle- and lower-level employees (including priests) and act

[53] *Commissioner, Hindu Religious Endowments, Madras v Sri Lakshmindra T.S. of Sri Shirur Mutt*, AIR 1954 SC 282.

[54] Rajeev Dhavan and Fali Nariman, 'The Supreme Court and Group Life' in BN Kirpal et al (eds), *Supreme But Not Infallible: Essays in Honour of the Supreme Court of India* (New Delhi, Oxford University Press, 2000) 258–64. See also Rajeev Dhavan, 'The Road to Xanadu: India's Quest for Secularism' in Gerald Larson (ed), *Religion and Personal Law in Secular India* (Bloomington, IN, Indiana University Press, 2001) 301–29.

as legal custodians of the temple. In the State of Kerala, this regulation extends to over a thousand temples; the State has a Cabinet-level temple portfolio, and its High Court has a 'temple bench' which meets bi-weekly to administer issues relating to Hindu temples. Scholars have disparaged this trend of 'bureaucratization of religion, with State appointed officers taking over the running of temples at the expense of traditional authorities'[55] and have argued that the de facto nationalisation of Hindu national religious endowments, temples and places of learning sits uneasily with both the guarantee of religious freedom and secularism. This measure has also created a backlash and contributed to the Hindu Right's argument that Hindus are disadvantaged by the mainstream institutions of governance.

It should equally be pointed out that the judiciary has aggravated members of minority communities with its approach to matters of free exercise of religion. In a landmark decision in *Mohd. Hanif Qureshi* (1958)[56] the Supreme Court had to decide whether Muslim butchers had a right to slaughter cows. While crafting a balanced judgment which preserved their right to carry on their trade, the judgment of the Supreme Court embarked on a study of the Holy Quran to decide that cow slaughter was not 'an essential practice' of the Muslim faith. In comparative contexts, judges have avoided doing this to maintain a separation between the secular and the religious. But Indian judges have taken the mandate to reform to mean that they can also become interpreters of religious faiths. Pratap Mehta argues that Indian judges 'engage in extensive scriptural exegesis' and seek to 'interpret the true meaning of religious traditions, and, conveniently enough, their interpretations and re-interpretations make religious traditions [fit] with modern ideals of social reform'.[57] This is what, arguably, was sought to be done in the infamous *Shah Bano* (1984) case, where the judges' attempt to so interpret the Holy Quran led to a severe backlash from the Muslim community who found this act blasphemous.

[55] Ronojoy Sen, 'Secularism and Religious Freedom' in Sujit Choudhry, Madhav Khosla and Pratap Mehta (eds), *The Oxford Handbook of the Indian Constitution* (Oxford, Oxford University Press, 2016) 885–902 at 892.

[56] *Mohd. Hanif Qureshi & Others v the State of Bihar* (1959) SCR 629.

[57] Pratap Mehta, 'Passion and Constraint: Courts and the Regulation of Public Meaning' in Rajeev Bhargava (ed), *Politics and Ethics in the Indian Constitution* (New Delhi, Oxford University Press, 2009) 326.

The other clear danger is that once judges arrogate to themselves the authority to 'become theologians'[58] there is also scope for judges with majoritarian sympathies to use their power to provide support for Hindu right wing parties. This is arguably what happened in the case of *Ramesh Y Prabhoo v P. K. Kunte* (1996).[59] The Supreme Court's judgment characterising Hinduism as a 'way of life' was 'promptly appropriated by the Hindu nationalists',[60] finding specific mention in the BJP's political manifesto for the General Elections in 1999, which resulted in the BJP going on to form the government at the centre.

The Supreme Court has had a similarly expansive role to play in moulding the jurisprudence that has evolved around the cultural and educational rights of minorities guaranteed under Articles 29–30. The field of Indian education has witnessed, since the colonial era, the existence of a significant number of private educational institutions—especially denominational schools of the Christian faith—that provided good-quality school and college education, particularly to the aspiring middle classes of Indians. Soon after independence, many governments began issuing a series of regulations that sought to undermine the autonomy of these private religious institutions of the minority faith, to bring them within the purview of State regulation. The minority educational institutions naturally sought to invoke their rights under Articles 29–30 to resist these governmental initiatives.

Dhavan and Nariman describe the evolution of the case law on the rights guaranteed under Articles 29–30 across two broad periods. From 1950 until about 1975 the Supreme Court resisted the 'over-assimilative, overly-regulative' attempts of State governments in the States of Bombay, Kerala and Gujarat in a series of decisions that sought to strike a balance between the rights of minority institutions and the justifiable claims of State institutions to regulate 'maladministration' in such schools and colleges.[61] It did so while strongly upholding the rights of autonomy of the minority institutions and struck down measures that sought to impose language restrictions or

[58] Dhavan and Nariman (n 54) 260.

[59] AIR 1958 SC 1918.

[60] Sen (n 55) 896–97.

[61] These included the following cases: *State of Bombay v Bombay Educational Society* (1955) 1 SCR 568; *In re Kerala Education Bill* (1959) SCR 995; *Gujarat University v Sri Krishna* (1963) Supp 1 SCR 112.

enable governments to nominate either students or people in the direct administration of these institutions. This trend began to change in the mid-1970s, when judges began to entertain the argument that the public interest demanded that minority institutions be able to adhere to standards of excellence, which was held to be a valid ground for State regulation. Dhavan and Nariman identify the decisions in *St. Xavier's case* (1975)[62] and the *Delhi (Frank Anthony School)* case (1986)[63] as turning points that characterised a second trend that was far more hostile to the autonomy rights of minority institutions. Covering decided cases up to 2000, Dhavan and Nariman are deeply critical of the latter trend of decisions, which, in their view, amounts to 'an ingress which has been spurred on for ideological reasons and a somewhat myopic view that minority institutions should play a less autonomous role in matters of education: that all persons must join a particular assimilationist version of the mainstream of Indian life'.[64] Since 2000 there have been a series of decisions in the education sector which have caused a great deal of confusion because of the intersection of issues relating to reservations, minority educational institutions and whether the rights of non-minority educational institutions have the same status as those of minority educational institutions. While this has caused needless confusion about the state of the doctrine across many issues, three major decisions have sought to uphold the autonomy rights of minority institutions under Articles 29 and 30. First, in *Ashoka Kumar Thakur v Union of India* (2008),[65] which dealt with the constitutional validity of Article 15(5), the Court upheld the exclusion of the applicability of reservations under Article 15(5) to minority educational institutions. In *Society for Unaided Private Schools of Rajasthan v Union of India* (2012)[66] a three-judge bench of the Supreme Court struck down a provision in the Right to Education Act 2009 which sought to impose a quota of 25 per cent of seats in all schools for children belonging to disadvantaged groups, on the ground that it could not apply to minority educational institutions in light of Article 30. Finally, in *Pramati Educational*

[62] *St. Xavier's College v State of Gujarat* (1975) 1 SCR 173.

[63] *Frank Anthony Public School Employees Association v Union of India* (1986) 4 SCC 707.

[64] Dhavan and Nariman (n 54) 269–70.

[65] *Ashoka Kumar Thakur v Union of India* (2008) 6 SCC 1.

[66] *Society for Unaided Private Schools of Rajasthan v Union of India* (2012) 6 SCC 1.

and Cultural Trust v Union of India (2014)[67] a five-judge bench of the Supreme Court reiterated the view that Article 15(5) was valid in so far as it excluded reservations in minority educational institutions from its ambit. While other issues relating to regulation of minority educational institutions remain unclear, what is clear is that they cannot be made subject to policies of reservation either under Article 15(5) or under the Right to Education Act 2009.[68]

To end, it is relevant to briefly address the extensive scholarly debate—and the legal and judicial discourse—over the nature and content of Indian secularism. To start with, it bears mentioning that the Preamble to the original Constitution did not contain the word 'secular', which was added by the Indira Gandhi Government through the infamous 42nd constitutional Amendment during the Emergency. There was, in fact, an attempt to incorporate the word 'secular' into the Constitution in the Constituent Assembly, when Brajeshwar Prasad moved an amendment to this effect on 17 October 1949. There was, at the same time, another amendment that sought to insert the phrase 'in the name of God' into the Preamble. Neither attempt succeeded, which gives us a sense of the collective ambivalence that the framers reflected on this issue.[69] Scholars such as Madan and Nandy have argued that Western notions of secularism are ill-suited to the Indian context, where people are deeply religious, and that Indian life is not amenable to any strict separation between the religious and public domains.[70] Those scholars who do consider India to be a secular state have noted its significant differences from the more conventional secular models in the US and France.[71] Some others have sought to conceptualise the Indian variant of secularism through formulations

[67] *Pramati Educational and Cultural Trust v Union of India* (2014) 8 SCC 1.

[68] K Vivek Reddy, 'Minority Educational Institutions' in Sujit Choudhry, Madhav Khosla and Pratap Mehta (eds), *The Oxford Handbook of the Indian Constitution* (Oxford, Oxford University Press, 2016) 921–42.

[69] CAD X 439–47. This is highlighted in Sen (n 55) 885.

[70] TN Madan, 'Secularism in its Place' (1987) 46 *Journal of Asian Studies* 747–59; Ashis Nandy, 'The Politics of Secularism and the Recovery of Religious Tolerance' in Veena Das (ed), *The Mirror of Violence* (New Delhi, Oxford University Press, 1990) 69–93.

[71] See, eg, Donald E Smith, *India as a Secular State* (Princeton, NJ, Princeton University Press, 1963).

that seek to capture its approach and constituent elements. Thus, for instance, Rajeev Bhargava has reconstructed from legal, judicial and political practice what he terms a model of 'principled distance' to capture the Indian experience of secularism.[72] Rajeev Dhavan, while focusing upon judicial resolution of religious disputes in particular, has characterised the Indian model of secularism as founded on three main elements: (i) the principle of religious freedom (which expansively protects religious practices, beliefs and freedoms); (ii) the principle of depoliticisation and celebratory neutrality (which prevents the State from being taken over by a single community while enabling it to give free rein to multiple religions and faiths); and (iii) the principle of social welfare and reform (which requires religions to be subject to reforms to rid them of gender-discriminatory and other constitutionally unacceptable prescriptions).[73] For its part, the Indian Supreme Court, in the case of *S. R. Bommai v Union of India* (1994)[74] held that 'secularism' is a part of the 'basic structure' of the Indian Constitution, elevating its status to a principle that cannot be tampered with by Parliament even in exercise of its plenary power.

V. CONCLUSION

This chapter has sought to provide an overview of: the five major markers of identity in Indian society; the way the Constitution has sought to regulate their effects; the relevant colonial and Constitution-making history in relation to these markers; and finally, the manner in which the principal institutions of the Constitution have sought to address the implications and practical workings of these five elements of the Indian identity. Together, these descriptive aspects hopefully capture the many complexities of multiculturalism in India, including the many opportunities and challenges it presents to the sustenance of a vibrant constitutional culture.

[72] Rajeev Bhargava, 'India's Secular Constitution' in Zoya Hasan, E Sridharanand and R Sudarshan (eds), *India's Living Constitution* (London, Anthem Press, 2005) 105–33.

[73] Dhavan (n 54).

[74] *S. R. Bommai v Union of India*, AIR 1994 SC 1918.

FURTHER READING

Bina Agarwal, *A Field of One's Own: Gender and Land Rights in South Asia* (Cambridge, Cambridge University Press, 1994).

Flavia Agnes, *Family Law I: Family Laws and Constitutional Claims* (New Delhi, Oxford University Press, 2011).

Rochana Bajpai, *Debating Difference: Group Rights and Liberal Democracy in India* (New Delhi, Oxford University Press, 2011).

Rajeev Dhavan, 'The Road to Xanadu: India's Quest for Secularism' in Gerald Larson (ed), *Religion and Personal Law in Secular India* (Bloomington, IN, Indiana University Press, 2001) 301–29.

Nicholas Dirks, *Castes of Mind: Colonialism and the Making of Modern India* (Princeton, NJ, Princeton University Press, 2001).

Marc Galanter, *Competing Equalities: Law and the Backward Classes in India* (New Delhi, Oxford University Press, 1984).

Gurpreet Mahajan and DL Seth (eds), *Minority Identities and Nation-State* (New Delhi, Oxford University Press, 1998).

Archana Parashar, *Family Law Reform and Women in India* (New Delhi, SAGE Publications, 1992).

Ronojoy Sen, *Articles of Faith: Religion, Secularism and the Indian Supreme Court* (New Delhi, Oxford University Press, 2010).

Nandini Sundar, *The Burning Forest: India's War in Bastar* (New Delhi, Juggernaut, 2016).

7

Constitutional Change

Textual provisions – Constitutional history – Constitutional practice of amendments – Role of constitutional interpretation – Constitutional change through constitutional moments

I. INTRODUCTION

THIS CHAPTER ANALYSES the ways in which constitutional change has occurred in India. In particular, the chapter considers the manner in which the formal text of the Constitution provides for amendments to its provisions; how the framers of the Constitution came upon that position; the practice of constitutional amendment in India; and how that position has evolved over time.

In constitutional theory, it has long been understood that, in Constitutions that empower judiciaries with the important power of judicial review over legislation, one of the important ways by which constitutional change occurs beyond the formal methods stipulated in the text is the mode of constitutional interpretation. This can sometimes extend to extraordinary degrees: writing about the US constitutional experience, Mark Tushnet asserts that constitutional interpretation by judges of the US Supreme Court accounts for 'a much larger portion' of constitutional change than the formal amendment process.[1] As we will see, judges in India too have considerable powers in relation to constitutional amendment, though the Indian Parliament has also exercised its power to amend the text of the Constitution frequently

[1] Mark Tushnet, *The Constitution of the United States of America: A Contextual Analysis* (Oxford, Hart Publishing, 2009) 237.

and with consequential effect. The Indian case, by design, is quite different from the US model but has raised its own peculiar conundrums. What is also interesting about the Indian constitutional experience is its evolution from a model that initially envisaged the amending power vested in Parliament as relatively absolute and unfettered, to one where implicit and explicit limitations on the amending power have been gradually accepted, largely as a result of interactions with other constitutional actors, and the judiciary in particular. Going beyond these two modes—of formal amendment specified in the text and constitutional interpretation—this chapter will also focus on change brought about through constitutional moments.

This chapter begins, in Section II, with an examination of the textual provisions relating to constitutional amendment, followed by a brief review of the views of the framers of the Constitution on the important question of constitutional change and how it was to be addressed and regulated. Section III provides a brief survey of the hundred-odd constitutional amendments that have been enacted since the adoption of the Constitution six decades and some years ago. The attempt will be to broadly understand the nature and type of amendments; the factors that have determined how often they have occurred; and the governments which initiated them. Section IV turns to the important question of the role of constitutional interpretation and the judiciary in regulating constitutional change, which has taken on extraordinary dimensions in India. Section V focuses on the importance of changes brought about in India since the early 1990s, which may count as a constitutional moment in Indian constitutional history.

II. RELEVANT CONSTITUTIONAL PROVISIONS AND CONSTITUTIONAL HISTORY

A. Textual Analysis of the Provisions Relating to Constitutional Amendment

Provisions which envisage constitutional amendment are, as is explained below, spread across the text of the Constitution of India. Nevertheless, Part XX of the Constitution is entitled 'Amendment of the Constitution'; it contains only one provision, Article 368. This provision has had a long and tortuous history and could be said to be one of the most frequently invoked and contentious provisions in the entire text. This is reflected in the fact that the text of the provision itself has become a battleground, with its present text being quite different now from its original form, following several amendments. Although this Part contains only one provision, other provisions also address the issue of constitutional amendment—they must be read together with Article 368 to avoid giving the impression that this provision alone regulates the amendment power.

The Constitution sets out a three-pronged amendment process for different categories of constitutional provisions.[2] The first category of constitutional provisions are those that were considered relatively less significant and can be amended by an ordinary law enacted by Parliament. They therefore require, as do ordinary laws, only a simple majority in Parliament followed by assent of the President. There are more than 20 such provisions, which are spread throughout the Constitution, including the following illustrative examples:[3] Articles 2, 3 and 4 (enabling the creation of new States and involving amendments to the First and Fourth Schedules), Article 125 read with Article 221 and the Second Schedule (enabling the raising of salaries of higher judiciary judges), and Article 169(3) (enabling the creation or abolition of Upper Chambers in the States).

It bears emphasising that the attribution of varying degrees of significance to these three categories may seem puzzling and particularistic when viewed from a comparative perspective. As noted in Chapter 3, the context of Indian federalism was fairly unique, resulting in a situation where the territorial sovereignty of the States in the Indian federation was not provided immunity. In most federal models, the fact that a constituent State can be amended out of existence without its consent or even involvement would be unacceptable.

[2] To obtain this understanding, one has to read across the text of the Constitution. Authors of leading constitutional commentaries explain this succinctly: Mahendra P Singh (ed), *V.N. Shukla's Constitution of India*, 12th edn (Lucknow, Eastern Book Co, 2013) 1070–72; MP Jain, *Indian Constitutional Law*, 5th edn (Lucknow, Lexis Nexis Butterworths Wadhwa Nagpur, 2009) 1617–20.

[3] For a fuller listing of the provisions in this category, see Jain (n 2) 1617–18.

However, in India, this reality represents the complex dynamics of federalism that required such an approach to issues of territory, although (as we shall see below), other issues of federalism are respected through the amendment process.

The second category of constitutional provisions includes all provisions except those mentioned in the first category and that are viewed as being of vital significance. This category is addressed by Article 368(2). In order to amend all such provisions, a Bill is to be introduced in either house of Parliament, and passed by a majority of its total membership and a majority of not less than two-thirds of the members of the house present and voting. Once this is done, the amendment has to receive the assent of the President, whereupon it has effect and the Constitution stands amended.

The third category of provisions, addressed by the latter part of Article 368(2), are those that are considered of high significance, bear upon the federal character of the Constitution and may otherwise also impact the interests of the States. For this reason, in addition to the supermajority requirement of those present and voting in the Union Parliament, amendments to this category of provisions are required to be ratified by at least half of the number of States (ie at least 15 States at present) before being presented for Presidential assent. Article 368(2) thus provides for further entrenchment of this category of provisions, which consists of six sets of provisions outlining:

(i) the manner of election of the President (Articles 54 and 55);
(ii) the extent of the executive power of the Union and the States (Articles 73 and 162);
(iii) the Supreme Court and High Courts (Articles 124–147 and 214–231);
(iv) the distribution of legislative, taxing and administrative powers between the Union and the States (Articles 245–255 and the three lists in the Seventh Schedule);
(v) the representation of States in the upper house of Parliament (the Fourth Schedule); and
(vi) the text of Article 368 itself.

An assessment of this three-pronged classification and its working will be conducted in a following section, after a brief examination of the drafting history of this provision.

B. The Relevant History of the Provisions Relating to Constitutional Amendment

The provisions relating to constitutional amendment had been extensively considered and debated before the Constituent Assembly was established in the mid-1940s. A brief survey of these positions helps situate the background considerations and thinking which informed the final choices of the framers and the strategic and structural choices reflected in the final version of the text that was adopted in 1950.

The nationalist drafts that were adopted prior to the Constituent Assembly sought to incorporate different sensibilities while approaching the question of altering the Constitution. In doing so, they anticipated the three modes eventually adopted, though they were motivated by different concerns. The Commonwealth of India Bill of 1925, which, as noted in Chapter 1, was a landmark event in the nationalist effort at Constitution making, had a single, short but clear provision on the subject of 'Alteration of the Constitution'. Section 46 stipulated that the power to alter the Constitution would vest with Parliament, albeit 'with the consent of the Provincial Legislatures'.[4] Since this preceded the formal incorporation of federalism in British India through the Government of India Act 1935, the provision is striking for its federal sensibility and willingness to incorporate the views of provinces on questions relating to constitutional amendment. However, the provision did not exhibit much nuance and revealed a mindset which assumed that the inputs of provinces would be relevant to *all* questions involving constitutional alteration or amendment. It also did not require any special majority rules and implied that alterations could be carried out by following the procedure for an ordinary law passed by Parliament. A mere three years later there was a clear shift in such thinking, as is revealed in the text of the provision relating to 'Amendment of the Constitution' in the Nehru Report of 1928. Section 87, ignoring the interests of the provincial legislatures that were recognised by other parts of the Report, chose to vest the power to alter or repeal any of the provisions in the Constitution solely with the Parliament.[5]

[4] 'The Commonwealth of India Bill, 1925' in B Shiva Rao (ed), *The Framing of India's Constitution* (Delhi, Universal Law Publishing, 2010) 48.

[5] The Nehru Report, 1928 in ibid 74.

However, it imposed an additional requirement by mandating a joint sitting of Parliament and the concurrence of two-thirds of the total membership of both houses.

Interestingly, Tej Bahadur Sapru was involved in both these initiatives. However, when he himself was tasked with drafting a Constitution nearly two decades later, the report of the Sapru Committee, published in 1945, showed a very different understanding of the power to amend the Constitution. Section 20 of the Constitution drafted by the Sapru Committee provided that only formal amendments could be passed akin to ordinary laws. Some significant provisions were to be immune from amendment for the first five years by being named in a schedule to the Constitution. Other significant provisions could be amended only after being publicly notified for six months, following which they would have to be passed by a two-thirds majority in Parliament and a similar number of provincial legislatures.[6] This very difficult amending process was in line with the Sapru Committee's overarching focus on maintaining communal harmony. This was a way of assuring the Muslim League and other minorities that their interests that were guaranteed in the Constitution would be safeguarded beyond the period of adoption by placing hurdles in the path of a Hindu majority that may be inclined to upset such guarantees.

By the time the question of amendment was taken up in the Constituent Assembly in June 1947, two broad positions had begun to crystallise.[7] The first was of those members who wanted to follow the procedures outlined in conventional Constitutions—the ones specifically discussed were those of the US, Canada, Australia and Switzerland—which made the process of amendment difficult and often involved actors beyond the Parliament, such as State legislatures and even the people, through devices such as referenda. The second position was represented by members who wanted the Parliament to be able to amend the Constitution relatively easily, acting on its own, similar to the position in the UK where constitutional amendments were secured through ordinary legislation. The position ultimately reflected

[6] Sapru Committee Report, Clause 20, xv. Full text available at <https://archive.org/details/saprucommittee035520mbp>.

[7] This is the way Granville Austin characterises the evolution of debates over the amending power, though he uses different terms. Granville Austin, *The Indian Constitution: Cornerstone of a Nation* (New Delhi, Oxford University Press, 1966) 257.

in Article 368—and the three modes that are now possible—is a compromise between these two broad positions.

Through the drafting process and in the debates on the draft Constitution on the floor of the Constituent Assembly, many views on the amending power were represented.[8] At one end were the views of members who sought guidance from existing Constitutions and devices such as supermajorities, referenda and plebiscites as a way of ensuring that the contents of the Constitution were not tampered with by subsequent Parliaments. At the other extreme was the view that the Constituent Assembly, having been indirectly elected and forced, by dint of circumstance, to act in haste, would not be justified in placing its decisions on a high pedestal beyond the amending power of a Parliament whose members would be directly elected by universal suffrage. Members holding this view wanted to make the Constitution easily amendable for a period of five or 10 years, during which Parliament could make amendments through a simple majority. This view was expressed, among others, by Prime Minister Nehru, giving it special force:[9]

> [W]hile we want this Constitution to be as solid and as permanent a structure as we can make it, nevertheless there is no permanence in Constitutions. There should be a certain flexibility. … [W]hen a new House … is elected in terms of this Constitution, and every adult in India—man and woman—has the right to vote, the House that emerges then will certainly be fully representative of every section of the Indian people. It is right that that House elected so—*under this Constitution of course it will have the right to do any thing*—should have an easy opportunity to make such changes as it wants to. … Therefore, while we make a Constitution which is sound and as basic as we can, it should also be flexible and for a period we should be in a position to change it with relatively facility.[10] [emphasis added]

This statement also exhibits Nehru's belief, in common with that of many members of his Cabinet and government, that the Parliament's power to amend the Constitution was complete and unquestionable. As we shall see, this view, which was shared by other leaders of

[8] For an overview of the wide-ranging debate, see ibid 257–64 and B Shiva Rao, *The Framing of India's Constitution* (New Delhi, Universal Law Publishing, 1968, reprinted 2010) vol 5, 'Amendment of the Constitution' 824–34.

[9] CAD VII 323.

[10] CAD VII 322–23.

government in the post-independence years, came to be questioned and, eventually, undermined. Given what followed later, it is interesting that some other members wanted special protections for the Fundamental Rights provisions and sought to immunise them completely from the amending power.[11]

In explaining the nature of, and motivation for, the finally adopted provision, Ambedkar asserted that the idea was to strike a balance between these various considerations. He noted that a considerable portion of the Constitution could be amended by Parliament through ordinary law, but to respect the federal values of the Constitution, a set of provisions which impacted federal power and relations had been made amendable only with the consent of the States. It is therefore clear that Nehru's desire for an arrangement that all provisions of the Constitution should be easily amendable for a specific period was not adopted in the final provision. Neither, however, was the stance of the opposite view, that *all* provisions should be made difficult to amend, including through the option of a referendum. Ambedkar also had a response to the view advocated by Nehru and some other members that the Constituent Assembly, being indirectly elected, was somehow lacking in legitimacy, especially in contrast with a future Parliament that would be elected on adult suffrage. His words have special importance in the contemporary period, where many Indians, disenchanted with the partisan politics of the time, are turning to the proceedings and debates of the Constituent Assembly for solutions to present-day institutional problems:

> The Constituent Assembly in making a Constitution has no partisan motive. Beyond securing a good and workable Constitution, it has no axe to grind. In considering the articles of the Constitution it has no eye on getting through a particular measure. The future Parliament, if it met as a Constituent Assembly, its members will be acting as partisans seeking to carry amendments to the Constitution to facilitate measures which they have failed to get through Parliament by reason of some article of the Constitution which has acted as an obstacle in their way. Parliament will have an axe to grind while the Constituent Assembly has none. That is the difference between the Constituent Assembly and the future Parliament. That explains why the Constituent Assembly though elected on limited franchise can be

[11] This is the view advanced by Dr PS Deshmukh during the final debates on the Draft Constitution in September 1949. See CAD VII 1646–48 at p 1647.

> trusted to pass the Constitution by simple majority and why Parliament though elected on adult suffrage cannot be trusted with the same power to amend it.[12]

In 1966, while reviewing the working of the Indian Constitution and its amending power in particular, Granville Austin offered the assessment that the provisions relating to amendment had proved to be 'one of the most ably conceived aspects of the Constitution'.[13] By 1966 the text of the Constitution had been amended 17 times, at the rate of more than one every year. This was, by comparative standards, a high rate even at the time. In the period immediately thereafter, the rate and nature of constitutional amendments increased sharply, causing some to question Austin's judgment. To understand why, we need to obtain a full sense of Indian constitutional practice in relation to the amending power up to the present, which is the subject of the next section of this chapter.

III. CONSTITUTIONAL PRACTICE IN RELATION TO THE AMENDING POWER IN INDIA: AN OVERVIEW AND ANALYSIS OF TRENDS (1950–2016)

As originally adopted and enforced on 26 January 1950, the Constitution of India consisted of 395 articles, spread across 22 parts, and eight schedules. Six-and-a-half decades onwards, in 2015, it stood at 448 articles, spread across 25 parts, and 12 schedules. This fact provides one indication of the quantity of changes brought about by invoking the power of amendment. In numerical terms, by September 2016, a total of 101 amendments had been successfully brought into force: this amounts to a rate of 1.53 amendments per year, which is relatively high by global standards of constitutional change.[14]

This number does not fully capture the extent of amendments since some of these individual amendments altered several different provisions of the Constitution. Thus, one has to distinguish between major amendments and minor, less consequential ones. Among the major

[12] CAD VII 33–34.

[13] Austin (n 7) 255.

[14] Shubhankar Dam, 'A British Misreading: Sir Ivor Jennings' Early Assessment of the Indian Constitution' in Harshan Kumarasingham (ed), *Constitution-making in Asia* (London, Routledge, 2016) 83.

amendments was the First Amendment to the Constitution (1951), enacted by the Provisional Parliament (while it was still a unicameral body) within a year of the coming into force of the Constitution and before the first general elections. This consequential amendment amended 10 existing provisions and introduced two new ones. Similarly, the Seventh Amendment to the Constitution (1956), enacted to implement the States Reorganisation Commission's recommendations for restructuring India's federal units on the basis of language, resulted in changes to multiple provisions of the Constitution. Arguably the most consequential amendment so far has been the 42nd Amendment (1976), introduced during the period of internal Emergency by the Indira Gandhi Government with the express purpose of centralising governance within the Union executive and reining in constitutional institutions such as the judiciary. This single initiative amended 55 provisions and introduced two new parts into the text of the Constitution. Among its many changes, it expressly inserted the ideas of socialism, secularism and integrity of the nation into the text of the Preamble, added a chapter on Fundamental Duties to which all citizens would have to adhere, and sought to make the Directive Principles more comprehensive and have priority over the Fundamental Rights. It had several provisions which sought to undermine and reduce the powers of the High Courts, including by giving the Parliament the power to set up tribunals and other courts where the executive would have a greater say over appointments and processes. It sought to more explicitly state the powers of the Prime Minister and the Council of Ministers in relation to the powers of the President by making the latter bound by the aid and advice of the former. There was also an attempt to insulate the power of constitutional amendment from judicial scrutiny.

Two years later, when the Janata Government came to power in the general elections held after the Emergency, it moved the 44th Amendment (1978), which reversed many of the worst excesses of the 42nd Amendment and was almost as extensive in scope. However, the 44th Amendment could not reverse all the objectionable portions of the 42nd Amendment since the Janata Government did not have the numerical strength in the Rajya Sabha where the Congress party still had a significant presence. The 44th Amendment also had its share of novel features: it sought to fortify the Constitution from abuses of emergency powers by strengthening constitutional safeguards such as requiring parliamentary approval for extensions of periods of formal

Emergency. Given the great conflict between the judiciary and Parliament over the scope and nature of the Fundamental Right to property, this Amendment removed the right from the Fundamental Rights chapter and moved it to another part where it would still retain the status of a constitutional right, but would not enjoy the immunities guaranteed to a Part III right. At the same time, it sought to fortify the right to freedom of the press and media.

A. A Rough Typology of Constitutional Amendments in India

The large number of constitutional amendments are difficult to classify into coherent categories as several of them were responses to very particular situations. However, a broad typology can be attempted for some of these amendments which share some common themes. The first broad type relates to amendments in relation to Fundamental Rights and specifically the right to property. As we shall see in greater detail in the next section, a large number of amendments in the early years revolved around the question of whether the Fundamental Rights could be diluted or otherwise undermined by Parliament and the executive in pursuit of their social goals through legislation. The specific right that was most affected was the right to property, enshrined in Article 19(1)(f) and Article 31 of the original Constitution. These provisions together provided that all citizens would have a right to property, which could be acquired by the State only after passing a law which specified the compensation to be paid. The broad trend of these amendments involved Parliament, motivated by a desire to secure land reforms, seeking to exclude the question of compensation for acquisition or requisitioning of property by the State from judicial review. Nearly all such attempts were challenged by individuals affected by these laws, resulting in judicial decisions which evolved from being initially deferential to becoming more adventurous over time. The trend began with the First Amendment (1951), which inserted Article 31B and the Ninth Schedule to immunise specifically named parliamentary laws relating to land reforms from judicial scrutiny in respect of violations of Fundamental Rights. The First Amendment contained a list of 13 laws that were so immunised by mentioning them by name in the Ninth Schedule. Since then, over the next three decades until the mid-1990s, there have been several amendments which have added to the original list, causing it to stand at 284 in 2016. Described by a distinguished constitutional scholar as 'a novel, innovative and drastic technique of constitutional amendment',[15] the mechanism of Article 31B read with the Ninth Schedule has recently been labelled a 'savings clause' and described as a 'unique' and 'exceptional' part of the Indian constitutional scheme.[16] As already noted, the status of the right to property itself was downgraded by converting it from a Fundamental Right into an ordinary constitutional right by the 44th Amendment (1978).

The second type of constitutional amendments would include a number of amendments that became necessary because of time limits specified in the text of the Constitution. Article 334 originally provided that reservation of seats (or quotas) for the representatives of the Scheduled Castes, the Scheduled Tribes and the Anglo-Indian community in the Lok Sabha and the State Legislative Assemblies would expire 10 years from the date of adoption of the Constitution. These reservations have been extended for another decade every 10 years and this trend does not seem likely to change in the foreseeable future. This has necessitated amendments to this single provision six times through the Eighth (1959), the 23rd (1969), the 45th (1980), the 62nd (1989), the 79th (1999) and the 95th Amendments (2009). It is notable that except for the 23rd Amendment, which also related to another provision, the other five amendments were enacted solely to change this single provision, and to only two words within it.

A third type of constitutional amendment in the 1980s was driven by the need of the Union government to impose and extend the period of emergency rule to address the 'troubles' following a secessionist movement in the State of Punjab, which required individual constitutional amendments at every stage. The fourth and final type is of amendments relating to the changing and growing number of States in India. As noted earlier in Chapter 3, the number of constituent States in the Indian federal model has been almost continuously changing—each addition or reorganisation required an amendment and they account for a significant number of amendments.

[15] MP Jain, *Indian Constitutional Law*, 5th edn (Gurgaon, Lexis Nexis Butterworths Wadhwa, 2009) 1290.

[16] Surya Deva, 'Ninth Schedule' in Sujit Choudhry, Madhav Khosla and Pratap Mehta (eds), *The Oxford Handbook of the Indian Constitution* (Oxford, Oxford University Press, 2016) 627–43.

Analysing the 101 amendments enacted up to September 2016 reveals that a fairly high number of them—40—fell into the third category of amendments envisaged by Article 368, and required the consent of the State legislatures. Of these 40 amendments, as many as 27 were secured prior to 1989 when the dominance of the Congress party came to an end. Thus, at least for the third category of amendments, there is a co-relation between the existence of a strong national party holding power at the centre and in several States, and the rate of constitutional amendments. Once the coalition era in Indian politics began in the early 1990s, the rate of constitutional amendments that required the consent and approval of States in addition to the Union has understandably fallen, given the difficulties involved in securing the support of the vast range of regional parties which now exists.

It remains to be seen whether the BJP's dominance in Parliament since the May 2014 general elections, coupled with its being the ruling government in several States, will lead to a situation similar to that during the Congress era, when amendments that also require the approval of State legislatures will see a resurgence. It is striking that in the two years it has been in power, the BJP-led government at the centre has been able to obtain the requisite support in the Union Parliament and the State legislatures for two major amendments falling within this third category, relating to the process of appointments in the higher judiciary (the 100th Constitutional Amendment, 2015) and the revamping of fiscal federal relations through the introduction of a General Sales Tax (the 101st Constitutional Amendment, 2016).

B. A Rough Quantitative Analysis of the Practice of Constitutional Amendments

A recent quantitative analysis of a different variable reveals that the number of amendments across decanal periods in India's postcolonial trajectory occurred at the following rates: 7 (1950–59); 15 (1960–69); 22 (1970–79); 18 (1980–89); 16 (1990–99); 16 (2000–2009); and 6 (2010–15).[17] After a gradual rate of seven in the first decade, the number has averaged 16 per decade since. As the analysis of the evolution of the Indian political landscape in Chapter 2 showed, the 1970s were

[17] Dam (n 14) 84.

a tumultuous decade in Indian constitutional politics and this was reflected also in the higher number of constitutional amendments (22). Shubhankar Dam's analysis shows that contrary to many other trends in Indian constitutional politics—such as that relating to the relative power of the judiciary, analysed in Chapter 4, which has been inversely proportional to the strength of the political executive—there is no direct co-relation between the nature of the political executive and the rate of constitutional amendments. So, while an elected government with a strong majority in Parliament could easily have moved constitutional amendments since it possessed the requisite two-thirds majority, that fact alone has not determined which governments moved constitutional amendments at greater rates. This is revealed by a comparison of the tenure of two governments in different periods. Prime Minister Nehru's Congress government, elected in the aftermath of the first general elections (1951–57) with a massive majority in the lower house of Parliament of 364 out of 489 seats, chose to move only seven constitutional amendments. By contrast, Prime Minister Narasimha Rao's minority Congress government successfully moved 10 constitutional amendments within a five-year period from 1991 to 1995 while enjoying the support of only 230 out of 532 MPs through skilful negotiations with other political parties. This included the enactment of the extremely significant 73rd and 74th amendments (1992), which, as noted in Chapter 3, brought in a third tier of governance institutions at the local level beyond the Union and State governments. Given its potential to change the dynamic of elections and the relative distribution of political power in India, it is at the very least surprising that a comparatively weak Central government was able to shepherd through such a landmark set of amendments.

IV. CONSTITUTIONAL INTERPRETATION AS A SOURCE OF CONSTITUTIONAL CHANGE[18]

The focus of this chapter now shifts to the significant role that the Indian judiciary has played in shaping the way constitutional

[18] Portions of this section have been drawn from my co-authored work: Douglas McDonald and Arun K Thiruvengadam, 'Comparative Law and the Role of the Judiciary' in Shaun Star (ed), *Australia and India: A Comparative Overview of the Law and Practice* (New Delhi, Universal Law Publishing and Lexis Nexis, 2016) 20–45.

amendments have occurred in India, and its role in changing the conception of amending power within the Indian and the global constitutional imagination. This relates primarily but not exclusively to the evolution of the doctrine of 'basis structure' or 'basic features' by the Indian Supreme Court. Some scholars treat this doctrine as covering the entire subject of constitutional amendment in India—the point of coming to the judicial role a bit later in this chapter is to draw attention to the many other issues in relation to the amending power in India that do not relate to the judiciary's intervention. It bears emphasis that while a significant portion of the 101 amendments covered in the previous section were prompted by judicial decisions, a considerable number, as we have noted, had very little to do with the judiciary's actions.

The broad narrative relating to the battles between the judiciary and Parliament on the issue of constitutional amendments has been summarised in Chapters 2 and 4. As is clear from that narrative, after starting from a position of deference, the judiciary slowly began asserting its interpretive authority, resulting in a battle of increasing intensity. These clashes extended across the first three decades of the working of the Constitution and are the focus of analysis here.

As noted earlier, while many of the framers who went on to join the first government of independent India under Prime Minister Nehru's Cabinet were keen to have a strong and independent judiciary, they expected the judiciary to have a limited role to play in the massive social engineering projects, including effecting land reforms that were to be initiated at the earliest opportunity. They were keen to convey this message to the judiciary when they perceived that some judges had not understood this constitutional compact clearly enough, and did so quite stridently through the First Amendment (1951) to the Constitution.

The trigger for the First Amendment were two sets of judicial decisions in relation to the right to freedom of speech and the right to property. Soon after the adoption of the Constitution in January 1950, three State governments imposed restrictions on speech and expression, which were challenged by the affected individuals before different High Courts. The Patna High Court struck down the restrictions in Bihar as violative of the fundamental right to speech. Another bench of the same High Court struck down a law of the Bihar legislature which sought to abolish zamindaris and bring about land reform.[19]

[19] The decisions of the Patna High Court were delivered in the cases of *In re Bharti Press*, AIR 1951 Pat 21 and *Kameshwar Singh v State of Bihar*, AIR 1951 Pat 91.

Both these issues irked many members of the Nehru Government, and they swiftly took steps to reverse the decisions of the High Courts by enacting the First Amendment (1951), which made changes to the rights to freedom of speech and expression, including the introduction of Article 31B and the Ninth Schedule.

What came to be known as the basic structure doctrine arose as a result of the evolution of the law on constitutional amendments across four successive cases relating to amendments made to the right to property. The first of these cases, *Shankari Prasad Singh v Union of India* (1952),[20] was a direct consequence of the First Amendment to the Constitution, and challenged the capacity of Parliament to violate the rights of freedom of speech and property of citizens through its provisions. The petitioner argued that the First Amendment violated Article 13(2) of the Constitution, which prohibited Parliament from violating the Fundamental Rights.

A five-judge bench of the Supreme Court delivered a unanimous judgment, authored by Sastri J, accepting the power of Parliament to amend the Constitution and to abrogate Fundamental Rights. The Court also relied on the distinction between constitutional law and ordinary legislation and the logic that an exercise of constituent power was not itself subject to challenge. Sastri J held that the power of Parliament to amend the Constitution under Article 368 was 'without any exception whatsoever'. The judgment of the Supreme Court may seem deferential but closer scrutiny of a set of cases decided at the same time shows that it was in keeping with other cases—including the free speech cases—where the Supreme Court adopted a textualist approach to constitutional interpretation which was consistent. As noted, the textual reading of Article 368 does indicate a seemingly unlimited power of constitutional amendment being vested in Parliament. However, in other cases, a textualist interpretation led the Court to strike down regulations which violated a strict reading of the guarantee of free speech. The interpretation accorded by the Court to the question of amending power is, therefore, consistent with what scholars have asserted was the dominant approach of constitutional interpretation during the Nehru era, which lasted from 1947 to 1964. It is also important to take a realistic view of the Court's approach, going beyond the

[20] *Shankari Prasad Singh v Union of India* 1952 (3) SCR 165.

interpretive consistency shown by it. It must be remembered that policies of social justice, including land reforms, were the driving force of the nationalist movement in the lead-up to independence and in the soaring rhetoric of the Objectives Resolution within the Constituent Assembly. The judges of the Court would have been only too aware of the importance of these policies for the Congress party and its nation-building efforts; some of them may well have felt obliged to be part of this nation-building effort by staying out of the way, at least in the initial phase when the credibility of the Nehru Government was high. This sentiment changed as time went on, and it is possible to read the changing trend across these cases in this light as well.

The next case challenging Parliament's untrammelled power of constitutional amendment arose 14 years later in the case of *Sajjan Singh v State of Rajasthan* (1965).[21] This involved a challenge to the 17th Amendment (1964), which had inserted 44 State laws (a number that originally stood at 124, of which 80 laws were deleted during the drafting process) into the Ninth Schedule to immunise them from judicial review. This case was also decided by a five-judge bench, headed by Chief Justice Gajendragadkar. Chief Justice Gajendragadkar's judgment for the majority of three judges reiterated the logic in *Shankari Prasad* to reject the constitutional challenge: that Parliament had the power to amend the Constitution, even if this led to violations of Fundamental Rights. This time, however, Hidayatullah and Mudholkar JJ issued partial dissents. Both judges, while agreeing with the effect of the majority judgment, expressed doubts about the untrammelled powers of Parliament to amend the Constitution. The separate judgment of Mudholkar J relied on a foreign authority for a crucial part of its reasoning. Mudholkar J's judgment mentions the possibility that there may be certain 'basic features' of the Constitution with which Parliament may not interfere through the exercise of the power under Article 368. This idea of 'basic features' subsequently served as the most significant contribution of *Kesavananda*. The Court's recognition of this notion in the later case was hence foreshadowed by Mudholkar J in *Sajjan Singh*. To illustrate his theme, Mudholkar J cited the judgment of Cornelius CJ in the Pakistan Supreme Court's decision in *Fazlul Quader Chowdhry v Mohd. Abdul Haque* (1963),[22] which held that franchise and form of

[21] *Sajjan Singh v State of Rajasthan*, AIR 1965 SC 845.

[22] *Fazlul Quader Chowdhry v Mohd. Abdul Haque*, 1963 PLD 486.

government were two aspects of the Constitution of Pakistan 1962 that could not be altered by the President of Pakistan. Although the result in *Sajjan Singh* was the same as *Shankari Prasad*, a lot had changed in the 15 years between the rulings. Nehru died while the 17th Amendment was being debated in Parliament and the case was heard while Prime Minister Shastri was in office. The deference shown by the *Shankari Prasad* case was already being questioned by several commentators—the fact that as many as 17 constitutional amendments had been enacted in the relatively short period of time and, more worryingly, the nature of the amendments, was causing disquiet. The two dissenting judges gave voice to these fears and also provided a way to work around the logic of Parliament's absolute power of constitutional amendment.

When this issue came up again for decision in the 1967 case of *Golak Nath v State of Punjab* (1967),[23] the political climate had changed considerably. Although *Golak Nath* was decided only two years after *Sajjan Singh*, there were significant differences. On the political front, Indira Gandhi was now the Prime Minister. At the helm of the Supreme Court was the maverick figure of Subba Rao CJ, who had replaced the pro-establishment, Nehruvian figure of Gajendragadkar CJ. Subba Rao CJ had shown himself in his years as a junior member of the Court to be a fiercely independent figure, who did not share the restrained view of the judiciary that many of his predecessors had embraced. At the time, Indira Gandhi was perceived as a weak ruler and had not yet established the firm command over governance that she was to wield in later years.

Golak Nath was decided by a bench of 11 judges of the Court. Unsurprisingly, the majority judgment was authored by Subba Rao CJ. Speaking for himself and four other judges, Rao CJ held that the prohibition in Article 13(2) would extend to constitutional amendments, thereby rendering Parliament powerless to violate any of the Fundamental Rights in exercise of its amending power. This ruling overturned the law laid down in *Shankari Prasad* and *Sajjan Singh*, amounting to a powerful assertion of the judiciary's power to authoritatively interpret the meaning of the Constitution against the will of Parliament (even where such will was expressed through the high power of constitutional amendment). The separate concurring judgment of Hidayatullah J

[23] *Golak Nath v State of Punjab*, AIR 1967 SC 1643.

(who had also dissented in *Sajjan Singh*) provided crucial support to Rao CJ's judgment. Five judges, speaking through three separate judgments, dissented from the majority's view and chose to uphold the reasoning endorsed in *Shankari Prasad* and *Sajjan Singh*. Significantly, to attend to a necessary consequence of his holding—that a number of Parliamentary laws enacted between 1950 and 1967 would be rendered unconstitutional as a result of his judgment—Rao CJ relied on and adapted the American doctrine of 'prospective over-ruling' to Indian conditions as part of his judgment. Similarly, Hidayatullah J's concurring judgment contains many references to case law and scholarly literature from several jurisdictions on the question of how the power of constitutional amendment is viewed in comparative constitutional law.

The decision in *Golak Nath* galvanised sections of the Congress Party. Prime Minister Indira Gandhi was spurred to take action against the Court and its 'anti-progressive' rulings. However, the precarious political situation at the time (the Congress had, in the fourth general elections held in 1967, won only 283 of 520 seats in the lower house of Parliament) convinced the Prime Minister to bide her time and win support from the people. After winning a massive mandate in the fifth general elections held in 1971 (when the Congress was returned to power with 350 of 520 seats in the lower house of Parliament), Indira Gandhi decided to launch an assault on the courts, and upon the *Golak Nath* ruling in particular.

With her renewed mandate in hand, Indira Gandhi's government enacted the 24th Amendment to the Constitution, which expressly sought to overturn *Golak Nath* by stating that the power of Parliament to amend the Constitution was unrestricted. Under this and ancillary amendments, the Kerala Land Reforms Act 1969 was included in the Ninth Schedule to the Constitution. Swami Kesavananda Bharati was a religious leader of a Math (temple) in Kerala, whose properties and grounds were sought to be acquired by the government of Kerala through the Kerala Land Reforms Act 1969. Consequently, the law was challenged by the religious leader, leading to the decision in April 1973 that is reported as *Kesavananda Bharati v Union of India* (1973).[24]

The decision in *Kesavananda* is the longest judgment, delivered by the largest bench, of the Indian Supreme Court to date. Eleven separate

[24] *Kesavananda Bharati v Union of India* (1973) 4 SCC 225.

judgments were issued by a bench of 13 judges. By a majority of 7:6, the Supreme Court overruled its decision in *Golak Nath* to the extent it had held that Parliament could not amend any of the Fundamental Rights provisions. While the majority upheld the government's argument that Parliament's power to amend the Constitution extended to all parts of the Constitution, it also held that this power did not extend to altering the 'basic features' or 'basic structure' of the Constitution. A minority of six judges held that Parliament's power to amend the Constitution was not subject to any limits. As a consequence of the majority judgment, the challenge to much of the 25th and 26th constitutional Amendments was held to be without force; these amendments were therefore upheld. At the same time, the majority struck down a portion of the 26th Amendment that excluded judicial review, finding this to be a violation of the 'basic structure' doctrine, to the extent that judicial review was a part of the basic features of the Constitution.

On its face, the ruling in *Kesavananda* represents a retreat from the more aggressive position adopted by the Supreme Court in *Golak Nath* (where the Court had held that Parliament could not amend any provision in the Fundamental Liberties chapter). Indeed, by upholding the majority of the 25th and 26th Amendments, the Court appeared to be meekly surrendering to the power of the executive and Parliament. However, by striking down a small portion of the 26th Amendment on the basis of the 'basic features' doctrine, the Court conferred upon itself the crucial power to decide which parts of the Constitution would be off limits for the exercise of such power. Over time, this power has proven to be highly significant and wide reaching; it has been exercised strategically by the Court to enhance its own stature as sole and ultimate interpreter of the Constitution. It is significant that the inspiration for one of the most crucial innovations made by the Court—the incorporation of the doctrine of 'basic features' or 'basic structure'—came from comparative law.

This is most evident in the crucial judgment of Khanna J, who provided the all-important seventh vote for what became the majority view. For the most part, Khanna's judgment hews the line adopted by the minority judges: he held, for instance, that the amending power of Parliament could extend to infringing the Fundamental Rights provisions as there was no wording in Article 368 to indicate otherwise. He also held that the amending power of Parliament could not be subject to any implied limitations, very much in line with the reasoning of the judges in the minority. However, he departed from the dissenters' logic to hold, with the majority, that the amending power was subject to the doctrine of basic structure. Khanna J's decision in many ways contradicts and rejects the reasoning adopted by many of the majority judgments, yet ends up agreeing with their result.

A significant portion of Khanna J's judgment is devoted to examining foreign and comparative law. For a crucial part of his argument, Khanna J relies on an argument made in an academic article published by the German scholar Dieter Conrad, who had visited India in 1965 (delivering, and subsequently publishing, a paper on the amending power). In his paper, Conrad relied on the German experience under the Weimar Constitution and during the regime of Adolf Hitler to make out a case for restricting the power of amending Constitutions. Though unknown to the common law world, the 'basic structure' limitation discussed by Conrad in his 1965 paper was well known in civil law countries. Among others, it had found expression in Article 79(3) of the Basic Law of the Federal Republic of Germany, adopted on 8 May 1949. This provision expressly bars amendments to the provisions concerning the federal structure and to the basic principles laid down in Articles 1 and 20 (on human rights and the democratic and social set-up). In his judgment, in holding the following, Khanna J relied upon Professor Conrad's logic to reason that:

> If the power of amendment does not comprehend the doing away of the entire Constitution but postulates retention or continuity of the existing Constitution, though in an amended form, [the] question arises as to what is the minimum of the existing Constitution which should be left intact in order to hold that the existing Constitution has been retained in an amended form and not done away with. In my opinion, the minimum required is that which relates to the basic structure or framework of the Constitution. If the basic structure is retained, the old Constitution would be considered to continue even though other provisions have undergone change. On the contrary, if the basic structure is changed, mere retention of some articles of the existing Constitution would not warrant a conclusion that the existing Constitution continues and survives.

In Austin's analysis, the Supreme Court in *Kesavananda* 'assert[ed] its institutional role vis-à-vis Parliament in constitutional matters and strengthen[ed] its power of judicial review through the basic structure doctrine'.[25] When the judgment in *Kesavananda* was first pronounced, it was met with outrage among constitutional scholars. Even its staunchest supporters—who emphasised that it was a pragmatic response and a way to tame the colossus that Indira Gandhi's government was in danger of becoming—had to concede that it was weak on legality, jurisprudence and textual support from the Constitution. However, over time, it seems that the pragmatism of the judgment has held sway and has allowed the doctrine to overcome its conceptual and jurisprudential deficiencies.

Across the next decade after the decision in *Kesavananda*, its central reasoning was reiterated in three major decisions of the Supreme Court. In the case of *Indira Nehru Gandhi v Raj Narain* (1975),[26] the Supreme Court struck down the 29th Amendment (1975), which sought to immunise Prime Minister Indira Gandhi's election dispute from judicial review on the ground that it violated the basic feature of democracy. Five years later, in the case of *Minerva Mills v Union of India* (1980),[27] the Supreme Court struck down the 42nd Amendment (1976) for violating the basic feature of a limited amending power. And finally, in the case of *Waman Rao v Union of India* (1980),[28] the Supreme Court held that laws inserted into the Ninth Schedule could be tested on the ground of exclusion of judicial review.

In later years, the basic structure doctrine was invoked by the Indian Supreme Court to assert that the features of secularism, judicial review and the individual rights to equality, life and fundamental freedoms (guaranteed by Articles 14, 21 and 19 respectively) were inviolable.[29] Over time, this doctrine has come to be one of the most momentous innovations of the Indian judiciary; it has allowed Indian judges to adopt radical strategies of initiating public interest litigation, using methods such as the creative remedy of continuing mandamus (through which it can keep a case alive even after it has been decided,

[25] Granville Austin, *Working a Democratic Constitution: A History of the Indian Experience* (New Delhi, Oxford University Press, 2000) 258.

[26] *Indira Nehru Gandhi v Raj Narain*, AIR 1975 SC 2299.

[27] *Minerva Mills v Union of India*, AIR 1980 SC 1789.

[28] *Waman Rao v Union of India* (1981) 2 SCC 363.

[29] For the cases in which these positions were taken, see Arvind P Datar, 'The Basic Structure Doctrine—A 37 year Journey' in Sanjay S Jain and Sathya Narayan (eds), *Basic Structure Constitutionalism: Revisiting* Kesavananda Bharati (Lucknow, Eastern Book Company, 2011) 159–67.

sometimes for decades, to ensure its implementation). While these powers had never been employed by any judiciary anywhere, the Indian judiciary could employ them because it had already reached for and enjoyed perhaps the greatest power any institution can enjoy in a constitutional democracy: the power to decide whether the constituent power of amendment can be invoked validly or not.

V. CONSTITUTIONAL CHANGE THROUGH CONSTITUTIONAL MOMENTS

In the US constitutional context, the American scholar Bruce Ackerman has argued that constitutional change occurs also through constitutional moments. As critics who have engaged with Ackerman's account in comparative perspective have noted, despite some failings, its great merit lies in alerting constitutional lawyers to periods of 'constitutional change, prompted by the failure of formal rules of constitutional amendment that are designed to constitute and regulate constitutional politics without becoming part of it'.[30] This is an interesting concept and it is arguable that the changes brought about by Prime Minister Narasimha Rao's Congress government in 1991 amount to such a period of constitutional change, although the changes heralded were not brought about either by using the formal constitutional provisions of amendment or through the mode of constitutional interpretation.

The advent of economic liberalisation in India in the early 1990s fundamentally altered the structure and operation of the State as it had evolved across the post-independence phase from the 1950s to the start of the 1990s. It has already been noted, in Chapter 5, how the advent of new regulatory institutions in the telecom, electricity, securities and other sectors has radically altered the balance of power between the traditional wings of government. Simultaneously, the creation and operation of these new institutional contexts is transforming the discourse of regulation, governance and policy making. There are other, more subtle ways, through which the changes since 1991 have made their presence felt. Ideas dating from the Nehruvian period—whether

[30] Sujit Choudhry, 'Ackerman's Higher Lawmaking in Comparative Constitutional Perspective: Constitutional Moments as Constitutional Failures?' [2008] 6 *International Journal of Constitutional Law* (I.CON) 192.

relating to economics or the relationship between religion, politics and governance—have become discredited and are openly challenged in ways that were difficult to imagine even as late as the 1980s.

VI. CONCLUSION

A recent comprehensive study of the processes of constitutional change across several jurisdictions concluded as follows in relation to the Indian constitutional experience: 'India's Constitution is probably the most sophisticated in establishing a great variety of procedures to adapt and change its arrangements based upon the careful selection of different matters (almost a model of variable rigidity or even flexible rigiditiy)'.[31] This assessment draws attention to the vision of the framers of the Indian Constitution, who crafted a three-pronged mode of constitutional amendment which sought to balance several factors, including the correct mix of rigidity and flexibility, but also the way India's particular models of national unity and federalism could be sustained over a period of time. While discussing matters of amendment, scholars both within and outside India tend to focus on the judicially developed doctrine of basic structure. While this doctrine is innovative and deserves attention, it often draws attention away from many other important issues relating to constitutional change in the Indian constitutional tradition, including through the process of constitutional moments. This chapter has sought to restore some balance in that skewed focus.

FURTHER READING

Granville Austin, *The Indian Constitution: Cornerstone of a Nation* (New Delhi, Oxford University Press, 1966).

Upendra Baxi, 'The Constitutional Quicksands of Kesavananda Bharati and the Twenty-Fifth Amendment' [1974] *Supreme Court Cases* 45.

[31] D Oliver and C Fusaro (eds), *How Constitutions Change: A Comparative Study* (Oxford, Hart Publishing, 2011) 425.

Gary J Jacobsohn, *Constitutional Identity* (Cambridge, MA, Harvard University Press, 2010).

Sanjay S Jain and Sathya Narayan (eds), *Basic Structure Constitutionalism: Revisiting* Kesavananda Bharati (Lucknow, Eastern Book Company, 2011).

Madhav Khosla, 'Constitutional Amendment' in Sujit Choudhry, Madhav Khosla and Pratap Mehta (eds), *The Oxford Handbook of the Indian Constitution* (Oxford, Oxford University Press, 2016) 232–50.

Sudhir Krishnaswamy, *Democracy and Constitutionalism in India: A Study of the Basic Structure Doctrine* (New Delhi, Oxford University Press, 2009).

Raju Ramachandran, 'The Supreme Court and the *Basic Structure* Doctrine' in BN Kirpal et al (eds), *Supreme But Not Infallible: Essays in Honour of the Supreme Court of India* (New Delhi, Oxford University Press, 2000).

SP Sathe, *Judicial Activism in India* (New Delhi, Oxford University Press, 2003).

PK Tripathi, *Some Insights into Fundamental Rights* (Bombay, University of Bombay, 1972).

Conclusion

Overview of Prime Minister Modi's influential term (2014–17) – Assessing India's constitutional journey across seven decades – Concluding reflections

I. INTRODUCTION

THIS FINAL CHAPTER has two broad objectives: to briefly update the narrative of the Indian constitutional order up to the present, and to offer an overall assessment of the project of constitutional democracy that was inaugurated in India in January 1950 and completes 67 years in 2017. The first part of the chapter focuses on the policies of Prime Minister Narendra Modi's government, which has been in power since mid-2014. Reactions to the Modi Government's policies enable an assessment of the perennial fears expressed both by external and internal commentators about the capacity of the Indian constitutional order to survive, given the many challenges it confronts. The second part of the chapter briefly summarises the views of some leading scholars on the trajectory of India's constitutional journey to conduct an assessment of its present and future.

A focus on the contemporary period is necessary because this book has, for reasons explained in the Introduction, focused on the overall trajectory of India's constitutional journey from the colonial era onwards. This has necessarily resulted in a very broad-brush treatment of specific constitutional developments in particular eras along the post-independence trajectory. A focus on the specific policies of Prime Minister Narendra Modi's government seeks to provide a counterweight to this general tendency. In addition, such a focus will help draw attention to a period of potentially crucial significance for the future development of the Indian constitutional order. This is because the policies of Prime Minister Narendra Modi's government have arguably already brought about significant changes in the legal, political and constitutional landscape of India.

In 2017 India completes 70 years of existence as an independent nation. This seems an opportune time to conduct an assessment of its experience with constitutionalism, at a time when constitutionalism as a foundational concept and practice is facing challenges in every major region of the world and there is deep concern and reflection on what makes for an enduring culture of constitutionalism.

II. A BRIEF OVERVIEW OF PRIME MINISTER MODI'S TENURE (2014–17) THROUGH A CONSTITUTIONAL LENS

Between April and May 2014 the citizens of India voted in a general election to elect a new Central government and a new Prime Minister to emerge from the 16th Lok Sabha that would be constituted as a result. As with each of the 15 general elections held in India since 1951–52, these were the largest elections ever held in human history. They were conducted under the supervision of the Election Commission of India, which, as noted earlier, is a crucial constitutional institution and has achieved a good measure of success in reducing electoral fraud and violence in India. Some numbers provided by the Election Commission help to get a sense of the scale of the event: a total of 814.5 million eligible voters cast votes for 543 parliamentary constituencies. In order to ensure that the elections were conducted fairly and smoothly, they had to be held across nine phases, and lasted five weeks, between 7 April and 14 May 2014.

The campaign of the Bharatiya Janata Party was spearheaded by Narendra Modi. Candidate Modi was a controversial choice for Prime Minister, given his tenure as the Chief Minister of the western state of Gujarat during the 2002 riots, which led to the killing of over a thousand Muslims and sparked universal outrage. This, combined with the general image of the BJP as a right wing party that caters primarily to its Hindu constituency, gave rise to fears among moderate Hindus and minorities that a victory for the BJP would imperil secularism and other values entrenched in the Constitution of India. (Such fears were likewise expressed throughout the 1999–2004 period when the BJP was the leading party in a coalition that ruled India from the Centre). The 2014 general election could, therefore, be viewed as having greater significance than usual.

When the results of the general election were announced on 16 May 2014, they fully met expectations of an extraordinary political event. The BJP garnered 282/554 Lok Sabha seats on its own, which is the largest number of seats won by a national party since 1984. Together with other parties in the National Democratic Alliance (NDA) coalition, the BJP government controls 336 seats in the 554-member lower house of Parliament. What is also striking is that the BJP under candidate Modi secured only 31.4 per cent of the overall vote. That this translated into a massive majority in Parliament is as much a function of India's constitutional design, which adopts a first-past-the-post system to declare a candidate as having won a constituency.

The 2014 general election was undoubtedly a watershed event in Indian political and constitutional history. Although the BJP heads a coalition government, it is the first Central government since 1989 to have a parliamentary majority of a single national party on its own. This makes the BJP Central government less susceptible to the pressures of its political allies than any Indian government has been in the past quarter-century. The result also confounded expectations of pundits who had assumed that Indian constitutional democracy had entered into a permanent phase of coalition governments since the early 1990s. At the time of writing, the BJP controls 70 out of the 243 seats in the upper house of Parliament. However, in state elections held since 2014, the BJP has continued its winning ways, and at the time of writing is in power in 16 out of the 20 States in India. This has the potential of being translated into a controlling majority in the upper house, which will give the BJP the power to push through legislative changes of its choosing.

This section briefly reviews some significant constitutional issues that have occurred between 2014 and 2017. They can be classified under the following heads: (i) judiciary–executive tensions; (ii) secularism controversies; (iii) civil liberties and related issues.

A. Judiciary–Executive Tensions

As noted in several chapters, the Indian judiciary has—perhaps in keeping with its constitutionally designed role—often had prickly relations with governments over time. Commentators have noted that the judiciary's expansive role from the late 1980s onwards—when coalition governments were noticeably weaker and less able to resist attempts to take over core governance functions—was always resented by the two other wings of government. However, little concrete action was taken to reverse this trend because of the political challenges involved. Meanwhile, the judiciary not only expanded its own powers through creative and sometimes outlandish acts of interpretation, but also took over almost entirely the important function of making appointments to the higher judiciary within India. It was therefore not altogether surprising that the Modi Government's first major policy initiative was an effort to clip the wings of the judiciary, by reclaiming the executive's primary role in making judicial appointments. The NDA Government initiated a constitutional amendment in Parliament to wrest back control in the process of appointment of judges in August 2014, and expeditiously completed the process of passing into law the Constitution (99th Amendment) Act 2014 and the accompanying National Judicial Appointments Commission Act 2014. It is significant that despite their differences with the government of the day on a number of issues, the major national and regional parties joined the government in endorsing the creation of the National Judicial Appointments Commission, a move that had extensive support across the political spectrum.

With almost equal alacrity, the Supreme Court of India expedited the hearings of the case filed by a lawyers' association which challenged the constitutional validity of these two actions of the legislature. On 16 October 2015 a five-judge Constitution bench of the Supreme Court struck down the constitutional amendment and the parliamentary law which established the National Judicial Appointments Commission as unconstitutional and void.[1] This created an impasse that extends to the time of writing. Both the government and judiciary seem quite set in their respective stances and it is not clear how the issue will be resolved in the near future.

These actions of the NDA Government seem to have had the desired effect in other respects—some commentators believe that the judiciary as a whole has respected considerations of separation of powers far more since 2014 and that judges have been more circumspect in issuing expansive orders. There is also the concern that some judges have consciously been toeing the line of the government, thereby acknowledging the soft power of a powerful executive.

[1] *Supreme Court Advocates-on-Record Association v Union of India* 2015 SCC Online SC 964.

B. Secularism Concerns

From the start of the NDA Government's term in May 2014, there have been persistent concerns that the balance in respect of issues of secularism has turned in favour of Hindu right wing groups, which have always demanded a greater space for their fundamentalist views and correspondingly, a lesser role and space for the views of minority groups that challenge the more stridently nationalist voices in the Indian public sphere. These issues have ranged from the relatively trivial dispute over the use of the original Preamble (which did not contain the word 'secularism') as part of an official Republic Day advertisement, to far more serious events involving the targeting of sections of religious minorities involving first the use of hate speech by prominent leaders associated with the Hindu Right, followed by acts of violence and murder. The lynching of a Muslim senior citizen following rumours that he had consumed beef in his home in September 2015 in Dadri, located very close to the national capital, was a particularly tragic case that has yet to be resolved. While the anti-cow slaughter movement has deep roots in Indian history extending back to the colonial era, the return to power of the NDA appears to have emboldened vigilante groups across the nation, resulting in large-scale reports of harassment of minority communities who eat beef. There have been similar reports of violence against young couples who have sought to have inter-religious alliances and marriages. Muslim and Christian communities, in particular, have reported an increase in incidences of acts of violence against them which are expressly motivated by religious difference. These figures have been confirmed by independent NGOs and press reports.

Such acts of violence and aggression have not been restricted to minority communities. Hindus who do not subscribe to fundamentalist views by, for instance, campaigning against superstition and advocating the virtues of scientific temper, have also been targeted. Across western and south India, a range of anti-superstition activists, many of whom were Hindu, have been targeted and in some cases murdered.

Hindu Right groups have a long history of seeking to control education processes in areas where they gain political control, including during the first stint of the NDA at the centre between 1999 and 2004. These trends have also witnessed an increase in recent years. Since the Central government has the prerogative of making important appointments to crucial educational ministries and institutions, there have been several instances of persons with ties to right wing Hindu organisations being appointed to important positions such as the Chairperson of the Indian Council of Historical Research and Vice Chancellors of important Central universities. In many states and even at the Central level, the Ministry of Human Resource Development has initiated policies which seek to revise school and university curricula to present a revisionist version of history that is closer to the understanding of the Hindu Right.

C. Civil Liberties Issues, Restrictions on Free Speech and Media Rights, etc

It is important to emphasise that in the recent past, nearly all Indian governments have been guilty of trampling on the civil liberties of citizens and other persons in India. However, the nature of these violations since 2014 has a distinct pattern, which can be attributed to the nature of cultural politics that the BJP is particularly adept at engaging in.

Since the latter half of 2014, Hindu right wing groups have begun taking strident nationalist positions and have policed those whom they view as 'anti-national' or unpatriotic. This has very often resulted in criminal legal action because many of India's antiquated laws that continue from colonial times enable prosecutions for offences like sedition and criminal defamation on minimal—even arbitrary—grounds. This in turn led to counter-movements such as the initiative in 2015 when a number of prominent artists and writers began returning governmentally conferred awards in protest against the rising intolerance in the country.

The demand for beef bans has become, as expected, more strident since the coming into power of the BJP Government at the centre. In March 2015 the State of Maharashtra banned the slaughter, sale, consumption and possession of beef by amending an existing law. The BJP had recently won State elections in Maharashtra and the implementation of the long-pending law was seen as a fulfilment of a campaign promise. Under the stringent law, those found selling or eating beef can face up to five years in jail as well as a fine that could extend up to Rs 10,000. This has been accompanied by vigilante groups setting upon people they suspect of eating beef or slaughtering cows, often without any real evidence to back up their claims. This has emboldened other groups, such as the band of young men in the southern State of Karnataka, who threaten headscarf-wearing female lecturers in local universities for engaging in 'unIndian' conduct.

More troubling have been government-led efforts, such as the imposition of a travel ban on a Greenpeace activist, Priya Pillai, who in January 2015 was stopped by an immigration officer at New Delhi airport while she was en route to address a British parliamentary committee on the anti-tribal activities of a British-registered company. Pillai filed a writ petition before the High Court of Delhi where the government argued that her 'anti-development' efforts would impede foreign investment in India and were therefore 'anti-national'. A single judge of the Delhi High court issued judgment in her favour and struck down the 'Look out Circular' issued in her name by the government. Shortly after this, the judge in question was transferred to the opposite end of the country, apparently against his wishes, giving rise to speculation that this was a direct effect of his courageous—and constitutionally correct—ruling.

This was not an isolated incident. Prominent NGOs that have run campaigns to bring justice to victims of the Gujarat 2002 riots have faced particularly harsh treatment from tax, foreign exchange and intelligence authorities. These include activists such as Teesta Setalvad (whose continuing regulatory struggles have brought a halt to her activist campaigns) and public interest law NGOs such as the Lawyers Collective. There have been similar government-led campaigns against a host of other NGOs, which have officially been justified as an attack on corruption through the use of foreign funds by governments and Northern NGOs.

On other fronts, too, basic constitutional values are under threat. The Modi Government has championed legislative Bills that seek to provide Hindus from around the world extensive and expedited citizenship rights, while the same are unavailable to Muslims in particular, but also to people of Indian origin who belong to other faiths. This risks adding a dangerous dimension of communalism to India's already complicated citizenship laws.

Media organisations have also been cowed under various pressures. Journalists who have been critical of key figures in government have been shunted out by their corporate backers, apparently because the latter did not want to risk the ire of the government. Media consolidation within a few corporate groups has had similar effects to the consolidation of the media in the US. Indeed, there seems to be a conscious mimicking of efforts to muzzle the free press in both large democratic societies.

Together, these various issues provide an overview of the factors which lead many commentators to believe that the Indian constitutional order is confronting fundamental challenges that may affect its ability to survive and endure.

III. ASSESSING INDIA'S CONSTITUTIONAL TRAJECTORY ACROSS SEVEN DECADES (1947–2017)

The fears expressed about the capacity of the Indian constitutional order to survive recall similar fears that have been expressed about politics in the Indian subcontinent as a whole across the last two centuries. In the early colonial period, it was India's many diversities—and the inherent instability they represented—which became an important justification for colonial rule in India. Many colonial figures believed that it was the imposition of English ideas of governance and rule of law that alone could keep India's warring tribes apart. Such figures also asserted that the persistence of colonial rule was a necessity in order to prevent the Hindu majority from oppressing the many minority faiths and cultures that existed in the Indian subcontinent. On the eve of independence in 1947, such fears were shared by many Indians themselves, including members of minority groups such as Muslims and Christians and by those in the Depressed Classes, who, while Hindu, feared that they would be victims of caste Hinduism in a free India.

The historian Ramachandra Guha has coined the term 'Unnatural nation' to characterise India's attempt at becoming a nation state.[2] As he details, India represented an anomaly because it sought to build a nation state without having what was considered essential for a nation: the presence of a single factor around which people could be mobilised and organised. Historically, this had occurred around a single religion or language, but given its multiplicities on these counts, independent India could not opt for a single pivot around which a national identity could be constructed. The framers of India's Constitution were treading

[2] Ramachandra Guha, *India After Gandhi* (London, Picador, 2007) xxi–xxvi and 744–71.

uncharted territory in seeking to build a nation on grounds other than the conventional prerequisites. India's survival as a constitutional order gains importance when viewed against the experience of its neighbours in South Asia, where such traditional markers of nationhood were pursued, often to disastrous effect. The state of Pakistan was created on the basis of religion, but broke apart on the question of language and these factors continue to be divisive in present-day Pakistan and Bangladesh. In the 1940s Ceylon was regarded as the colony most likely to succeed as an independent nation in Asia, given its relatively high levels of human development, the robust state of the colonial economy in Ceylon, and the absence of violence in the transfer of power from the British to the indigenous political elite. However, the preference for a single language by the national leaders of Sri Lanka in the initial years of independence led to simmering tensions that culminated in a long civil war which has left the nation in a perilous state, even though recent events provide hope for a strong constitutional vision.

Along similar lines, the political scientist Sudipta Kaviraj has noted that the Indian experience at seeking to build a democratic governmental order defied all the preconditions that political theory lays down for the success of democratic government, based, of course, upon the rise of democratic forms in the modern West. These preconditions go beyond those identified by Guha above to cover the following: 'the presence of a strong bureaucratic state, capitalist production, industrialization, the secularization of society (or at least the prior existence of a secular state) and relative economic prosperity'.[3] Kaviraj suggests that the Indian experience should cause scholars of political theory to view these supposed preconditions as historically contingent factors that accompanied the rise of West European democracies that may not apply to other contexts. In this sense, the Indian experience may be revelatory of important insights from the perspective of post-colonial societies.

Historians of post-independence India have noted that the journey of Indian constitutionalism has been riddled throughout with obstacles, hurdles and severe challenges.[4] Independence in 1947 was

[3] Sudipta Kaviraj, *The Enchantment of Democracy and India* (New Delhi, Permanent Black, 2011) 2.

[4] The summary overview in this paragraph draws from the recent writings of Ramachandra Guha, whose several books on post-independence India cover

accompanied by the horrors of Partition, which posed manifold legal, political, administrative, financial and human costs in the short run and continues to extract a heavy psychological cost in the contemporary moment. Soon after the adoption of the Constitution in 1950, the nation had to confront the challenge of linguistic claims, which was resolved by acceding to demands for the creation of territorial units or States on the basis of language. Around the same time, the Naga insurgency in the north-east picked up steam, leading to concerns that there would be similar upsurges across the region. In the 1960s anti-Hindi protests in the State of Tamil Nadu created mass unrest; this was accompanied by the rise of the Naxalite movement in the States of West Bengal and Andhra Pradesh. The 1970s witnessed the imposition of the internal Emergency, which is still regarded as the darkest hour of India's constitutional democracy. The 1980s were witness to violent separatist movements in the states of Punjab and Assam. Religious and caste identities were brought into sharp conflict in the 1990s, a period which also saw the introduction of policies of economic liberalisation that brought about massive changes in the way Indian governance had worked itself out across the first four decades between 1950 and 1990. These changes caused disruption on a wide scale that affected poor, marginalised and working class communities in particular. The Gujarat riots of 2002 and a slew of farmer suicides are but two major markers of the 2000s. The 2010s, while still unfolding, have witnessed a widespread mistrust of elected leaders, particularly during the scandal-ridden tenure of the UPA Government from 2009 to 2014, which caused commentators to describe the period as a low point for constitutional governance and trust in public authorities in India.

A. Longitudinal Assessments of Indian Society and Its Constitutional Politics

This section provides an overview of assessments of India's democratic and constitutional journey by distinguished observers—both foreign and Indian—at different points of time. This historical and

this subject repeatedly. I draw in particular on two of these books: Ramachandra Guha, *Patriots and Partisans* (New Delhi, Allen Lane, 2012) and Guha, *Democrats and Dissenters* (New Delhi, Allen Lane, 2016).

scholarly perspective on the task of assessing India's experience will enable an assessment of India's Constitution in the contemporary period with an eye towards gaps and challenges that will have to be tackled in the future.

Scholars who study the constitutional politics of India have often had to confront the following puzzle: how is it that a country with so many contending social forces, characterised by high levels of everyday strife, struggle and violence, has nevertheless remained united politically, has retained a fairly stable parliamentary democracy, and has been largely successful economically?

Some scholars have suggested that at least part of the solution is to be found in India's constitutional design. Granville Austin—whose scholarship has informed the analysis of several chapters in this volume—offered two assessments of Indian constitutional democracy across two different periods. The first, offered in 1966 at the time of the publication of his classic work on the making of the Indian Constitution, was much more positive. Writing nearly two decades after independence, Austin declared that the Indian Constitution had 'worked well' and endorsed the view that it was, indeed, a 'signal success'.[5] Austin backed up this claim by noting that there were many indications that the Indian Constitution had been effective. The first piece of evidence he offered was 'the smoothness with which a successor government to that of Prime Minister Nehru was chosen' upon his death in 1964. Austin highlighted the importance of this factor by making a comparative reference—to the smothering of democracy in Ghana 'by the very factors that protected it in India, a charismatic leader and a mass party'.[6] Secondly, Austin emphasised that the Constitution had anticipated difficulties in respect of the linguistic division of States and the issue had been resolved within the framework of the Constitution. He noted other examples where the institutions envisaged by the Constitution had worked to head off crises. Austin's third claim was that the Indian Constitution 'had provided a framework for social and political development, a rational institutional basis for political behaviour'. By doing so, Austin asserted, 'a strong, positive counterforce to political

[5] Granville Austin, *The Indian Constitution: Cornerstone of a Nation* (New Delhi, Oxford University Press, 1966) 308.

[6] ibid 329.

and social authoritarianism had been established'.[7] Austin attributed these successes principally to the fact that the Indian Constitution had been 'framed by Indians, and in the excellence of the framing process itself'.[8] Austin's somewhat grandiose praise for the Indian experiment with constitutionalism has been contested by scholars such as Upendra Baxi who note many problems in Austin's analysis.[9] What is indisputable, however, is that Austin's comparative assessment of India's constitutional order was accurate—by even surviving into its 20th year, India had already bucked the trend of constitutional failures across post-colonial Asia and Africa. In the mid-1960s there were very few examples of vibrant constitutional orders that had lasted beyond the initial exuberance of decolonisation and the rapid burst of Constitution making in the aftermath of the Second World War.

Austin offered a second, more sober assessment of Indian constitutionalism when he published his second book in 2000, which analysed the working of the Indian Constitution from 1950–1985. Writing at a time when the Constitution was marking its 50th year, Austin maintained his view that it had served the Indian people well. He argued that the Constitution had enabled the successful pursuit of the three primary goals of its founders—'establishing the institutions and spirit of democracy; pursuing a social revolution to better the lot of the mass of Indians; and preserving and enhancing the country's integrity and unity'. He was particularly appreciative of the fact that the interdependence of these three goals was well-understood, and each element was regarded as important in its own right. He argued that Indians should be commended for pursuing both democracy and the social revolution simultaneously, and not at the expense of the other, as had occurred in many other nations. He noted that this was particularly salutary in a country whose 'population that in 1950 was about 250 million [had] grown to nearly a billion persons' by 2000, and was marked by 'diversities and disparities without number'. Give this, he argued, the country's political stability and its relatively open society were considerable achievements which were attributable, 'above all' to its Constitution.

7 ibid 310.

8 ibid.

9 Upendra Baxi, 'The Little Done, the Vast Undone: Reflection on Reading Granville Austin's The Indian Constitution' (1967) 9 *Journal of the Indian Law Institute* 323–430.

Austin however conceded that the Emergency had been a 'terrible distortion'. He also noted that while representative democracy had been reasonably pursued, the social revolution 'has gone nowhere near far enough'. Striking a rare note of stridency, Austin argued that '[t]he meagre efforts by government and society's 'haves' to extend liberty and socio-economic reform to the 'have-nots' should be cause for national shame'.[10] Austin's views on issues of economic development—a principal preoccupation of the framers, as evident in their call for a social revolution—are worth noting. He was broadly critical of the achievements of four decades of socialist policy, wryly commenting on the paradox that 'socialism has impaired progress in [achieving] the social revolution'. However, he was equally critical of the policies of economic liberalisation that had, by 2000, been in place for almost a decade. He argued that 'economic liberalization needs to be accompanied by occupational safety and health, and other protections for workers in the private sector'. He was critical of the fact that 'Capitalism in India [was] in a very exploitative stage'. While remaining positive about the prospects of the Constitution on the occasion of its golden jubilee, Austin concluded that the most important objective for the near future was the securing of 'extensive social and economic reform'.[11]

Austin's views emphasise an aspect of Indian constitutionalism that may well be exceptional when compared to the experience of constitutionalism historically. The framers of the Indian Constitution were seeking to pursue the goals of constitutional democracy and economic development simultaneously in a post-colonial setting, something which was quite unprecedented in the annals of constitutionalism. As Upendra Baxi emphasises, the Indian Constitution sough to pursue four goals: *rights*, *justice*, *development* and *governance*. Each of these, he asserts, was intertwined with the other and resulted in contradictory pulls and pushes.[12] The retention of the colonial civil service and the structure and practices of the colonial police led to the replication of colonial practices of closed models of top-down governance, which

[10] Granville Austin, *Working a Democratic Constitution: A History of the Indian Experience* (New Delhi, Oxford University Press, 2000) 633.

[11] ibid 668.

[12] Upendra Baxi, 'A Known but Indifferent Judge: Situating Ronald Dworkin in Contemporary Indian Jurisprudence' (2003) 1(4) *International Journal of Constitutional Law* (I.CON) 557–89, 582.

continue to sit uneasily with a constitutional culture that promises transparency and accountability.[13] Here, the use of repressive laws dating from the colonial period and the adoption of newer anti-terror laws, which manifest continuing colonial attitudes to oppress the people of Kashmir, self-determination movements in several states in the north-east, and the continuing armed struggle of Maoist groups, stand out as jarring notes in an orchestral consensus around progressive constitutional values.

Somewhat paradoxically, the Indian State is chastised by social welfare activists for *doing little* to meet constitutional mandates in relation to provision of social welfare, while simultaneously attracting criticism from civil rights activists for *over-using and abusing* constitutional powers in relation to national security to oppress other populations. These contradictory practices, Baxi emphasises, are equally enabled by the conflicting objectives sought to be attained by the framers of India's Constitution.

What has complicated the journey of the Indian legal and political order as it has approached these objectives are the massive changes occurring alongside. Guha has described India as undergoing five revolutions—on the urban, industrial, national, democratic and social fronts—simultaneously. The 250 million people who inhabited the territory of India in 1947 are now 1.2 billion in number. What was a rural, agriculture-based economy has moved towards industry and services, marked by massive urbanisation, especially in more recent times. A political culture that was feudal and based on hierarchy and deference has now become participatory and adversarial. Social systems built on patriarchal and community-oriented edifices that were deeply exclusionary have had to respect the assertion of individual rights as well as those of groups that had been historically subordinated, including women, the lower castes and tribal groups.[14]

India was one of the early examples of this simultaneous pursuit of constitutionalism and development, which later become emblematic of post-colonial Constitutions. Such a trend continues in the present, as is borne out by the provisions of the 2015 Constitution of Nepal, several

[13] Upendra Baxi, *The Crisis of the Indian Legal System* (New Delhi, Vikas Publishing House, 1982) 1–57.

[14] Ramachandra Guha, *Makers of Modern India* (New Delhi, Penguin India, 2010) 4–5.

of which exhort the Nepalese State to pursue multi-dimensional developmental goals, and appear inspired by the Indian precedent.[15]

Given the significance of the twinned objectives of constitutionalism and development for the Indian constitutional order, this brief survey concludes with the views of the developmental economists Jean Dreze and Amartya Sen, who have jointly tracked India's progress in securing its constitutionally ordained democratic and developmental objectives for nearly three decades. Starting with an initial focus on governmental policies relating to famines, hunger and starvation, their scholarship has gradually taken on a broader focus, extending eventually to a vast range of issues at the core of democracy, governance and development in India.[16] I focus here on their most recent book, *An Uncertain Glory*, published in 2013, which places significant emphasis on India's constitutional vision and policy.

Dreze and Sen note that constitutional democracy in India has had major achievements, including on the economic front. As economists, they have a deep appreciation of the fact that the Indian economy has gradually evolved from the low rates of growth during the colonial era (when GDP rates were as low as 0.9 per cent) to moderate rates in the period from 1950 to 1980 (when GDP rates hovered around 3 per cent) to increasingly higher rates from 1980 to 1991 (average GDP rate of 5.2 per cent), 1990 to 2001 (average GDP rate of 5.9 per cent) and 2000 to 2011 (average GDP rate of 7.6 per cent), while maintaining and consolidating democratic forms of governance in one of the poorest countries of the world. Other nations, especially in Asia, have achieved far higher GDP rates, but have often done so by compromising on principles of constitutional governance, especially in the crucial formative years, the effects of which have arguably continued to afflict them even after their later embrace of forms of constitutional democracy. This makes, for Dreze and Sen, India's embrace—and sustenance—of full-blown constitutional democracy from the outset a considerable achievement.

[15] See Constitution of Nepal 2015 (specifically, the provisions of Part 4 (Articles 49–55) relating to 'Directive Principles, Policies and Responsibilities of the State').

[16] The most important books that detail this trajectory are: Jean Dreze and AK Sen, *Hunger and Public Action* (Oxford, Clarendon, 1989); *India: Economic Development and Social Opportunity* (Delhi, Oxford University Press, 1995); *India: Development and Participation* (Oxford, Oxford University Press, 2002); and *An Uncertain Glory: India and its Contradictions* (London, Allan Lane, 2013).

Dreze and Sen note that the changes in Indian economic conditions are also reflected in social factors, gauged through changes in human development indicators:

> Life expectancy in India today (about 66 years) is more than twice what it was in 1951 (32 years); infant mortality is about one fourth what it used to be (44 per thousand live birth today as opposed to 180 in 1951); and the female literacy rate has gone up from 9 per cent to 65 per cent.[17]

Having noted these accomplishments, Dreze and Sen then focus on the many failings of India's legal, political and constitutional order, which are, for them, manifold and deeply troubling. Earlier it was noted that many of India's accomplishments in the constitutional sphere have to be appreciated by adopting a comparative approach. When one views the many failures of constitutional democracy after the enthusiastic embrace of constitutionalism across Asia and Africa in the aftermath of decolonisation, a more radiant hue is imparted to India's mixed but relatively more positive experience with constitutional democracy. Dreze and Sen seek to assess India's developmental achievements through a similar comparative analysis, to quite the opposite effect. Having noted that India's human development indices have progressively improved when contrasted with the very low levels that they began with at independence in 1947, Dreze and Sen draw attention to the fact that India has not fared particularly well when viewed through a comparative lens. India's human development indicators place it among some of the poorest countries of the world. On counts such as mean years of schooling and access to sanitation facilities, India's human development scores are worse than those of Vietnam, Moldova and Uzbekistan. Dreze and Sen emphasise that in recent years India's scores have been lower than those of other South Asian countries whose scores have been improving at a faster rate than those of India, which has far higher levels of GDP per capita. While Bangladesh continues to be much poorer than India, it has overtaken India on counts such as life expectancy, child survival, enhanced immunisation rates and reduced fertility rates. While India's growing geopolitical power is acknowledged by its being included in groups such as the BRICS (a bloc including

[17] Dreze and Sen, *An Uncertain Glory* (n 16) 5.

Brazil, Russia, India, China and South Africa), it fares quite poorly when compared to these nations in human development terms. While each of the other four nations has universal or near-universal literacy in the younger age groups, one-fifth of all Indian men between the ages of 15 and 24 and one-fifth of women in this age group were unable to read and write in 2006. The figures regarding immunisation of children are similarly lopsided.

What is striking is that India has some of the lowest allocation of funds for public support, social welfare or economic redistribution, even among low-income countries. This underscores the very low investment in welfare systems by India's political leaders historically, from Nehru to Modi. This is particularly damning given the many provisions in the Constitution that relate to providing for the social welfare of the poorest and most marginalised sections of India's population. Dreze and Sen are particularly harsh in their critique of successive Indian governments' approach to the crucial issues of education and health care, both of which are in a state of severe crisis in the contemporary period. They focus in particular on issues of inequality and the lack of discussion about crucial issues in the media and other democratic spaces. Dreze and Sen highlight the issue of open defecation, which is more widespread in India than in any other nation: as late as 2011, half of Indian houses did not have a functioning toilet. These facts detailing extreme poverty and suffering are, for Dreze and Sen, deeply worrying because they indicate a complete absence of voice of those suffering from such concerns. They also note the equally worrying tendency in the years since liberalisation signalling 'the biases of public policy towards privileged interests … including the neglect of agriculture and rural development, the tolerance of environmental plunder for private gain, and the showering of public subsidies on privileged groups'.[18]

Dreze and Sen conclude with a ringing endorsement of India's choice of a constitutional democratic model while strongly rejecting the idea that an authoritarian regime would deliver better results in the context of India's vast multiplicities. While appreciative of India's many hard-fought achievements in the democratic arena, they highlight

[18] ibid 286.

issues which the institutions of democracy have continued to neglect—particularly in relation to the worst-off in Indian society—and issue a call for action on these fronts.

Dreze and Sen's focus on changes in Indian policy making in the last quarter-century since liberalisation is significant and worth emphasising. Although they remain strong supporters of liberal economic policies, many others have noted the deleterious effects of a combination of distressing policy choices that dominate the legal and political spheres in the contemporary period. These have resulted in a mix of pro-market policies, combined with continuing low levels of public investment in social welfare goals, regressive labour laws which leave workers in several spheres unprotected or open to exploitation, and a general lack of systemic means to impose accountability upon state or corporate activity that leads to political and societal corruption on a massive scale.[19]

What these recent analyses highlight is the crisis of legal, political and constitutional institutions in India.[20] Given the demographic and environmental projections for India's future, these challenges are only going to be exacerbated in the short and medium term. There is, unquestionably, a deep sense of distrust in India's democratic institutions. This is perhaps inevitable in any constitutional order, but the gap between the Constitution's high normative foundations and the lows reached in the practice of everyday politics in India are only increasing over time. It is this context which makes the appeal of strongman politics, which promises to provide quick fixes to long-standing problems, stronger. For those who aspire to continue along the path of constitutional means, the challenge will be to resuscitate constitutional institutions and principles to ensure that the allure of authoritarian politics is resisted.

[19] There is a growing body of journalistic literature which covers this narrative through well-chosen case studies and vignettes. See, eg, Neelesh Misra and Rahul Pandita, *The Absent State* (Delhi, Hachette India, 2010) and Josy Joseph, *A Feast of Vultures* (Noida, Uttar Pradesh, Harper Collins, 2016).

[20] A recent volume which focuses on various aspects of the crisis of public institutions in India is Devesh Kapur, Pratap Mehta and Milan Vaishnav (eds), *Rethinking Public Institutions in India* (New Delhi, Oxford University Press, 2017).

IV. CONCLUDING REFLECTIONS

In reviewing the Indian constitutional experience, one is struck by the sense of adventure, hope and optimism displayed by its framers, who lived through some of the darkest periods of world and South Asian history. It was perhaps inevitable that the nearly seven-decade-long experience of the working of the Constitution of India has not witnessed the realisation of many of the aspirations of the framing generation. Still, what is remarkable about that vision—regardless of whether one views it as successful or not—is the fact that the terms of the constitutional discourse set by the framing generation are still acknowledged by principal constitutional actors in the contemporary period as relevant and significant. This is so even as that vision has become obsolete in some respects and new issues that were not originally envisaged have become salient in the contemporary moment.

The contemporary moment is of great significance for the health and future of constitutional government in India. Prime Minister Modi's style of governance runs counter to much of what has preceded it in India's post-independence history, and some of his methods have drawn praise and admiration from many quarters of the Indian public. Yet, for constitutionalists—as the first section of this chapter has sought to demonstrate—there are many worrying concerns. Whatever may be the merits of his government's achievements, even his supporters will admit that the Modi Government does not adhere to constitutional values that counsel the virtues of moderation, proceeding after consulting all affected interests and making every effort to be inclusive. Swift, decisive, often secretive actions which seek to 'shock and awe' appear to be the methods of choice of the Modi Government. Given that post-independence governance in India, even at its best, has continued the tendencies of colonial forms of governance, this new style of governance marks a disturbing trend where such methods are hailed rather than criticised. To be fair, and to ward off the charge of 'presentism', India's constitutional journey has seen far darker times, such as during the Emergency, when the situation was much more bleak. It may well be that constitutional government in India will survive this phase too. However, given the turmoil of the last few years, it is reasonable to observe that Indian constitutionalism may be undergoing a particularly significant churning, which has the potential to change quite drastically the way citizens and government engage with each other as they move forward towards a common future.

At this critical juncture in the journey of Indian constitutionalism it becomes even more important that there is a renewed debate and understanding about the nature and scope of the constitutional culture that was ushered in by the new constitutional order in 1950, and what the contours of this order are at the present time. This requires both a turn to constitutional history and a deeper understanding of contemporary politics to gain a deeper insight into the paradoxes of the contemporary period, where elections are throwing up populist figures who claim to stand aside from party politics and ask voters to trust in their ability to bring about foundational change through the force of their personalities. Consequently, there is a rise in authoritarianism and in the concentration of political power in the hands of specific individuals. Some of this can be understood through an exploration of India's peculiar mix of institutions and the complex politics that have led to the current state. Such an understanding can also be aided by looking at comparative law and politics since similar phenomena and leaders are rising in many other parts of the world. There is thus a need to simultaneously probe the local and the global contexts to deepen understanding and formulate responses, both in institutional and political terms. This book has attempted to throw light on the former dimension. Other books in the series it is part of, and whose sensibilities it has drawn upon, can help illuminate the latter dimension.

As we near the end of the second decade of the twenty-first century, there is a growing sense that the shift towards authoritarianism in every region of the world will result in a major intellectual and societal turmoil that will call for new thinking on issues of constitutionalism. This final chapter has sought to emphasise that on the occasion of the 70th anniversary of the independence of India, India's constitutional order confronts some challenges that are very similar to those that are being confronted elsewhere. At the same time, some of the challenges presented here are very particular to the Indian variant of constitutionalism, which may not have exact parallels elsewhere. Nevertheless, what is common is the need to revisit the history of constitutionalism and constitutional practice, both in India and elsewhere, to find ways to address the gaps that have been demonstrated to exist between the aspirations of the original constitutional vision and the lived reality and experiences of constitutional practice.

FURTHER READING

Rajeev Dhavan, *The Constitution of India: Miracle, Surrender, Hope* (Gurgaon, Universal Law Publishing, 2017).

Ramachandra Guha, *India after Gandhi: The History of the World's Largest Democracy* (New Delhi, Picador India, 10th anniversary edition, 2017).

Devesh Kapur, Pratap Mehta and Milan Vaishnav (eds), *Rethinking Public Institutions in India* (New Delhi, Oxford University Press, 2017).

Index

Introductory Note

References such as '178–79' indicate (not necessarily continuous) discussion of a topic across a range of pages. Wherever possible in the case of topics with many references, these have either been divided into sub-topics or only the most significant discussions of the topic are listed. Because the entire work is about the 'Constitution of India', the use of this term (and certain others which occur constantly throughout the book) as an entry point has been restricted. Information will be found under the corresponding detailed topics.